# Rediscovering Value

## LEADING THE 3-D ENTERPRISE TO SUSTAINABLE SUCCESS

Geary A. Rummler
Alan J. Ramias
Cherie L. Wilkins

Foreword by
Michael DeNoma

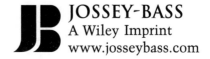

JOSSEY-BASS
A Wiley Imprint
www.josseybass.com

Published by Jossey-Bass
A Wiley Imprint
989 Market Street, San Francisco, CA 94103-1741—www.josseybass.com

Jossey-Bass books and products are available through most bookstores. To contact Jossey-Bass directly call our Customer Care Department within the U.S. at 800-956-7739, outside the U.S. at 317-572-3986, or fax 317-572-4002.

Jossey-Bass also publishes its books in a variety of electronic formats. Some content that appears in print may not be available in electronic books.

**Library of Congress Cataloging-in-Publication Data**
Rummler, Geary A.
    Rediscovering value: leading the 3-D enterprise to sustainable success / Geary A. Rummler, Alan J. Ramias, Cherie L. Wilkins.
      p.   cm.
    Includes bibliographical references and index.
    ISBN 978-0-470-19233-7 (cloth)
      1. Organizational effectiveness.   2. Industrial management.   3. System analysis.
  4. Performance.   5. Value added.   I. Ramias, Alan J.   II. Wilkins, Cherie L.   III. Title.
    HD58.9.R86   2011
    658.4–dc22

                                         2010045734

Printed in the United States of America
FIRST EDITION
*HB Printing* 10 9 8 7 6 5 4 3 2 1

# CONTENTS

## PART ONE The 3-D Concept

## PART TWO The CEO's Agenda

# LIST OF FIGURES AND TABLES

## Figures

## Tables

To Geary Rummler, my partner, friend, and wise guide through many years;
to my partners at PDL, Cherie Wilkins, and Rick Rummler, whose loyalty
and dedication to our team keep me in the game; and to
my dear wife, Lory, who keeps my days bright.

—Alan J. Ramias


To Geary, my mentor, partner, and friend, who set me on this path, and to Chip,
my husband and silent partner, who walks it all with me.

—Cherie L. Wilkins

I met Geary Rummler in 1991 while a member of one of several task forces pressed into service at Citibank to pull the bank back from the abyss it was being pulled into during those difficult days. I came to know of RBG (as the firm was called then) from exceptional comments about Geary and his approach in interviews with senior executives from Motorola, GE, and ABB. The interviews were part of an urgent benchmarking exercise we were conducting to determine how successful organizations had survived their life-threatening challenges.

Answering my subsequent phone call for help, Geary pressed a team of three consultants, one of whom was his son Rick, into service two days later. Diagnosis and then the actions to fix the largest mortgage business in the United States were under way within a matter of weeks, and we expanded the use of the tools across the bank over the following eighteen months.

Success there with the tools and approach was followed by success in dealing with performance and strategic challenges at Hutchison Whampoa in Hong Kong, particularly in the retail division as it attempted to move into China.

The thinking of Geary and his partners has continued to evolve and improve over the past two decades. The notions and methods around the 3-D Enterprise presented in this latest work expand on their systemic model of an organization and offer managers and executives a robust approach and toolkit for dealing with complex performance challenges in this extraordinary world in which we all now live.

Improving the performance of an organization is not easy. To paraphrase a number of philosophers, the major challenge any executive or manager (and especially any CEO) faces is that his or her experience of the reality of the organization is not the same as the reality itself. How then does an executive: (1) develop a more accurate and complete representation of the organization; (2) identify critical business issues and improvement opportunities across this system; (3) design a way forward; and (4) install the feedback and measurement mechanisms necessary to ensure the organizational system delivers the performance and stays on course?

This is where this book comes into its own. This approach is not simplification on the near side of complexity (the kind of simplification that Einstein said he would pay nothing for); but rather it's perhaps closer to simplification on the far side of complexity (that he stated he would pay anything for).

As we have seen in this latest financial crisis, complex systems fail in unpredictable ways. Executives need to rethink the way in which we are managing organizations; giving focus and time to the management of each dimension—resources *and* value. This balanced approach to management is essential to being able to adapt and succeed in these volatile economic times.

Geary Rummler was the real deal in providing managers tools to improve performance. And, amazingly, across decades of management fads and "one-book wonders," he remained the real deal up until his untimely death in 2008. I'm thankful that he's been followed by his partners, Alan Ramias, Cherie Wilkins, and son Rick Rummler.

Michael DeNoma
*President and CEO*
*Chinatrust Bank, Taiwan*

## ACKNOWLEDGMENTS

For contributing to the concepts and methodology:

Mark Munley

Klaus Wittkuhn

For providing opportunities to develop the ideas in their organizations:

Steve Hassenfelt—for whole enterprise Performance Planned and Managed system design

Richard King and Bert Kerstetter—for management system design and application of the Rummler Process Methodology to custom application development

Mark Munley—for management system design in a service-based industry

Rick Rummler (Geary's brother)—for early opportunities to apply the management system design toolset

Joyce Wells—for whole business redesign

For helping in the writing of this book:

Mike DeNoma

Lorena Lanese

Mark Munley

Keith Reece

Rick Rummler

Dave Stanalosavitch

Klaus Wittkuhn

Special Thanks:

To Mike DeNoma, for writing the Foreword

To Leslie Stephen, for another wonderful editing job

To Matt Davis, Lindsay Morton, and Nina Kreiden, for their expert help during publication

## ABOUT THE AUTHORS

**Dr. Geary A. Rummler** was the founding partner of the Performance Design Lab (PDL), where he was continuing his life-long work on organizational performance improvement in complex systems. He died on October 29, 2008.

At the time of his death, Geary was working with his partners on two books. One was this book; the other addresses process improvement and is written specifically for practitioners. Entitled *White Space Revisited: Creating Value Through Process*, it is a companion book to this one. The intention is that these two books provide a thorough look at both management of organizations for value and the use of process management and improvement.

Prior to founding the Performance Design Lab, Geary was the founding partner of the Rummler-Brache Group (RBG), an organization that became a leader in the business process improvement and management business in the 1980s and 1990s. Prior to that, Geary was president of the Kepner-Tregoe Strategy Group, specialists in strategic decision making; co-founder (with Thomas F. Gilbert) and president of Praxis Corporation, an innovator in the analysis and improvement of human performance; and co-founder (with George S. Odiorne) and director of the University of Michigan's Center for Programmed Learning for Business.

Geary was a pioneer in the application of instructional and performance technologies to organizations and brought this experience to the issue of organization effectiveness. His clients in the private sector included the sales, service, and manufacturing functions of the aircraft, automobile, steel, food, rubber, office equipment, pharmaceutical, telecommunications, chemical, and petroleum industries, as well as the retail, banking, and airline industries. He also worked with such federal agencies as IRS, SSA, HUD, GAO, and DOT. Geary's research and consulting took him to Europe, Japan, Korea, Malaysia, China, and Mexico.

In addition to consulting, teaching, and presenting at conferences, Geary published a steady stream of articles and a variety of books, on topics ranging from labor relations to the development of instructional systems. His articles appeared in numerous professional and management journals and handbooks. In 1988, he co-authored *Training and Development: A Guide for Professionals*, with George S. Odiorne. In 1990, he co-authored *Improving Performance: How to Manage the White Space on the Organization Chart*, with Alan P. Brache. Geary received his MBA and Ph.D. from the University of Michigan and served as

- The national president of the International Society for Performance Improvement (ISPI)
- A member of the Board of Directors of the American Society of Training and Development (ASTD)
- A member of the Editorial Board of *Training* magazine

  Geary's professional accomplishments include:

- Induction into the Human Resource Development Hall of Fame in 1986
- The Distinguished Professional Achievement Award from ISPI in 1992
- The Enterprise Reengineering Excellence Award from *Enterprise Reengineering* magazine in 1996
- The Distinguished Contribution Award for Workplace Learning and Performance from ASTD in 1999
- The Life-Time Achievement Award from the Organization Behavior Management Network in 1999

**Alan J. Ramias** is a partner at PDL. He was employed by Motorola for ten years as an internal consultant on organizational performance. As a member of the team that founded Motorola University, he was the first person to introduce Geary Rummler's pioneering concepts in process improvement and management to business units within Motorola. Alan advocated for and led several of the first groundbreaking projects in process improvement that evolved to the invention of Six Sigma, and Motorola's winning of the first Malcolm Baldrige Award in 1988.

After joining RBG in 1991, Alan led major successful performance improvement engagements within Fortune 500 companies. His experience spanned several industries and the full spectrum of corporate functions and processes, such as strategic planning, manufacturing, product development, financial management, and supply chain. Major clients included Shell, Hewlett-Packard, 3M, Citibank, Motorola, Steelcase, Citgo, Hermann Miller, Louisiana-Pacific, and Bank One. After leading many high-profile projects, he became a partner and Managing Director of Consulting Services at RBG. He led development of much of RBG's products and services and was responsible for selecting, training, and mentoring RBG's consultant teams. He joined PDL in 2005.

Alan can be reached at aramias@thepdlab.com.


**Cherie L. Wilkins** is a partner with PDL. She specializes in the design of measurement and management systems and the application of performance logic methodology to strategy formulation and performance improvement. She has helped many companies define their process architectures and link them with business strategy. She has extensive consulting experience in the financial services, retail, chemical, petroleum, and manufacturing industries. Recently, she has been helping IT organizations improve their alignment with the businesses they serve. In Cherie's fifteen years of consulting experience, she has brought a full range of performance solutions to such clients as Louisiana-Pacific, Chevron, DuPont, CIGNA, Meredith Publishing, US Trust, Charles Schwab, CEMEX, NavAir–US Navy, and Idaho National Laboratory.

Prior to joining PDL, Cherie was involved in technology development and process improvement consulting with RBG. Before joining RBG, she specialized in consulting for internal communications to organizations undergoing large-scale change efforts. Prior to that, Cherie worked eight years in the television industry, five of those with the *MacNeil/Lehrer NewsHour*.

Cherie can be reached at cwilkins@thepdlab.com.

# INTRODUCTION

To describe the complexities of organizations, and the roles and behavior of people who build and run those organizations, writers on business subjects often turn to metaphors of systems, systems builders, and "the system."

On the positive side, for example, there is *Built to Last*, by Jim Collins and Jerry Porras, describing the patient, strategic builder of organizations that produce long-term value as a "clock builder."[1]

Then there are the not-so-positive, such as Gary Hamel in *Leading the Revolution*,[2] pointing out how today's organizations often pledge allegiance to business models that are rapidly "decaying" while the world innovates around them, and how many employees often brag that their most important achievement is how they "beat the system."

And reinforcing the point that organizations do behave according to some discernable systems principles, there has been in the past decade or so a whole genre of books on complexity theory, making the argument that organizations and economies operate according to rules of systems behavior.

## OBJECTIVES AND PURPOSE OF THIS BOOK

We too subscribe to the notion that organizations are like complex systems and operate according to systems principles along somewhat predictable paths. We believe, like Collins and Porras, that business leaders should be builders of organizational systems whose aim is production of lasting value, while also deploring, with Hamel, the fact that in many organizations the systems in place tend to thwart organizational purpose. Our objectives in this subject area are twofold:

- To describe the basic systems, or dimensions, inside organizations and their internal dynamics, because we think it's those dimensions—of value and resources—that are often misunderstood and become misaligned or unbalanced and thus at odds with each other, leading to irrational organizational practices.

- To describe what can be done to change an unbalanced organizational system, providing as much practical advice and as many useful tools as we can without making this a recipe book or a technical manual.

We were part of the process "revolution" that began in the early 1980s. The impetus for that movement was the realization that in every industry, functional silos were a major impediment to organizational success. Our guiding metaphor was the "white space" between silos on organization charts, founded on the belief that redesigning the work that connects and transcends silos was key to delivering value in the eyes of customers.

But process improvement has never been enough by itself. Management has always been the critical element in conquering white space. And thus this book, which is about designing the dimension of management itself. In these pages, we explain why we think creating a balance between value and resources and achieving sustainable success require a fundamental rethinking of the very act of organizational management. The result would be what we might call a "3-D Enterprise," an organization in which the dimensions of value and resources are kept in balance by the third dimension of effective management.

## AUDIENCE AND STRUCTURE

This book is written for the executive and executive teams. We don't know any organization that has successfully undertaken a journey such as we describe here without leadership from the very top. Should this book inspire you to lead your own organization on such a journey, our companion book *White Space Revisited* was written for the people inside your organization who can help you.[3]

This book is organized into three parts.

In **Part One** we introduce the three dimensions and examine the effects of the current imbalance between the value and resource dimensions.

In **Part Two** we present and describe the executive agenda for making the transition to a 3-D Enterprise. Along the way, you will hear the story of Belding, Inc., and its new CEO who drives the move to a 3-D Enterprise. While Belding is fictitious, we have seen each of Belding's issues in numerous client companies, and everything that the CEO does to address the issues has been done in reality by our clients.

In **Part Three** readers who want more detailed assistance will find lengthy descriptions of the templates and tools we use to develop management systems for organizations, using content from the Belding case. And for those who want more of the story, we return to Belding and grant them a grand "do-over" in order to see how things would be different in a mature 3-D Enterprise.

## A NOTE ON THE RUMMLER LEGACY

When we set out to publish our observations about the state of process improvement and management, we knew that we needed to write two books. *White Space Revisited* was written for practitioners who would need the details and tools to support organizations that elect to become 3-D Enterprises. This book is for the executive who must understand and lead the 3-D journey, and thus is meant to be less technical but more concentrated on the role and behavior of the top executive and managers.

So these two books were planned together. *White Space Revisited* was largely written when we lost co-author Dr. Geary Rummler, who passed away in October 2008. But the concepts, tools, and Belding case already existed, so this is very much his work, his thinking, his purpose carried out.

# The 3-D Concept

In Part One we propose the central notion of this book: that every organization consists of three dimensions—the value dimension, the resource dimension, and the management dimension. The first chapter introduces the general concept and the reasons why leaders need to understand the purpose and importance of all three dimensions.

The remaining chapters are devoted to a more detailed discussion of each dimension. We describe the value dimension and its critical importance to achieving the objectives of an organization. The resource dimension is characterized as dominant in most organizations; the reasons for this are described as well as the ill effects of resource dominance on organizational effectiveness. Finally, the management dimension is introduced as the mechanism for ensuring that the other two dimensions are thoughtfully designed and kept in optimal balance.

Our purpose is to make clear that all three dimensions of an organization are critical to success. While recognizing that the emphasis on resource management has put many organizations out of whack, there *is* a way to create and sustain proper balance. The aim of this entire book is to describe that way.

# Three Dimensions of an Organization

In the Introduction we alluded to the rise of the "process movement" in the 1980s and 1990s and its effect on organizational performance—the promise versus the reality. Where did all of the past efforts really miss the mark? It was not a failure of an idea; it was a failure to implement it properly. The fundamental notion that value is delivered to customers only through the cross-functional work system is still the correct and relevant notion. Implied in that notion is the need to manage the delivery of value across those functions—that is an essential but often missing or deficient act of management. Failure to address this remains the biggest failure of the whole movement. Now with ever-more dynamic markets and business environments, the need to get a handle on defining and managing value is more challenging than ever. But it remains the critical priority for success.

In this chapter we try to answer the question of what the act of management is supposed to be. We look at the three dimensions of an organization as constituting what managers must design and continually keep in proper balance.

## SOME BASIC ASSUMPTIONS ABOUT ORGANIZATIONS

Despite a vast broadening of the language, concepts, and tools of "process," there has been insufficient progress in transforming organizations into well-designed and well-managed institutions. Much of the momentum of the initial work in the 1980s that established process as a legitimate business concept has been followed with a trail of misfires and misapplications of potentially powerful techniques and tools.

The root cause of this lack of progress is that most people still do not really recognize and understand that organizations are systems; consequently they don't realize the implications for how organizations should be planned, designed, and managed. Many managers and employees are familiar enough with notions of process to talk about "their process" but don't see the connections of that process to a larger architecture of processes that must be deliberately designed and managed. Despite lip service to "systems thinking," many don't get—in a practical, applied sense—that work processes and resources are part of a larger organizational system and therefore cannot be tinkered with in isolation.

As a natural course of being in a particular part of a given organization and possessed of a particular set of skills, managers and employees are still fundamentally grounded in their own discipline or functional area (Engineering, Sales, Manufacturing, Customer Service, Product Development, Finance, HR, etc.) and tend not to look beyond their departmental boundaries, nor are they encouraged and enabled to do so. And, if anything, technology has abetted their functional myopia.

The correction to this myopia is to return to the underlying assumptions about organizations as systems. Our starting point for understanding and characterizing any organization is to try to understand it as a system. But a system to do what? Answering that question is a very helpful way of diagnosing what is happening in an organization and evaluating what needs to change in order for it to improve.

All organizations—public or private, large or small—exist to provide value. For all the myriad activities and complexities of any organization, what it must fundamentally produce is something of value to someone other than itself, or it will not be in business long. In short, a business is a system that exists to provide value to customers and financial stakeholders. Per the diagram in Figure 1.1, there are four key requirements for a business to provide value to its constituents:

1. Understanding the value to be delivered to its dual constituency.

2. Designing and maintaining a value-adding work system that has been engineered and optimized to produce the valued product/service.

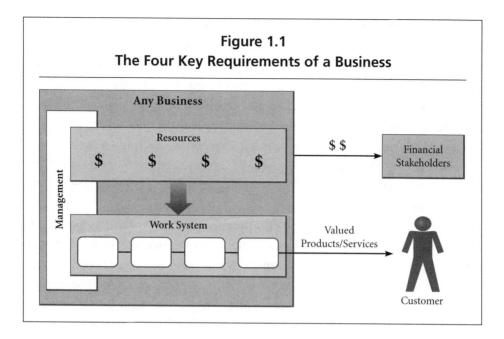

**Figure 1.1**
**The Four Key Requirements of a Business**

Any Business

Management

Resources

$   $   $   $

$ $

Financial Stakeholders

Work System

Valued Products/Services

Customer

3. Resources to perform that work, which starts with capital and expense dollars that are converted into people, technology, equipment, facilities, and materials.

4. Management of the integration of resources and the work system to produce the desired value.

The diagram in Figure 1.1 represents the ideal relationship among these four elements. What actually happens in many, if not most, businesses today is woefully out of balance. Following is a summary of what happens to the four elements in many organizations.

## Imbalance of Value Delivery and Stakeholder Value

Many companies are failing to manage a balance between the value delivered to customers and that delivered to financial stakeholders. Increasingly, there is a short-term emphasis on delivering value to financial stakeholders (return on investment). What seems to be lost is the inescapable fact that the return to financial stakeholders is ultimately totally dependent on the value (in the form of valued products/services) delivered to the customer. This shift in priorities regarding delivery of value drives a corresponding shift in priorities within the organization: To satisfy the continual demand for short-term financial results, control of resources has become the primary internal priority.

## Lack of Visibility of the Value-Adding Work System

A major reason the resource element is prominent in business is because, by contrast, the work and work system are virtually invisible to the human eye. With the exception of a few engineering drawings in a manufacturing or process operation, there is no agreed-upon end-to-end articulation of the value-adding work required to produce a valued product or service, from product/service inception, through marketing and selling, to delivery and support. Even when such a drawing may exist, it tends not to be a tool used by management to understand and guide the organization. Process understanding may reside at lower levels of the organization but not at the top.

Further, what little definition of the work and work system has been done tends to be confined to individual functional resource buckets. The work specification is under the control of each function or department, constrained by their given resources and their particular parochial view of the business. These costly work activities quickly evolve within the siloed functional areas into what many organizational observers then call "culture," which is really many little individual, self-absorbed, rigidified cultures whose goal becomes self-preservation. In many cases these insular functional resource buckets are further reinforced by legacy technology systems and applications provided by an often obliging IT organization. The IT organization reinforces a silo view of work when it organizes itself to mirror the resource buckets on the organization chart.

## Single-Minded Attention to the Resource Dimension

The most dominant element in most organizations today has become resources, for several reasons:

One major reason we have already stated: the priority given the return to financial stakeholders. Resources are where the money is. This emphasis on resources exacerbates a fundamental misunderstanding of cause and effect among our four requirements of a business. Many organizations behave as if there is a direct connection between resource management and returns to financial stakeholders. In the short term, there often is. But the longer-term reality is this: When things are working as they should inside an organization, resources make their contributions within value-creating work systems that provide products and services to customers, which in turn results in earnings to be distributed to financial stakeholders. There is no viable long-term shortcut to results.

A second reason for the fixation on resources is their daily visibility in any organization. Resources—people, facilities, equipment, technology—are visible and are represented in the form of the ubiquitous organization chart. The organization chart of a business is in most cases a high-level view of the allocation of critical resources across the organization. Each function shown on the organization chart is a "resource bucket," backed by a corresponding capital and expense budget. The visibility of the budget structure is understandable, given that dollars are the lifeblood of a business, and in any well-run enterprise every nickel must be accounted for. The dollars are distributed at the beginning of the year and their utilization tracked and accounted for very publicly every month. Heads roll if resource utilization doesn't tally with resource allocation at the end of the year.

## One-Dimensional Management

The third and final reason why there is such an imbalance between resources and value-adding work systems in business today is the relentless emphasis on resource management. Resource ownership represents status and power for executives and managers at every level of the organization. The bigger the resource bucket controlled, the greater the presumed value of the executive. Yes, there have been many experiments with virtual teams, lateral promotions, managers without staffs, and the like, but clear away the rhetoric, and it's clear that power games regarding headcount have not changed in corporations.

As ready evidence of this bias, note the annual planning and budgeting ritual—easily extending over four to six months of a year and consuming a quarter or more of management time annually. Add to this the time spent monthly, quarterly, and annually, at every level of the organization, examining "budget actual versus plan" and pursuing endless initiatives to close any gaps between the two, and you easily come up with 85 percent of management time being focused on resource management. Add to that the untold hours of effort by numerous staff organizations assigned to crank out mountains of analyses and PowerPoint charts designed to protect the backsides of various and sundry managers, and you have organizations that expend enormous energy to manage only half the equation.

Meanwhile, the little attention paid to work and work systems is carried out down within the functions and usually is focused on how to get more work with fewer resources. And all the while, the truth is that resources can be wisely managed *only* in the context of the value-adding work required to deliver products and services.

But how do we make this happen? How do we get "resources" back in balance with "work"? Resource management is "front of mind" for every executive or manager in any business sweating how they will stay within budget. ("Who's paying for that? It sure as hell is not coming out of *my* budget!") In contrast, the value-adding work required to keep the enterprise in business is invisible—buried in virtually independent functional resource buckets. Like Rodney Dangerfield, "work" gets no respect!

A starting point for rebalancing the management of work and resources is to *think differently about the contribution of work.*

## THE VALUE MACHINE

Let's reorient ourselves to our picture of the ideal components of a business, shown in Figure 1.2. In that depiction, we start with the assertion that a business is

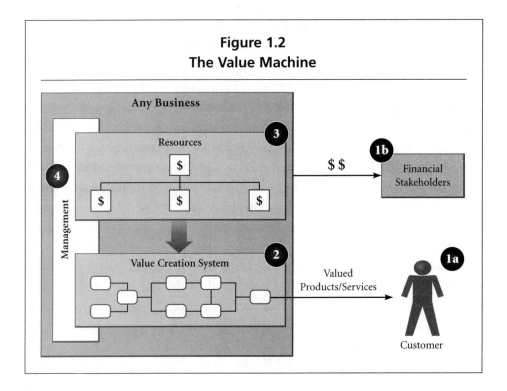

**Figure 1.2**
**The Value Machine**

fundamentally a value-producing machine (a Value Machine, for short) that exists to produce valued products and services for customers (1a) and a return to financial stakeholders (1b). When we look inside the machine, we see two fundamental components that must be managed in concert to produce the desired results:

- The end-to-end Value Creation System (VCS) (2), which effectively and efficiently converts customer needs and desires into products and services that those customers value and will pay for. In this context, we are no longer viewing work as resource-consuming activities but rather as a carefully designed set of value-adding outputs leading to products and services. This system of *value-adding* work is the backbone of the business. The business is only as good as this Value Creation System.
- The resources (3) necessary to fuel the VCS.

The primary acts of management (4) are to properly allocate and manage those scarce resources across the Value Creation System so as to effectively and efficiently produce the desired products and services.

So this means there are really three critical dimensions to business performance, two of which must be managed in concert by the third:

- The value dimension (the system of value-adding work that delivers products and services to customers)
- The resource dimension (the scarce resources required to perform the value-adding work of the enterprise)
- The management dimension (the processes, practices, and policies in place to design and manage the other two dimensions and to make the inevitable tradeoffs between them)

Up to this point, the world over, management has been skewed in the direction of the resource dimension, with inconsistent results. There is ample evidence of this imbalance between resources versus value creation, including:

- Endless cycles of reorganization that fail to work because the only thing being reorganized is the names on the functional resource buckets. There is seldom any change in the end-to-end value-adding work required to deliver the end product or service. In most cases, functional sub-optimization of the end-to-end work system continues unabated.

- Failed product/service launches because key functions can't or don't participate in the design, development, and proper preparation of the organization for the launch, because of their functional resource constraints and inward focus on their own activities.

- Customer outrage at companies that try to keep costs in line by skimping on resources (think of help desks and outsourced technical support) instead of properly delivering value.

- Slow and expensive attempts to adapt to changes in the market and business environment. It takes a crisis or imminent failure to align the internally focused functions and redirect their priorities.

- Downsizing death-spirals as companies try to resource-manage themselves back to profitability. The resulting chaos in the value dimension is ignored by everyone but the customer.

And what is life like for the manager inside an organization where the fixation is on resources? The manager who must get work done, define objectives and carry out plans, develop employees, and meet budget goals? Here is a description from one middle manager:

> You know, they do this survey every year of manager performance, and there's this one item in the survey, "How well does this manager MTB [manage to budget]?" And it's always the lowest-ranked item in the survey, for all of us. And how can we do any better? We don't control the work we are asked to do; it's just piled on us without rhyme or reason. We should be sitting down and asking, "What work should we be doing?" And then schedule the work so it is, one, achievable, and two, can be done with a minimum of personal pain and waste. But instead we just pile it on.
>
> And so who gets the rewards and the promotions? It's those managers who pull rabbits out of hats, who figure out some way to work the system to get out a reasonable amount of work, or at least look like they did it. But you know, you can only do that for so long—you can't always work a miracle, and after a while you get so cynical you just stop trying anyway.

It is time to begin managing both the value dimension and the resource dimension. It most definitely should not be a case of resource *versus* value.

The only way a business is going to survive in the future is the wise allocation of critical, scarce resources *in the context* of its unique Value Creation System. However, we are quick to acknowledge that this task is easier said than done. Forces driving an emphasis on resources are many, including:

- The functional structure of organizations
- The formal accounting, budgeting, and planning systems
- The desire for some accountability, which is easier to approximate with a focus on functional silos and their resources

Add to these reinforcers the fact that we are asking for a fundamental rethinking of the act of management, and you can see the challenge is significant.

## OUTLINE OF THIS BOOK

This book, then, is about the three dimensions of organization, and, more important, about changing the act of management for a balanced focus on both value and resources. Management can only succeed when based upon a clear and complete understanding of what has to be managed. Our contention is that management of the Value Machine has been insufficiently understood and addressed, to the detriment of organizational results and value to the customer.

In the next several chapters, we will explain in more detail the value and resource dimensions and then further address management, providing a model and explanation of the roles of management vis-à-vis the other two dimensions.

Then we provide a case study of an organization and its handling of multiple crises, first when it takes a resource-fixated approach and then when it applies a balanced-management approach.

In the final section of this book, we provide a full set of documents related to the case study for those who want to see the details of this management approach.

# The Value Dimension

Any organization that fails to provide value to customers will cease to exist. Any manager who fails to understand that should cease to be employed! And yet how easy it is for managers inside complex organizations to lose sight of this fundamental truism and default back to a simple focus on resources in their turf.

In Chapter 1 we introduced the notion of two dimensions in every organization that must be designed and managed in concert in order to achieve the short-term and long-term objectives of leaders and stakeholders. We proposed that every organization exists to deliver valued products and services, which requires careful design and continuous optimization of both dimensions. Making the organization as lean and efficient a value-producing machine as possible, using the available resources, is the constant challenge of leadership.

In this chapter we will describe the value dimension in more detail, defining its components and discussing how leaders can begin to make the value dimension of their organization more visible, which is a necessary first step to designing and managing it.

The value dimension is critical because it's the means by which anything is ever achieved in an organization. It's the wiring of the organization's internal processes to execute strategy, accomplish organizational goals, satisfy customers, create and deliver goods and services. Of course, these ultimate goals cannot be achieved by any one functional area but must be accomplished through collaboration across departments, divisions, regions, external partners, and so on, which is why the organization's cross-functional processes are most important.

Because the value dimension is so critical, it is vital for leaders to have a clear understanding of how their organization's value dimension is designed and whether it is working effectively. The questions every leader needs to ask are whether the value dimension is constructed to achieve the aims of the organization; whether it is optimized to achieve results with as little organizational friction and waste of resources as possible; whether the innumerable activities of employees are achieving outcomes of worth; and whether customer needs are being met and long-term value is being reliably produced. All these things are hard to judge without having a clear understanding of just what is going on inside the organization where the work is taking place. What can be done to make the value dimension understandable and manageable?

- Step 1 is to make it visible.
- Step 2 is to determine how well it is working—that is, whether it is achieving results with optimal resource usage.
- Step 3 is to redesign it when necessary to achieve desired results.
- Step 4 is to manage it together with the resource dimension
  - To make tradeoff decisions
  - To optimize performance
  - To redirect efforts as necessary for long-term value

In this chapter we will focus on the first step—how to make the value dimension visible as a first step in accomplishing the others.

## DEFINITION OF A PROCESS

The value dimension consists of an organization's business processes. So before we begin our detailed examination of the value dimension, we need to ask, "Just what is a process?" The reality in most organizations today is that no two people in a given organization would define its processes in the same way. That is a problem because an organization must have a common understanding of the relationship of its work to value. Unfortunately, current definitions of "process" are vague enough to cause an unhealthy level of variation.

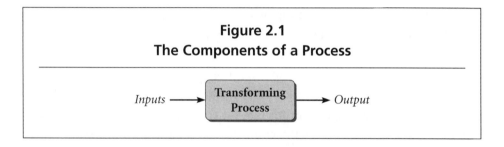

**Figure 2.1**
**The Components of a Process**

Inputs → Transforming Process → Output

The commonly held definition of process, as shown in Figure 2.1, is limited to these components:

- A desired output
- Inputs that will be transformed into the desired output
- A system of work that transforms inputs into output

Described this way, the emphasis is on sequence (inputs turned into output). And that is certainly one of the important elements of a process. Our own definition of a process begins with these words:

*"A process is a construct for organizing value-adding work to achieve a business-value milestone."*

That is, a process is a way of organizing tasks in order to produce something of value. Producing that valuable product or service meets some business goal or milestone. So first of all, a process is about getting organized. Harking back to one of the classic definitions of management (Plan/Organize/Lead/Control), organizing work is one of the essential acts of management.

But there are additional attributes of a process to add to our definition.

There is often more than one way a process can be performed. A process should be designed so that it can be effectively and efficiently **performed**. Most process improvement methodologies are focused on this attribute of process design.

A process should also be organized so it can be effectively **managed**. The major emphasis on process design has usually been effective and efficient *performance* of the work—but effective *management* of the work is just as important. In addition to efficiency and effectiveness, the work must also be designed and organized to give management *visibility* into the process and some *control* over its performance.

The need for management visibility and control can be incredibly challenging when the work is being performed in multiple places, in different parts of the world, perhaps, or when the work has been outsourced. The design of an effective management system on top of such work processes is absolutely critical and takes as much thought and creativity as design of the work itself.

However, when there is too much control built into processes, the management system can itself be a root cause of poor performance in work processes. A classic example is the Product Development process that is so burdened with project reviews and multiple sign-offs that the company fails to get its new products to market in time to beat the competition. Organizing work so it can be effectively managed is a critical criterion for intelligent work design.

Finally, wherever practical, work should be organized to provide the business with *a competitive advantage*. This criterion is adapted from the work of Michael Porter, who has said:

- "A company outperforms rivals only if it can establish a difference that it can preserve. Ultimately, all differences between companies . . . derive from the hundreds of activities required to create, produce, sell, and deliver their products and services."

- "The essence of strategy is in the activities—choosing to perform activities differently or to perform different activities than rivals."

- "Competitive advantage comes from the way . . . activities fit and reinforce one another."[1]

So this is our definition:

PROCESS is a construct for organizing value-adding work to achieve a business-valued milestone so it

    Can be *performed* effectively and efficiently

    Can be *managed* effectively

    Offers the potential for a *competitive advantage*

There is an important assumption underlying this definition of process—that a process is not some God-given sequence of work, chiseled in stone. Processes can be designed in different ways to meet the same criteria.

Why should this matter to executives? When process performance first gained widespread acceptance and visibility, it was usually viewed as "strategic" or central to an organization's success. Now, twenty-five years later, the perception among many executive teams is that processes are akin to procedures and are only of interest when there is a need to prove regulatory compliance or achieve certification in an industry standard. So process has been relegated to the province of "process experts" in process excellence groups, quality groups, IT, or other lower levels of the organization.

But we believe it is critical that senior leaders take back the responsibility for defining, designing, and managing the organization's key processes. Why? First, the definition and prioritization of processes are very much strategic actions if processes are defined and considered as units of value delivery. Second, to be effectively designed and managed, processes need to be defined top down, not bottom up. The very definition of business processes is a strategic choice that cannot be delegated, because you are defining the points where competitive advantage is to be found in the organization.

When left without senior executive guidance, process definition and management tend to fall into the same white-space trap as resource management. Unless told otherwise, managers will view their business processes as beginning and ending at the boundaries of the functional silos they individually manage, even though the critical processes—the ones that create and deliver value—are inevitably cross-functional and must be defined and managed as such.

So process definition is strategically important. And with this definition of process, we can take a closer look inside the value dimension and try to answer our question of how to make it visible.

## THE VALUE CREATION SYSTEM

Every organization exists to produce and deliver products and services of value to someone outside the organization—that is, a market. To provide those valued products/services, the organization needs a way to design, produce, and deliver them to the market. So if we look inside any organization, we will see something like the diagram in Figure 2.2.

Inside every organization, the value dimension consists of an internal Value Creation System. What does this system consist of? Taking a closer look, we find

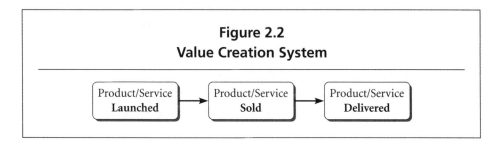

**Figure 2.2**
**Value Creation System**

Product/Service **Launched** → Product/Service **Sold** → Product/Service **Delivered** that it consists of sets, or "sub-systems," of business processes that work together to transform inputs into those outputs that the market wants.

In looking at many different companies we have found that, regardless of a given organization's line of business and its industry-specific terminology, it will always have the same large groups of processes:

- It will have a set of processes devoted to creating its products or services. We call this sub-system "Product/Service Launched." The processes in this collection include researching new product or service concepts, designing new products or services, performing product development, launching the new product or service into the marketplace, extending or replacing existing products or services, and, finally, sun-setting them.

- It will also have a set of processes devoted to selling its products and services. These processes include doing market research, promoting products and services, selling and closing a sale, and managing the customer relationship. We call this sub-system "Product/Service Sold."

- It will have a third sub-system that we label "Product/Service Delivered." This includes all the processes required to get a product or service to the customer, including the order fulfillment process, manufacturing (when relevant), shipping, ongoing customer service, and any other follow-up processes.

In Figure 2.2, these sub-systems are shown in a simple sequence, but in reality, they overlap in time because some of their processes are repeated again and again. For example, a given product may be invented once, but it is sold again and again and delivered to many different customers. The "Customer Relationship Maintained" process is included in Product/Service Sold, but it spans the entire life cycle of a given customer, so it overlaps with Delivered.

Every organization has a Value Creation System. There are numerous variations, but the general concept holds up pretty nicely as a way of describing any organization at a very high level. Nevertheless, we often run into objections and potential exceptions. Here are a few of the most common ones (with our rejoinders supplied):

- *The concept of a Value Creation System applies to businesses but not to non-profit organizations, government agencies, and the like.* (On the contrary, every organization has to provide something of value, so it must have the equivalent of a Product/Service Launched sub-system, and it has to deliver those products or services, so Delivered also exists. What is less clear for such an organization is whether it has a Product/Service Sold sub-system. But even a government agency has to make visible its services, so it does perform the equivalent of marketing and promoting, and some of its services may in fact have to be sold at a price to citizens.)

- *This concept oversimplifies a big organization because there are many products and services.* (We fully agree that a big company usually has multiple Value Creation Systems, each one designed to create, sell, and deliver a product/service. How all of those systems are designed and organized is a major organizational challenge, but the starting point is to identify the Value Creation System, or systems, that exist.)

- *Some businesses don't start by creating a product. They first have to have a committed customer.* (Point taken. A maker of fighter jets for the federal government, for example, can't just go spend millions of dollars on a new jet design; it first has to get a contract with the military. So in that case, the Sold sub-system precedes the Launched sub-system.)

- *The Delivered sub-system includes the "Customer Service" process, but in our business, customer service after a product/service is rendered is critical.* (Where it makes sense to emphasize a process buried inside Launched, Sold, or Delivered by calling it out as a separate sub-system, by all means, do so. So, for example, in Figure 2.3, "Customer Support Provided" is called out as a major sub-system of its own. Why do that? Well, one reason would be that a particular process fits the Michael Porter definition of bringing a competitive advantage.)

- *This model does not apply because we have chosen to outsource much of our Value Creation System to partners.* (You may have outsourced to external resources, but it is still your Value Creation System and you still need to understand and manage all of it.)

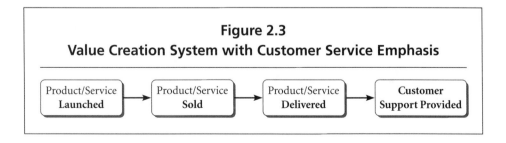

**Figure 2.3**
**Value Creation System with Customer Service Emphasis**

| Product/Service Launched | → | Product/Service Sold | → | Product/Service Delivered | → | Customer Support Provided |

With the above caveats, we can use the notion of a Value Creation System as the highest-level depiction of any organization's value dimension. Now let's go into further detail.

When we go inside a given organization to find its value dimension, we find that it is not as simple as the three boxes we have depicted in Figure 2.2. In fact, the Value Creation System is a whole hierarchy of detail because work is performed at multiple levels, as shown in Figure 2.4.

This view of an organization's value dimension depicts how work is accomplished, from the very highest level of the business down to sub-processes. It shows that there are multiple levels of processes inside a complex organization. A business is made up of processing sub-systems, which in turn are made of processes; processes are made of sub-processes; and sub-processes are made of tasks.

Why does this matter? In order to design and manage the value dimension, one must understand its complexity. This is not creating complexity; it is revealing it. Without this view of an organization's internal processes, the tendency is either to stay at too high a level for design work (that is, the whole business) or at too low a level (that is, down to individual jobs, tasks, and technologies).

A view of the entire value dimension of an organization allows you to:

• Understand the whole and then to decompose it into logical levels
• Align the parts for desired performance
• Evaluate the effectiveness and efficiency of an organization's value dimension
• Gauge the value dimension against an organization's strategy

We will say more about the usefulness of modeling an organization's value dimension after we have explored the resource dimension in the next chapter.

# Figure 2.4
## An Organization's Value Dimension

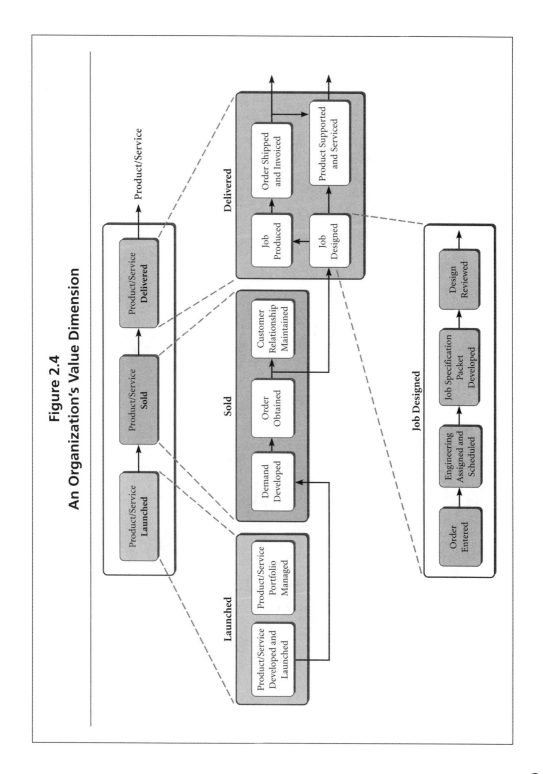

# The Resource Dimension

The resource dimension is just as vital as the value dimension because without resources to execute the strategy, no value can be produced. And resources have to be organized—typically into functional specialties, geographical groupings, or areas of responsibility. These "silos" exist for very valid reasons, including the hiring, care, and nurturing of expertise, the development of best practices, the utilization of complex tools, equipment, facilities, the focus on market segments, and so on.

But many of the problems of organizational performance are traceable to an over-emphasis on the resource dimension to the detriment of the value dimension. The resource dimension has become so dominant that it has subsumed the value dimension. The "process" or value view has been co-opted down into the functions. "By golly, if I have to map and improve processes, they are going to be my processes!" And so we now have mostly a functional view of process. This chapter will cover how the resource dimension has come to dominate the attention of management and how that fixation has negatively affected organizational performance.

## SILOS AND ORGANIZATIONAL EVOLUTION

When organizations are newly created, there generally is little tension between the value and resource dimensions. A small company is quite naturally all about providing value to customers. Its very survival depends on being lean, intensely focused, and capable of delivering on its promises. But with success comes complexity: the addition of management and staff specialists to provide professional practices; the divvying up of territories and customers into groupings; the physical expansion from one place to many. One of the greatest leadership challenges becomes allocating enterprise and business goals and resources (budget dollars, headcount, etc.) among the various lines of business and functional domains (such as Marketing, Sales, HR, Finance, etc.) in support of enterprise goals. The functional domains seem to have an unquenchable thirst for resources and each promises "important" but difficult-to-quantify returns. The desire for more resources often becomes more competitive than the desire to outperform external competitors.

As the organization grows and becomes more complex, leadership may attempt to continue a focus on customers and value but can become increasingly frustrated by the lack of a shared focus by the many members of the organization. Countless millions of dollars and thousands of initiatives have been launched to try to address this dichotomy, with little lasting effect. The need to focus on value receives more attention when profits drop but tends to be forgotten again when profitability returns. In most organizations, this loss of shared attention to value becomes permanent, and the siloed nature of functional areas and their internal politics and competition become the natural state.

In some notorious cases, the silo mentality has invaded the highest levels—the business units and the value produced by the enterprise as a whole became secondary to the "success" of the areas that individual leaders controlled. It is in these organizations that the Achilles' heel of siloed organizations became most visible—siloed functions can be very effective in scaling to meet largely static missions, but they often are the most significant barrier to change when the organization and functional missions are in transition. In organizations marked by large-scale silo behavior, it takes a "burning platform" or bankruptcy, or both, to refocus the organization or even significant parts of it on value and customers (think GM, Kodak, and Blockbuster, among others).

The siloed nature of organizations can also create an environment of reluctance to change in order to meet the shifting needs of existing customers as well as requirements posed by new customers, products, and business ideas. Growth in complex organizations is often accomplished only by acquiring new customers, products, and businesses because it becomes so hard to grow a new line of business from within. But even with acquisitions, there is a major risk of "tissue rejection" by the existing siloed functions.

It can seem like the only way to grasp the reality of business is to turn to "Dilbert." As illustrated in Figure 3.1, this is the environment that most of today's managers and executives grew up in. Everywhere are functional silos grasping for resources and guessing at their relationships to real value and the customer. This is a natural result of trying to take something good—the establishment of functional areas to foster capability development and increase scalability—and turning them into the way we run an entire organization.

## LIFE IN THE RESOURCE DIMENSION

So what is the effect on the inside, where executives and managers are dutifully trying to carry out their organizational mission?

Susan manages an IT services organization for a large corporation. All of the work her department performs is accomplished via projects, which are requested by the managers of the other departments that make up the corporation. This project-oriented cycle begins each autumn, when the department heads are required to participate in "portfolio planning" sessions. Each department head submits a list of requests for things he or she would like from IT (such as new applications, upgrades, system fixes). The requests, when developed into detailed

**Figure 3.1**
**The Dilbert Reality of Functional Silos**

Copyright © Scott Adams/Distributed by United Feature Syndicate, Inc.

project plans, can range from simple maintenance items to major multi-year development efforts.

Using a set of seemingly rational criteria, the senior department heads and the IT leaders, with lots of help from Finance, choose and fund those projects deemed most important and useful to the company. That approved list is then deployed to the IT functions, including Susan and her troops, who provide their particular expertise.

*So, Susan, how's this working for you?*

Susan says, "It could make sense if any of the people who decide on these projects had a clue what kind of work it takes to execute their projects. But they don't. They make their decisions in a complete vacuum about how much work it's going to take, what kinds of resources are needed versus what's actually available, how long it will actually take versus when they want it."

*You mean they actually don't know what resources are required?*

"Well sure, they sort of know. When they were at my level, they certainly had to know. But when some project is being labeled as critical, and it's championed by some senior VP who is used to getting his way, the whole effort to be rational about choosing projects just gets swamped by politics. So promises are made that can't be met. Sometimes everybody knows it; sometimes only we know it but nobody asks us."

*Then what happens?*

"Then the projects are executed. And as it becomes clear that deadlines are going to be missed because the resources are just not there, the juggling and dicing of work projects sometimes gets frantic."

*So you're tracking the progress on these projects?*

"Oh, God, yes. We track the [expletive] out of these projects. Every day, huge spreadsheet, me, my boss, my customers, and my managers, all looking at where every hour is being spent, where every resource is spending time, where it's all going, why we are getting so behind. And meanwhile, new projects are being piled on top of the ones that we originally committed to. Having this kind of data makes some people think we are managing the work, but really, we're just tracking the mismanagement, the fantasy versus the reality."

*What could be done differently?*

"If these senior leaders would just take the time to understand, really understand, what work can be accomplished, in the time available, with the resources available. Really understand how to produce quality results and commit to that and only that."

*What can you do to make that happen?*

"Me? I can't. I do what I can. I plan the best I can. I defend myself and my people against unreasonable requests and unwarranted changes. But change this system? Not unless I make it to that senior position myself, and even then I gotta wonder. We've done this same planning cycle forever. Right now I can only influence my little corner of the world."

This is the resource-dominated way to run a business, seen through the eyes of a middle manager for whom the real work of the organization tends to be well understood (she knows what she should be accomplishing), but the ability to manage all the variables is not possible. Susan is trapped in that middle state, between the top of the organization, where the dreams and plans originate, and the innards, where the work products are churned out. She is accountable for but not always capable of achieving what she is tasked to accomplish year after year. The environment in which she functions is a breeding ground for cynicism and mistrust of the aims, even the competence, of the company's leadership.

It might seem that the straightforward solution to Susan's problems is better project planning and management. But in fact her organization has quite an elaborate, sophisticated project management system. The uncontrolled demands simply overrun any attempts at rational planning and resource management.

And it is not just the managers at Susan's level for whom resource domination is an issue.

Barry is the VP in charge of a very healthy line of business in a chemicals company. He has P&L responsibility worldwide. Corporate has been on a cost-cutting mission for years, although they talk the growth game. They have asked for a 20 percent reduction in budget by each line of business this year. Barry knows that his operations, which are focused on their cash-cow business (producing products for the home consumer market), are as lean as he can make them. He knows where the cuts will have to come from. All of those resources are developing applications of his product for the industrial segment—where their growth will come from in the next five years. He boldly told Corporate that they would be sacrificing future growth for current cash flow. Barry's argument was effective, and he was made exempt from this year's cuts.

Fast-forward to the next year. The same request for cuts comes down from Corporate again. This time, Barry cannot escape the cuts. His business never really did get the growth in the industrial segment that he had counted on. The cash-cow consumer business has slipped over the edge into commodity as more competitor products enter the field. Now Corporate looks at its underperforming businesses and asks for more cuts because they are not meeting projected growth and earnings goals. They sell off the "non-core" product lines (incidentally, the ones with greatest future potential). The return to the shareholder has to come from somewhere, they say. This death spiral has in fact been going on for the past ten years. The glory days of this once-thriving business are long gone. It is only a matter of time.

No single manager can change this situation. A resource-dominated organization tends to become self-perpetuating. The planning and budgeting processes focus attention on resources, and the management tracking and reporting systems reinforce the focus on plans versus actual. It all makes perfect sense if the plans are based on organizational realities, such as how much work can be accomplished with the resources available and what kind of work is value-adding. But you can't see that reality if you lack a picture of the value dimension. And you can't produce value if the way to survive is to camouflage the sometimes-dire truth.

## WHY THE RESOURCE DIMENSION PREDOMINATES

There are lots of reasons why the resource dimension rules organizational behavior (and consequently, why it would be so difficult to alter), but here are some of the most powerful:

- The resource dimension is far more tangible than the value dimension. You can see people, materials, facilities—stuff—and have a sense of ownership over it. It's far harder to have a sense of ownership over work you are not doing, or over a horizontal work system. As we said in our definition of process in Chapter 2, a process is a "construct," not a real thing.

- Many managers measure their own achievements and worth in terms of the resources they are given (or view themselves as having earned). And, in fact, managerial positions and related compensation are in large part determined by how many resources are under one's command and how much budget one controls. (Just ask any Compensation and Benefits department what formulas they use.) Career paths for most are defined up through the silo—not across silos. This naturally leads to territory-building. The more resources a manager has, the more important that person is, to himself and to others, and the more salary and benefits he is likely to be rewarded with.

- Much of the organizational apparatus in place to manage and control (that is, the management system) is geared to overseeing the resource dimension (HR, the budgeting and financial systems, capital funding, and management, virtually all of the contributing functions); "management" is virtually defined as management of resources. In fact, the whole chart of accounts is a setup of resource buckets.

- Being able to control resources is an expression of power. It may run contrary to some of the stronger aspects of human nature to maintain a horizontal view of the organization versus a vertical one, if you have any amount of valuable resources within your control. The vertical view is about what is "mine"; the horizontal view is more about what is not mine.

- And what is not mine I cannot control. So I am uncomfortable if you hold me accountable for performance that includes or is impacted by resources that are not mine (such as process performance that crosses functional boundaries). The natural tendency is to insist that those resources report to you as well, if indeed you are to be held accountable. We have heard many a manager insist on those terms for process ownership. This isn't pettiness; it's a logical survival strategy.

- Managers are groomed to be resource managers from the start of their careers and are judged by their ability to manage resources, whether human, financial, or physical. It is, for many, what managers do. The effect is to create organizations in which power games are prevalent and lots of time and energy are spent trying to accrue resources and outmaneuver other managers, who are viewed as competitors—all of which takes attention away from the real business and the real competitors and customers. We will all do what gets us rewarded—and avoid things that will get us fired.

- This way of viewing organizational life has been fixed in place forever. It is "the way it is"; it is organizational culture at its most obdurate. It is perhaps the most natural way of viewing an organization and how it operates. Organizations that are heavily laden with resource-oriented processes, policies, and procedures (an example being where the budgeting process is the single biggest activity of all managers) become incapable of fast adaptation. The resource dimension doesn't just overshadow the value dimension—it obliterates it eventually.

- Some people have a strong need to maintain an "us versus them" outlook. It reinforces their sense of identity and group cohesion, at the expense of the larger but more abstract organization. In his book, *The Need to Have Enemies and Allies*,[1] psychoanalyst Vamik Volkan describes the psychological need of some people for "enemies"; the need can be so overwhelming as to sabotage any efforts to resolve conflicts because of the threat to self-identity. Volkan believes this phenomenon is a fundamental aspect of the human condition, impossible to eradicate but manageable through collaborative techniques such as identifying common ground and building alliances—techniques quite similar to ones you will see applied later in this book in the Belding case.

## THE PERSISTENCE OF FUNCTIONAL SILOS

Where do some of these reasons for resource predominance reveal themselves most clearly? In the structure of organizations into functions (the silos or stovepipes). The resource dimension exists in silos. By "function," we mean more than departments. It includes regions, divisions, even things like teams—anything that constitutes groupings of resources that take on some permanence. Silos reinforce the resource dimension mentality

- To focus on internal concerns
- To become self-perpetuating
- To become territorial
- To ignore the greater good

A lot of managers do recognize the cross-functional view and its value, but it is hard to maintain that view with all of the pressures upon them to manage the resource dimension.

By now it's an old cliché that functional silos exist in organizations, causing the development of myopic little sub-cultures, all busily devoted to their own optimization often at the expense of the larger organization's goals and values. Geary Rummler and Alan Brache wrote about the pernicious effects of functional silos in their 1990 book, *Improving Performance*, and the theme has been recounted in countless other books and articles since then.[2]

What Rummler and Brache pointed out is that the important work of organizations must happen cross-functionally, but the functional silos tend to hoard their resources and resist cooperating across functional lines. They described this contradiction as two views of an organization, illustrated in Figure 3.2: (1) the vertical, which focuses on the structure of resources, formal authority, and chain of command, and (2) the horizontal, which reveals that organizations are actually value-creating systems that convert inputs into outputs by using the

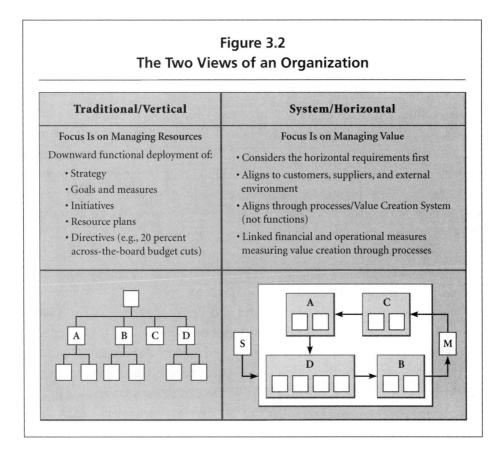

**Figure 3.2**
**The Two Views of an Organization**

| Traditional/Vertical | System/Horizontal |
|---|---|
| Focus Is on Managing Resources | Focus Is on Managing Value |
| Downward functional deployment of:<br>• Strategy<br>• Goals and measures<br>• Initiatives<br>• Resource plans<br>• Directives (e.g., 20 percent across-the-board budget cuts) | • Considers the horizontal requirements first<br>• Aligns to customers, suppliers, and external environment<br>• Aligns through processes/Value Creation System (not functions)<br>• Linked financial and operational measures measuring value creation through processes |

organization's resources across functions. Unfortunately, the vertical view still tends to dominate managerial attention.

So the insight about functional silos is not new. But here's the rub: despite the general acknowledgement of the bad effects of silos, little has been done about them.

In his 2004 book, *The Fiefdom Syndrome*, Robert J. Herbold, a former COO at Microsoft, describes the power of turf protection in stifling creativity, undermining necessary change, and rewarding blind loyalty, the effects of which he saw in his days as a senior executive. "The fiefdom syndrome," Herbold writes, "stems from the inclination of managers and employees to become fixated on their own activities, their own careers, their own territory or turf to the detriment of those around them."[3] What is frustrating to top executives who recognize the bad effects of silos is their own inability to change matters.

It can be mind-boggling to witness the power of functional silos against even the most capable executives. We watched one key client of ours, a senior VP in charge of a critically important product group in a large corporation, try to lasso his executive team and pull them in the same direction. Three team members were heads of product divisions and a fourth was in charge of a components section that supplied the product divisions with parts to sell. For several months in a row, the executive team looked at a steady decline in revenues and profits, which neatly correlated with the predictions of industry watchers that the market was in freefall. No matter, the components chief just kept on building parts and the product divisions just kept on stockpiling inventories, even as the business dried up. Each month the SVP would scream at his staff to stop building inventory, to no avail. They just kept on building, right up to the point at which the entire group almost went out of business and some people were fired. Why such blind behavior? Because each of those product division leaders earned a bonus for building, not for shipping, products. And so did the components chief. For each of them, the horizon ended just outside his door.

Despite his title and status, the SVP did not control the bonus system (which was eventually changed) and did not control all the variables that drove management decisions and behavior. He seemed helpless, despite all his yelling.

That recipe for sub-optimization is also what Susan was describing in her role at mid-management level. The only way she can get her projects done is by juggling the necessarily competing demands of different functional departments and by successfully managing projects across organizational lines. When there is a lack of cooperation about the priorities among her customers (and there is almost always a lack of cooperation), she cannot succeed at pleasing anyone. What she sees time and again is a pretense at cooperation and coordination while the functional department heads put all their efforts into getting their own projects done, regardless of what anyone else might want and whether resources are actually available.

Even when managers become frustrated with the fixation on the resource dimension, there is little they can do about it. It is impossible to change matters from the bottom up because the resource dimension is so grounded in organizational policy, practices, and culture. This goes a long way toward explaining the sense of helplessness that some managers express when considering whether anything can be changed in their organizations—so much appears fixed in place and, to keep their own jobs, they must concentrate on demonstrating their ability to manage the resource dimension.

The frustration of those, like Susan and Barry, who are required to work across the organization demonstrates the difficulty of trying to maintain a value-centered, cross-functional view. IT is often trying to implement technology that will serve more than one fiefdom, but it is reduced to getting the requirements from each function and then creating a design that serves the sum of all functions—instead of providing a solution that efficiently supports value creation.

The fixation on resources and tendencies of functional silos to hoard resources and focus on their own glory are made possible in part because the value dimension is so invisible. When there is no common understanding of and commitment to the work that must be performed to produce value, there is no compelling reason to look above one's own close interests. Managers spend most of their time and energies on things related to the resource dimension (staffing, budgeting, purchasing, etc.), leaving less time for understanding or designing and managing the value dimension.

The dependency on resource-fixated management to manage the design and execution of work in organizations has been and will continue to be a major impediment to business and enterprise success. A common refrain we hear these days from frustrated individuals in underperforming organizations is, "You don't understand: we are a VERY siloed organization." In our view, the markets most organizations exist in are becoming more dynamic and turbulent, not less. As a result, there is a need for a different model for managing the performance of organizations.

So once again, making the value dimension visible is one of the most necessary acts of management, serving as a potential gateway to reducing the silo mentality in an organization.

In Chapter 4 we begin to explain that model, using an extended example.

# Managerial Practices in a One-Dimensional Organization

chapter
FOUR

W̲e are not so naïve as to suggest that in this day and age any organization has failed to recognize the existence of the value dimension at some
level. The issue is the failure to evolve the management system in such a way as
to capitalize on that recognition of value. Instead, despite efforts to define and
improve processes or value streams, management usually defaults to resource
management. Managers end up trying to manage value though the resource
dimension—a rather misguided notion, one that prevents them from proactively
recognizing new opportunities to enhance value and limits their ability to align
in response to a business challenge.

In this chapter we will walk through a case example that illustrates how a
resource-fixated organization tends to be led. In later chapters we show how it
would be different if top management utilized a balanced approach to the two
dimensions. The purpose of the case is to illustrate the features and benefits of
two-dimensional management with a close-up view of managerial practices in a
fictitious company called Belding Engineering Corp.

Our objectives are to

- Demonstrate that there are substantial differences between the two approaches
to management

- Convince you that the two-dimensional approach is vastly superior to the resource-fixated approach
- Provide you with enough specifics that the differences are not theoretical but practical, attainable, and repeatable

Let's start with a quick overview of what management at Belding looked liked before it underwent some major changes.

## INTRODUCTION TO BELDING

In business for ten years, Belding invents, designs, manufactures, and sells equipment that facilitates internal communications for organizations. It started with one highly successful electronic product and has added an additional product every three years, for a total of three. Two new products are scheduled for introduction next year. Belding is a wholly owned subsidiary of a large holding company we will call "Corporate." However, Belding does have all the functional departments you would normally see in a stand-alone company.

The vertical organization is shown in Figure 4.1. It represents the resource dimension of Belding.

Some of the company's current issues include the following:

- Revenues continue to grow, but for the past two years, growth has been at a rate less than the overall growth of the industry.
- Profits have been in serious decline for the past three years. This reduced profitability has begun to hamper plans for future expansion.
- Customer complaints are on the rise, primarily due to missing promised delivery dates and products not meeting customer specifications.
- General turnover has been rising for the past two years. Several key middle managers have left in the past twelve months.

## CURRENT PERFORMANCE PLANNING SYSTEM

Performance planning consists of an annual planning process, accomplished over a four-month period. The major steps are

1. Belding's CEO, Lindsay Maxwell, receives earnings guidelines and expectations from Corporate.

## Figure 4.1
## The Belding Engineering Corporate Structure

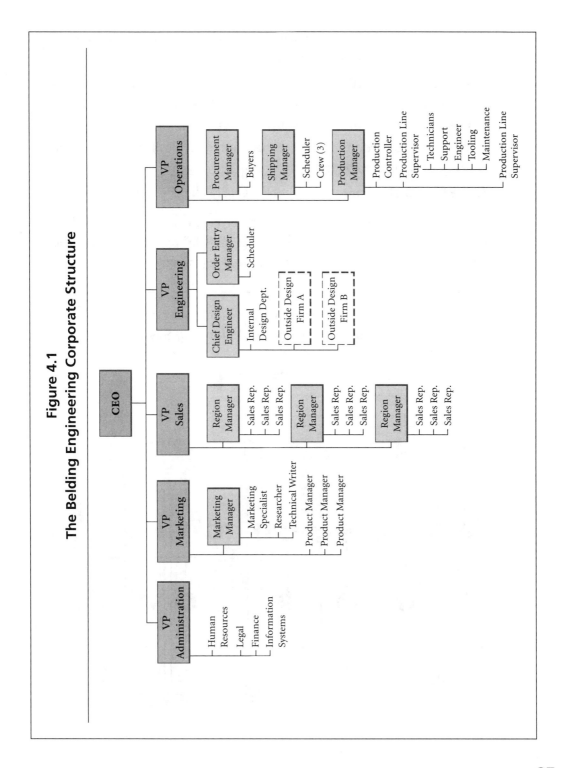

2. Maxwell and the Director of Finance meet individually with VPs to discuss operating and budget goals for each function for the next year.

3. VPs and their functions prepare draft budgets for the next fiscal year (total and by month). These proposed budgets are sent to the Director of Finance, who consolidates them into a draft Belding budget.

4. The CEO and Director of Finance then meet individually with each VP to bring each proposed budget "into line."

5. The Finance Department publishes the final Belding budget.

The current planning system is illustrated in Figure 4.2, which shows how Belding thinks of planning as being about vertical "silo" resource planning and allocation instead of horizontal process performance planning.

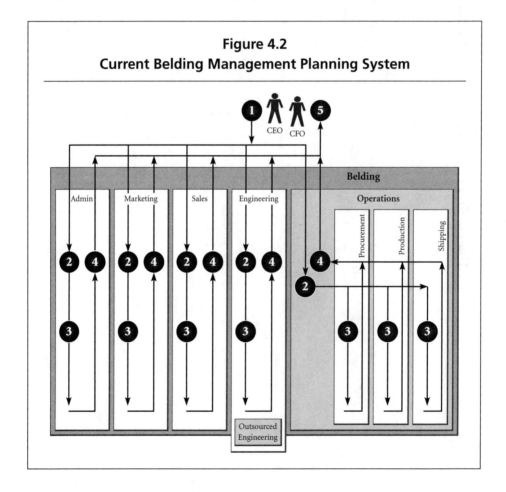

**Figure 4.2**
**Current Belding Management Planning System**

In a typical resource-fixated organization like Belding, performance planning is a straightforward matter of vertical alignment. Enterprise goals are set at the top and converted into functional goals. Functional goals are then elaborated in plans and budgets and then cascaded down to sub-functions. These sub-function goals then become the basis for setting performance objectives for individuals. During the course of the performance year, at established intervals each management level evaluates planned versus actual and takes action to close gaps.

There are several shortcomings with this approach, which all stem from the lack of visibility of the value dimension and the cross-functional processes that produce value:

- The approach assumes work occurs inside buckets of functions and jobs, failing to recognize the interdependence of work between jobs and functions.

- Performance goals are pinned down to single areas or individuals for the purpose of defining accountability, which fails to recognize that most significant work is necessarily linked across jobs and functions to create and deliver a product/service that customers value. These measures of work within each bucket tend to drive sub-optimization of total organizational performance.

- This approach also tends not to distinguish between value-adding work and activities. The focus is on what individual performers spend their time doing but not necessarily on whether their performance is of value to organizational objectives and customer needs.

## CURRENT PERFORMANCE MANAGEMENT SYSTEM

Performance management at Belding consists of the following:

1. Maxwell holds a monthly Operations Review with the VPs and a quarterly one-day "retreat."

2. The Ops Review agenda includes a review of company budget, sales performance, and shipments. Gaps between planned and actual performance are discussed, along with possible corrective and preventive actions.

3. Follow-up meetings are held with individual VPs as appropriate to pursue follow-up actions.

The function performance measures at the monthly Operations Review are summarized in Table 4.1. As you can see, what is being measured is primarily

**Table 4.1**
**Function Performance Metrics**

| | |
|---|---|
| **Finance** | Administration budget (Plan/Actual) |
| **Marketing** | Marketing budget (Plan/Actual) |
| **Sales** | Revenues (Plan/Actual);<br>Sales budget (Plan/Actual) |
| **Engineering** | New product development projects (Plan/Actual);<br>Engineering budget (Plan/Actual) |
| **Operations** | Units shipped (Plan/Actual);<br>Cost per unit shipped (Plan/Actual);<br>Operations budget (Plan/Actual) |
| **Procurement** | Materials costs per unit shipped (Plan/Actual);<br>Procurement budget (Plan/Actual) |
| **Production** | Production cost per unit shipped (Plan/Actual);<br>Production budget (Plan/Actual) |
| **Shipping** | Shipping cost per unit shipped (Plan/Actual);<br>Shipping budget (Plan/Actual) |
| **IT** | Number of projects (Plan/Actual);<br>Project budgets (Plan/Actual) |

resource consumption (dollars, materials, operating costs). Aside from the number of New Product Development projects and number of units shipped, there is little to show what value the company is producing for its market. That myopia, of course, can play havoc with managerial decision making when times get tough, which is happening at Belding.

Now let's follow the actions of Belding's management team as a wave of bad news hits the company, and you will see how a resource-oriented management system tends to function.

## Scenario 1

At the quarterly management offsite meeting, Sales reported that customer complaints about late deliveries had "skyrocketed." To make matters worse, the VP of

Operations announced that shipping costs had gotten "out of control" and there were also alarming jumps in materials costs and labor overtime. Alarmed by this news (but with no data at hand), the management team decided on the following actions:

- A materials task force was initiated to look into the cause of escalating materials costs.

- A quality awareness campaign was initiated to determine the best way to convey a sense of responsibility for quality to the Belding workforce.

- The VP of Operations called a "Come to Jesus" meeting with his managers and:

  - Ordered a stop to all overtime unless he personally approved it

  - Set a limit on monthly shipping charges, using the same period from last year as the "benchmark"

These actions were initiated with a great show of determination. Managers were for a time everywhere, especially in the quality campaign, giving speeches about "Job One" and encouraging everyone to "think quality."

Now, going forward about three months, here's what resulted from the management actions:

- The materials task force generated a report outlining all the areas where materials costs are, or potentially could be, an issue. They recommended a number of general actions ("We should . . .") for controlling costs; but without good data, they actually had not pinpointed the cause of the current problem.

- The quality awareness campaign went into a stall when some leaders began to argue that training was necessary because few members of the workforce were aware of the principle that you cannot inspect quality into the product or that there were a number of Japanese quality improvement tools and approaches that might be helpful. A task force then spent a couple of months interviewing possible training vendors. They made their pick and presented it to CEO Maxwell, who tabled the proposal due to a lack of funds.

- In Operations, production jobs started to back up because labor demand exceeded supply. An expeditor system had to be put into place to see that the jobs of key customers were at least placed at the "head of the line." Meanwhile, due to the decision to limit shipping charges, late deliveries skyrocketed, increasing customer complaints even more. After five weeks of this, the VP of Operations reversed his decision.

## Our Diagnosis

In this scenario, the management team is reacting to bad news in a not uncommon riot of action. They don't know what is wrong, so they do a lot of different things, hoping they will either hit on something successful or, even more voodoo-like, that the actions will add up to some kind of "comprehensive solution." The mantra of "Just do it!" and its variant, "Do something even if it's wrong," has taken hold in many management suites, where it has become more important to be seen as taking action than to apply a fact-based, and thoroughly designed, solution.

If we pick apart each of the individual actions, they were all flawed and all based on assumptions imbedded in the resource dimension:

- The materials task force had no real, solid data and no way to objectively analyze what was causing the cost increases, so they mucked around for a time hoping to be seen as doing a thorough job, then threw in the towel and wrote a report. Without a clear view of how costs are accumulated during the work processes, what you are stuck with is "cost buckets," which sum up costs into usually pretty arbitrary categories. Without a value dimension view of the work, this is mostly just adding of costs, not analysis.

- The quality campaign, like most rhetoric in fad-weary corporations these days, was doomed from the start. It had no clear purpose other than to "rally the troops" (meaning make them suspicious of management's motives) and, once again, focused on the resource dimension—this time the "people." Once it was realized that some money would have to be spent to put real tools behind the rhetoric, the campaign vanished. (Nothing in American business has become more debased than the line, "People are our most important asset.")

- The seesawing actions inside Operations (no overtime, work backing up, expediting, even worse production, and reversal of the decision) demonstrated to one and all that nobody really understood the work system in place and what the effects of pushing down on one lever (overtime) would be on other parts of that system. Without a clear view of the value dimension, the variables of an organization's performance system can be viewed as just a bunch of free-floating elements that can be safely fiddled with, and improvement is a matter of triggering simple one-to-one cause-effect reactions.

## Scenario 2

The company's profit-and-loss statement has recorded a steady and significant increase in materials costs while revenues have remained flat. At the monthly management meeting, Maxwell tells the VP of Operations to "get a handle" on the materials problem.

Following the meeting, the VP of Operations asked the Procurement Manager to take action to reduce materials costs. In turn, the Procurement Manager decided to target the cost-of-parts inventory. Historically, parts with long lead times were procured and placed in inventory based on the quarterly sales forecast. Since the forecast does not specify the product mix, Procurement assumes a mix based on annual sales plan percentages, a practice that goes back to the company's beginning.

This time the Procurement Manager decided to adjust the forecast order volume downward for parts with long lead times, reasoning that this was a root cause of inventory costs' being tied up the longest, and based on his first-hand knowledge of how far off the forecast the actual orders have been in recent months.

For a time, this seemed to work. The P&L reflected lower materials costs while revenues remained steady. But then in Month 3, revenues dropped because shipments were delayed as some orders had to wait for parts not in inventory. Procurement then had to readjust inventory levels for long lead times, and expedited procurement was needed to clear the production backlog, increasing materials costs above the level that triggered the CEO's alarm to begin with.

## Our Diagnosis

Once again, there is a lack of understanding of the variables that affect organizational performance. What we see here, though, is the hellish reality of many middle managers tasked to solve a problem with the means within their control, but the actions they take can have consequences well outside their own areas. Without understanding what affects what, the Procurement Manager takes an action in panic that causes a chain of negative events, which in this case comes back to bite him.

## Scenario 3

At Belding's annual planning meeting, the management team determined that a major contributor to its loss of market share was the eighteen to twenty-four months it took to get new products to market (especially given that some newer competitors were cranking out new products in half that time).

Wanting to get a handle on this new products situation, CEO Maxwell asked that the process be defined. People from the Corporate Performance Department helped draw a cross-functional process map (that is, a "swimlane" chart), as shown in Figure 4.3.

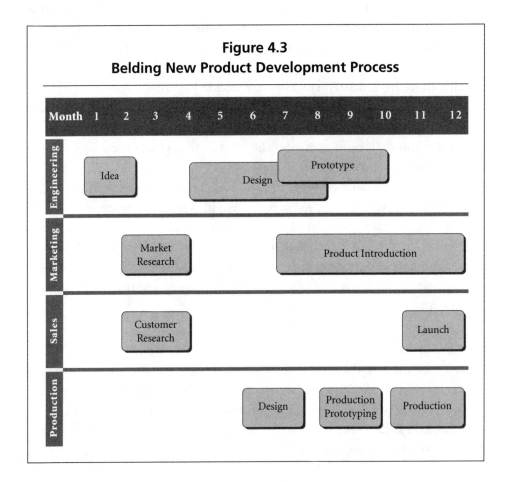

**Figure 4.3**
**Belding New Product Development Process**

With this picture in hand, Maxwell then sat down with each VP and established (sometimes with rather forceful "negotiation") a set of goals and the time
targets for each (Table 4.2).

Then what happened? Let's take the functional areas one at a time:

- Engineering did accomplish the design of the next new product in four
  months as planned, but the idea-gathering phase took longer than expected
  (it was kind of chaotic), and prototyping was greatly underestimated because
  the design had to be redone during that phase.

- In Marketing, research took three months instead of two. Product introduction did happen in four months as planned, but it was not very effective because Marketing could not get technical specs from Engineering
  in time.

- In Sales, customer research simply didn't happen (they weren't sure what they
  were supposed to do) so Marketing didn't get any customer data. And launch
  took four months instead of two because Sales could not get the information
  from Engineering and Marketing for two months.

## Table 4.2
## New Product Development Function Goals

| Function | Plan (in Months) | |
| --- | --- | --- |
| Engineering | Idea | 2 |
| | Design | 4 |
| | Prototype | 3 |
| Marketing | Market research | 2 |
| | Product introduction | 4 |
| Sales | Customer research | 2 |
| | Launch | 2 |
| Production | Design | 2 |
| | Production prototyping | 2 |
| | Production | 2 |

**TOTAL ELAPSED TIME: 12 MONTHS**

- In Production, design did not happen. Engineering did not involve Production in the design phase because they did not want to take the charge for Production people eating up Engineering time against their budget. Production prototyping took five months instead of two because Production had to design much of their production process "on the fly," since they were not involved in the product design. Production was also twice as long as expected because of delays in getting critical parts due to redesigns during the prototyping phase. The actuals are shown in Table 4.3.

## Our Diagnosis

First, there was the CEO, who appropriated a tool without understanding its value. A swimlane chart of a business process is potentially extremely useful for understanding how a given process works, how participants must interact with each other to accomplish the work and improve such a process in a systematic, rational way. But in this case it was employed simply to bludgeon the VPs into accepting the goals Maxwell wanted, even if they were unrealistic.

### Table 4.3
### New Product Development Function Goals vs. Actual Results

| Function | Plan (in Months) | | Actual |
|---|---|---|---|
| Engineering | Idea | 2 | 3 |
| | Design | 4 | 4 |
| | Prototype | 3 | 6 |
| Marketing | Market research | 2 | 3 |
| | Product introduction | 4 | 4 |
| Sales | Customer research | 2 | 0 |
| | Launch | 2 | 4 |
| Production | Design | 2 | 0 |
| | Production prototyping | 2 | 5 |
| | Production | 2 | 4 |

**TOTAL ELAPSED TIME: 19 MONTHS**

Then there were the heads of the functional areas, each fixated on his or her own turf. Their unwillingness to collaborate damaged the process at every stage. A primary objective in cross-functional process improvement is to improve collaboration across the participating organizations, but that does not happen by diktat or exhortation. It requires a close-up understanding of how the process works today and a genuine agreement to improve its performance across all functions. Simple resistance can stymie good intentions.

This is a classic example of an attempt to manage the value dimension through the resource dimension. We have seen countless attempts at process improvement that have gone this route: Leaders recognize the importance of the value dimension and launch the effort to make it visible. At this point: things often go wrong. Having defined the cross-functional process and all of its flaws, they take a divide-and-conquer approach to designing and implementing the solutions within their respective functional silos. "Okay, I get it—now leave me alone to go fix it back at home." Even in cases where they have collaborated on the fixes, they then retreat back to their old way of managing—resource management. They tend not to recognize the need to manage cross-functionally this now-visible value-creating process. In the rare case when a process management system is installed, it is not integrated with the resource management system. In either case, the improvement in process performance is not sustainable and quickly succumbs to functional sub-optimization or some other change in the business environment for which it has no capability to adapt quickly and across the silos.

## Scenario 4

This year's budget was finalized during Q4 of last year, after much discussion about strategy and how the functional areas were supposed to support that strategy. However, during January and February, it became clear that assumptions about revenues were overly optimistic.

In March, all functions were ordered to cut their budgets by 10 percent for the remainder of the year. In reaction, each function decided on its own which activities, programs, and initiatives it would delete in order to reach the 10 percent reduction in budget. Meanwhile, Corporate reissued the annual budget reflecting the 10 percent across-the-board cut in planned expenditures for the remaining three quarters.

Here are the decisions of the individual functions and the impact on Belding of those actions:

- Finance held up its introduction of the new Oracle system, which served to continue the lack of key management information available in Engineering and Production.

- Engineering did not implement a planned "partnership" program with the external design organizations it uses to develop critical component designs. The result is that those external companies continue to misunderstand or fail to achieve Belding's exacting design standards.

- Sales cut back on hiring new sales reps. Turnover for the remainder of the year resulted in several unfilled sales territories for up to six months. This action caused lost sales but, even more important, opened the door to greater competition in those territories where Belding's presence virtually disappeared. Sales also eliminated training for the new sales reps it had already hired, which meant those reps were less technically competent and took longer to learn the job.

- In Procurement, the supplier certification program was put on hold, which meant that incoming materials were still highly variable and overly costly. Procurement also held up its inventory optimization program, so materials shortages continue to plague Production.

- In Production, a hold on capital expenditures to support new products was initiated. As a result, a new product was put on hold in the production proto-typing stages because of lack of production capacity.

- And finally in Shipping, plans for new automation were put on hold. These changes would have sped up packaging time and addressed some costly problems with in-transit damage, but those problems simply continued, resulting in customer complaints and expensive on-site repairs.

## Our Diagnosis

Is such a nightmarish scenario hard to believe? Not really. This is the virtually inevitable result of two very common management behaviors. One is across-the-board cost-cutting. It's done all the time. It seems to come partly from the bizarre notion that because the managers of the functions where costs must be reduced are "owners" of those functions, it would be unseemly and dictatorial for the CEO to make discriminations; therefore, it is easier to treat all departments as if they are equals and make the cuts the same everywhere. It is also this hands-off policy that led Maxwell to let the functions decide for themselves exactly how they should reduce expenses.

The other reason, however, is because making appropriate budget cuts would take so much effort and require so much real, detailed knowledge of how the business system works that it is simply easier to hit all areas with the same ax. Is this management? More like abdication. The systemic effects of some of the reductions (such as failing to hire more sales reps) are not seen or understood for months, but the impacts are potentially strategic. Yet who decided to stop hiring reps? The Sales VP—alone and for good reasons if you were sitting in that chair. But from a company viewpoint the effect turns out to be catastrophic.

## Scenario 5

At the last quarterly offsite meeting, the VP of Administration made a presentation about the number of improvement initiatives currently under way within Belding. As examples of the issue, the VP cited the following:

1. There were six projects initiated by Corporate, including studies of accounting practices, executive compensation, and overtime policies.

2. There were several projects initiated within Belding, including

   - Improving the "spirit of innovation"
   - Changing the corporate culture to make employees less risk averse
   - Improving earnings forecasting

3. There were twenty projects mandated by various government agencies.

4. Within various Belding functional areas, there were countless improvement projects, including twelve Six Sigma efforts in Operations and metrics development programs in Engineering and Shipping.

The VP of Administration then pointed out that this list did not even include the continual product-related changes being made to "stay in business." A quick ballpark estimate was that these projects were consuming as much as 30 percent of all management time annually.

This presentation created discussion but no action, as a quick flutter of reasons were given for the importance of just about every improvement effort. The consequence of this inaction was that, far from the removal of any initiatives, one or two continued to be started up per month, adding more reasons for the overworked, burned-out, cynical attitudes of managers and employees alike.

## Our Diagnosis

In a company dominated by functional silos, setting priorities for initiatives can be virtually impossible. Everybody has his or her own preferences, and without an overriding interest in funding only those projects that benefit the entire company (which would be projects that increase value creation capability), each function is free to focus wherever it wishes. Sometimes initiatives are kept quiet, so people in other areas don't even know the kinds of resources that are being expended. Employees are yanked in a dozen directions; the most competent employees are tasked to be on as many different initiatives as possible; and the entire enterprise is getting little out of all the activity.

## Scenario 6

The biggest initiative of all at Belding was an attempt to overhaul its legacy systems. Everyone in the company was unhappy with the antiquated order management system that contributed to late and inaccurate customer shipments. There were also numerous complaints about the database that underpinned Belding's accounting and financial management processes. An IT vendor was brought in to look at these systems, and, at considerable expense, the vendor instead developed a "vision" of the entire technology platform that would "transform" Belding's future. CEO Maxwell and staff became very excited about the vision and funded a broad-based project to update all of Belding's IT systems. While the CIO supported this plan, several key people in IT quit in protest, feeling their opinions had been ignored in favor of the vendor's.

Then ensued months of project work led by the vendor but consuming many hours of employee time. In the meantime, the vendor held a cherished position at the management table, giving highly polished updates at every monthly meeting and performing dazzling technology demos at several quarterly offsite meetings. Then, after eighteen months, the first pieces of software were piloted and bombed miserably. The frantic vendor made some changes in staffing and revamped the offending software, then ran another trial. The results were no better. Now questions cropped up about how much the vendor was owed since his product was defective.

In an emergency offsite, the management team concluded that it had spent $37 million on the IT transformation thus far and had nothing to show for it. Not wanting word to reach the street about this disaster, they decided to quietly pay off the vendor and continue the project with internal resources. After another hard slog of six months, the internal IT staff threw up their hands and the transformation project was stopped altogether.

## Our Diagnosis

This unfortunate scenario is commonplace. In the resource dimension, technology may be more poorly managed than any other resource. Managers who are not technology experts themselves are often all too willing to let the IT specialists lead them down shining pathways to disaster. There are many stories about the failures of IT at a cost of hundreds of millions of dollars at a clip. But we know about these incidents only because they took place inside public agencies. Most IT blunders go unreported. Senior executives often do all they can to prevent the story from leaking to the outside world because they are panicked at the possibility their stock will take a hit. (And, you know, it probably would. We know of a company that did report a giant IT fiasco and its stock price plunged 50 percent.)

What Belding management did not do here was *lead* the technology effort; instead, it allowed experts too much autonomy until it was too late. We also suspect that management was lax in specifying exactly what it did want from this "transformation"—and a lack of specifics just opens the door to a fixation on technology for its own sake, instead of focusing on the value that is supposed to be delivered or enhanced with this project.

## The Final Scenario

It was inevitable. At the last Belding offsite, the Corporate liaison announced that Corporate was "fed up" with Belding's consistent underperformance, which had resulted in Corporate's missing its earnings projections. On Wall Street, analysts were recommending "hold" or "sell." This problem was serious enough that Corporate now considered "accuracy of earnings projections" as counting for 60 percent of the bonus for CEO Maxwell.

After this disastrous confrontation, Maxwell formed a task force of vice presidents to make a recommendation on how to make earnings projections more reliable. The task force met several times during the quarter but had no recommendations to make at the second quarter offsite meeting, when Belding once again missed its earnings projection.

At the end of the second quarter, CEO Maxwell was shown the door. S.K. Owens was then brought in to turn Belding Engineering Corporation around.

## PERFORMANCE MANAGEMENT MODEL

To summarize what is going on at Belding, here is a model of management that we use when assessing, designing, or improving management systems. The model, shown in Figure 4.4, consists of three components:

1. **Performance Planned**—Goals and plans are set and communicated to the performer.

2. **Performance Executed**—The "performer" (an individual, an enabling technology, or a combination of these) delivers the desired performance prescribed in the goals and plans.

3. **Performance Managed**—As performers do their assigned work, they are supported with training, tools, materials, and anything else required. Actual performance is monitored against the goals and plans, and, if a negative deviation is detected, it is analyzed and then followed up with appropriate action to get performance back on track.

In addition to providing goals and plans to Performance Executed, the Performance Planned component also makes available the necessary resources (human, financial, and other) to support goal achievement. This is the appropriate deployment of the resource dimension, as driven by value-creation goals.

The resources (whether people, technology, or a combination) that do the work are always a very visible component of this fundamental performance system, which is why resource management gets such attention. However, the Performance Planned and Performance Managed components tend to be less visible. But this combination (the Performance Planned and Managed system) is the mechanism whereby the organization is both an effective value-creating system and an adaptive learning system.

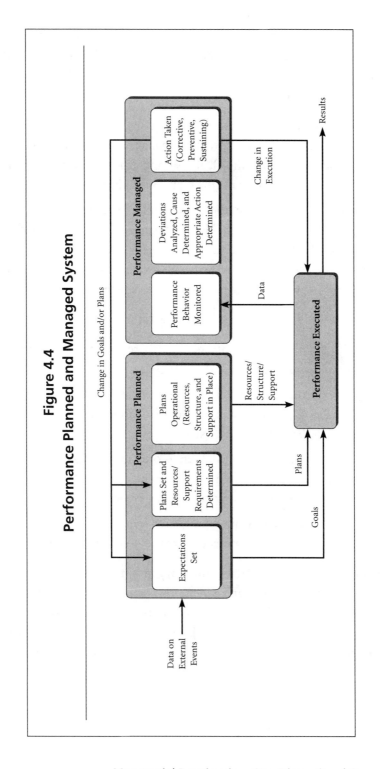

**Figure 4.4**
**Performance Planned and Managed System**

Management forms the critical central cortex of the organizational system. Management is the "intelligence" that keeps the system in balance and the organization on track.

The critical actions of management are

1. Alignment of the organization's goals, strategies, and priorities with the reality of the super-system (that is, management of the **adaptive system** through strategy formulation), and setting expectations for all components of the organizational system (the planning component)

2. Effective and efficient operation of the internal processing system to meet customer and financial stakeholder needs (that is, management of the **processing system** through value creation management), closing any gaps between performance expectations and actual performance (the management component), and supporting performers as they execute the assigned work

Instead, at Belding, what is happening now is the following:

1. There is no concept of an internal Value Creation System and the need to manage value-adding work and resources.

2. Within Performance Planned, there is vertical deployment of goals within functional stovepipes, an almost exclusive emphasis on resource management, and no Value Creation System or process goals.

3. Within Performance Managed, there is only functional area and individual performance monitoring and management, no cost data by product, and no horizontal process performance management.

4. There is unmanaged "white space" between functions and between the sub-systems of Product Launched, Product Sold, and Product Delivered.

This concludes the first part of our story about Belding. In the next chapters we lay out a view of management that integrates the value dimension with the resource dimension for a balanced approach to decision making that was entirely absent from CEO Maxwell's performance. Then we will return to Belding Engineering to see how it can be led differently, with far better results.

# PART TWO

# The CEO's Agenda

In Part Two we use the Belding case to describe an approach to management that ensures a proper balance of the value and resource dimensions. A new CEO, S.K. Owens, embarks on a quest to bring Belding back to performance excellence, and we follow him as he crafts and executes an agenda to achieve that objective.

The chapters in this section are organized according to the steps that Owens takes to bring about a revival of Belding's fortunes. We follow him as he learns about the problems facing Belding, develops a plan of action, and begins the initial efforts to introduce a different way of thinking about and managing the business. We continue to watch as he builds on his initial success and creates a complete management system for addressing the flaws in the current organization and sustaining a new way of managing.

Our purpose is to provide a concrete example of how a senior executive can go about introducing two-dimension management in a practical manner, a few steps at a time and bringing along his team. While not every detail of Owens' story will fit every situation, his approach is typical of what it takes to rethink and rebuild an organization for effective 3-D performance.

# chapter FIVE

# Two-Dimension Management

M anaging in a way that allows us to bust through the impenetrable functional silos and begin to see and make the important tradeoffs that bring the resource and value dimensions into optimal balance is not just a tweaking of the existing organization management system. It is a fundamental re-think of the act of management. It challenges the paradigms that every manager has been taught.

In this chapter we outline an approach to management that balances the value and resource dimensions. By providing a means of making the necessary tradeoff decisions that such an ongoing balancing act requires, this approach breaks down the walls around functional silos and reduces their negative effects on organizational performance.

We track S.K. Owens as he begins a turnaround of Belding and derives a method for installing a two-dimension management system. Owens has been chosen because he has a reputation within Corporate for salvaging poorly operating organizations. His approach to addressing Belding's problems is as important as the end result of having a balanced management system, because he has to deal with a host of obstacles that threaten to derail his effort at every turn. So we will watch how he uses his experience with organization revitalization.

## THE CEO'S AGENDA

In his first weeks on the job, Owens does the usual routine of a new leader. He takes stock of the situation by holding talks with his senior leadership team members, with various mid-level managers, with customers and suppliers, with a number of identified "opinion-makers," and with random employees. He comes away both sobered by the challenges and convinced he can lead Belding to success.

He is sitting at his desk, turning over in his mind what he has learned, gradually formulating his approach. An advocate of simple lists, he first jots down what he views as the major problems. That list is shown in Figure 5.1.

To address Belding's managerial deficiencies, a new management system must be put in place, at whose foundation is the recognition that both the value and resource dimensions must be defined and optimized. Based on his experiences with other organizations, Owens was convinced that he needed to take a strong, commanding role in directing this transformation. It would take a kind of "visionary dictatorship" on his part to drive the organization forward, or it would just be human nature to slide backward to resource-dominated behaviors.

Expecting people to quickly become open and willing to collaborate, share resources and objectives, and admit mistakes would not be "natural." It took years to inculcate the culture he saw at Belding. So it would require very strong leadership

---

**Figure 5.1**
**Owens' List of Major Problems at Belding**

*Problems*

1. Heavily stovepiped; nobody sees the whole business.
2. Senior Leaders are not a team.
3. They haven't seen any other way to manage.
4. Lack of good information.
5. Fixation on cost control, resource management.
6. Value creation system invisible.
7. Everybody trying to solve problems in their own areas.

---

until the vision was systematized. Too many managers put in something and expect quick financial returns; Owens knew he would have to be persistent.

Also, before putting in anything new, Owens would also have to make visible the value dimension. If he tried to simply talk about the concept, most people wouldn't understand. If he talked too much without accomplishing anything, people would get annoyed and turned off. So he would have to use techniques for educating the Belding employees about two-dimension management that were non-theoretical but instead practical and concrete and hands-on: learning while doing.

So now Owens creates a list of the steps he decides are necessary to implement this new way of running the business (Figure 5.2).

He fiddles with the sequence for a while and then concludes that some of the initial steps are concurrent and quite possibly would be accomplished in stages. But eventually he is satisfied that he has a starting point.

## DEFINE THE NEED FOR ACTION

Having accomplished with due diligence his interviews and examination of company data, Owens knew that the staff of Belding was quite well aware of the company's deep trouble. His very presence signaled that a major redirection was about to happen, and the sense of impending loss was everywhere.

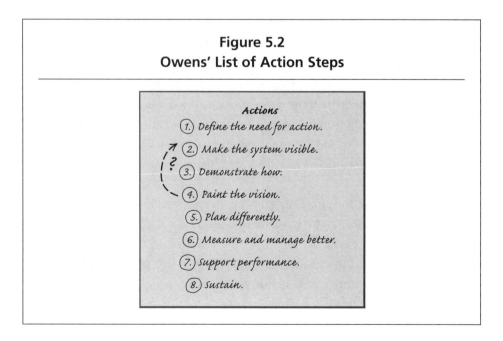

**Figure 5.2**
**Owens' List of Action Steps**

*Actions*
1. Define the need for action.
2. Make the system visible.
3. Demonstrate how.
4. Paint the vision.
5. Plan differently.
6. Measure and manage better.
7. Support performance.
8. Sustain.

It was not a matter of gathering more data so much as mustering a reasonable level of commitment to making a change, reducing that sense of dread enough to keep people from simply freezing in place or starting to leave, and, frankly, selling himself as a responsible, capable, level-headed leader who had the company's long-term interests in mind rather than being a head-chopper.

So Owens organized what he called a "sensing" session to get input and ideas about improving the organization. His idea was based on the "work-out" sessions made famous by Jack Welch at GE, or what others have called "big room" sessions. The notion is to gather together everyone in an organization (either literally everyone, if possible, or in some logical groupings, such as by business unit) and ask them to advise top management. Owens and his senior leaders were there along with every available employee who could be spared just short of shutting down the business for two days.

Owens introduced the session, described its purpose, described his role and that of his senior leaders (which was mostly to ask questions and listen), and then proposed an agenda intended to find answers to two questions:

1. What is broken and needs to be fixed?

2. How would you fix those things?

Owens used facilitators to lead small groups as he wandered around listening and occasionally asking a question or posing a possible idea. But mostly he watched the behavior of executives, managers, and employees, gauging their understanding, readiness for change, and ability to lead.

At the end of the session, when all the ideas had been presented, Owens closed simply by stating that the problems identified were real, needed to be fixed, would be fixed, would require changes in organization and personal behavior, and that he would personally come to various people with requests for commitment. At this point he asked for a general commitment from every person in the room.

Owens then made the first tiny step on the approach he intended to take when he stated that one of the fundamental problems at Belding was "a lack of agreement about the business: how it operates, how it should operate, what to fix, what to keep. You can see that from the big pile of problems and ideas you churned out. It sometimes sounded like you work in entirely different organizations." That got some heads nodding. "You can't fix things together if you don't understand them the same way . . . if you can't see them the same way. So we need to start by making 'it' more visible, that is, the business. What the business is, and how it needs to operate. That's what you'll be hearing more about in coming weeks. That's what I'll be coming to some of you for help with—making this business visible."

In the next several chapters, we continue following Owens as he leads the Belding organization through his agenda. We will keep the description of his actions at a general level, but for those who want the details, in Part Three of this book we have compiled the completed versions of all the templates and tools Owens applies to Belding.

# Making the System Visible

O wens' first challenge is making the value dimension visible so it can be designed and linked to resources, which then allows the two dimensions to be managed in concert. There are three major contributors to the invisibility of the value dimension:

- Relatively few people in any business have a full view of work beyond their functional walls. With such a restricted view of work, the cost of work is more visible than its value. Since few have a clear view of the final result of work and the cross-functional chain of work required to achieve the final objective, work is seen mostly as cost.

- There is little perceived need to understand and manage the cross-functional chain of work that produces valued products and services. Few have been tipped to the fact that the Value Creation System of a business can and should be managed. The management discussion of the past twenty years has been about value propositions, value chains, and value streams; nowhere has anyone talked about *managing* value creation.

- There has been no framework, methodology, or tools available to help business managers get their heads around the complexity of the work required to develop, market, and deliver products and services.

The starting point to articulating the value dimension is to understand that a business is a system to produce value—a Value Machine. When we start with this perspective of a business, we arrive at a very different place than if we start with the traditional resource view of an organization.

As explained in Chapter 1, the basic premise is that a business organization is a system that exists to produce value to customers in the form of products or services, and to financial stakeholders in the form of a return on their investment. A business must first consistently meet the needs of customers before it can consistently meet the needs of investors. The reverse order does not work, and trying to make it work has ensured the demise of quite a few organizations. Unfortunately, the tendency to see organizations largely in terms of the resource dimension has been fostered in particular by investors, who tend to focus on managing resources as the surest way to provide a return to financial stakeholders.

The alternative when looking inside a business to see how it works is to focus not on the organization chart but on the internal system of critical processes that must work together to provide value:

- The Value Creation System, representing the work that directly produces the products and services of the enterprise or business
- Contributing processing sub-systems, such as those hosted by HR, IT, and Finance, which support the Value Creation System
- The management system, which represents the managerial tasks required to keep the enterprise aligned externally and internally

Thus the design of an organization's process architecture (that is, the structure of all the key processes in an organization), rather than single processes, is the key to effective, sustainable organizational performance. This system of processes within Belding is what Owens knew he had to make visible so that his language about "value creation," the "three dimensions," and the "organization as a system" would make sense instead of sounding theoretical.

## THE VALUE CREATION HIERARCHY

The model that Owens intends to use to create this understanding is what we call the "Value Creation Hierarchy." As the name implies, this is a multi-level view of the work system of an organization, which combines the value and resource dimensions. We showed some of this model in Chapter 2 when describing the value dimension. But now we put both a "top" and a "bottom" on that model. Figure 6.1 shows this five-level model.

# Figure 6.1
## The Value Creation Hierarchy

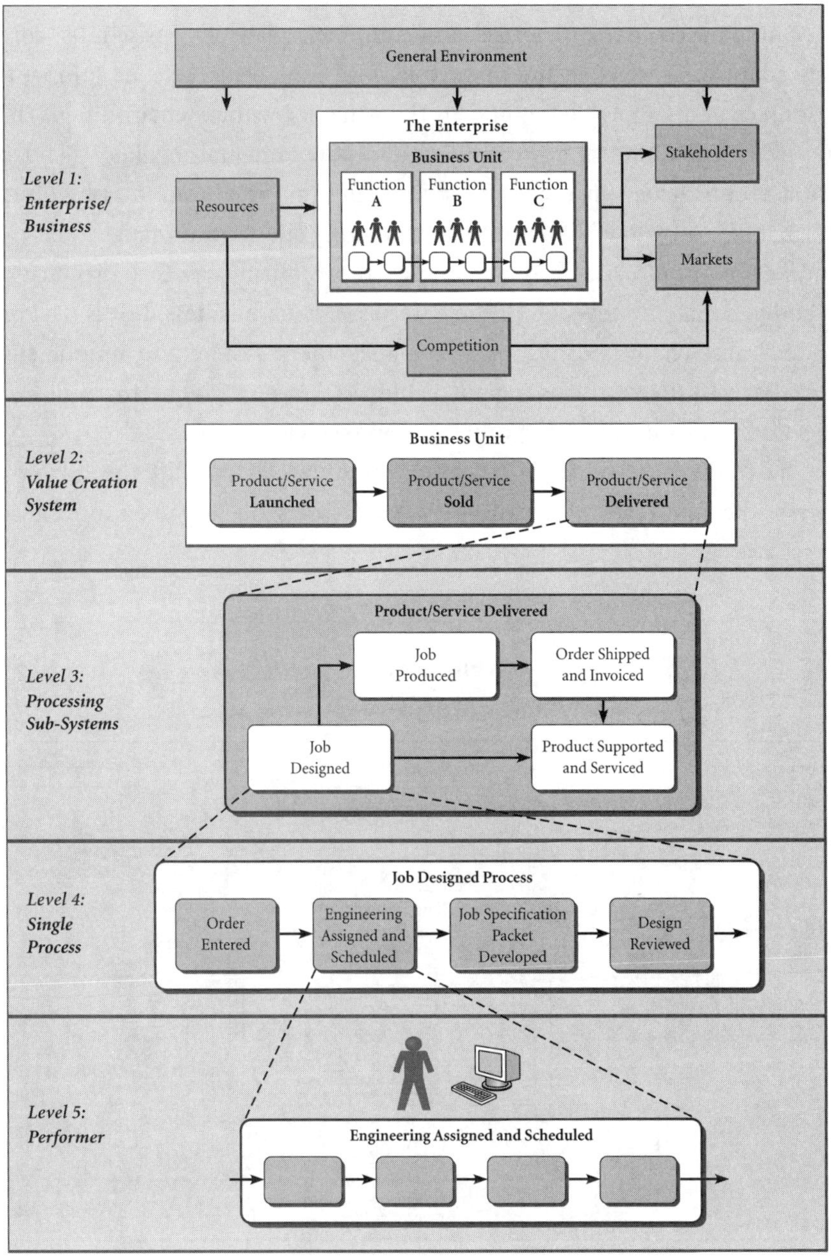

**Level 1:**
*Enterprise/
Business*

General Environment

The Enterprise

Business Unit

Function A
Function B
Function C

Resources

Stakeholders

Markets

Competition

**Level 2:**
*Value Creation
System*

Business Unit

Product/Service Launched

Product/Service Sold

Product/Service Delivered

**Level 3:**
*Processing
Sub-Systems*

Product/Service Delivered

Job Produced

Order Shipped and Invoiced

Job Designed

Product Supported and Serviced

**Level 4:**
*Single
Process*

Job Designed Process

Order Entered

Engineering Assigned and Scheduled

Job Specification Packet Developed

Design Reviewed

**Level 5:**
*Performer*

Engineering Assigned and Scheduled

## Level 1: Enterprise/Business

At the top is an entire enterprise or business, as shown in Figure 6.2. Outside the enterprise are elements of what we call the super-system. In providing goods and services valued by customers, the business uses key resources such as capital, technology, human resources, materials, and equipment. The enterprise must continuously adapt to changes in the marketplace, in capital markets, in competition, in resources and supply chain, and in the general business environment of the economy, culture, natural environment, and governmental/regulatory and geopolitical events. This super-system surrounding the organization is its ultimate performance reality to which it must continuously adapt or ultimately fail.

Inside the "Enterprise" box are one or more businesses that produce outputs and generate the revenue of the enterprise. Each business unit is part of an extended value chain and has its own management system and unique super-system. Each business unit is a giant Value Machine and is the first link in the connection of process results to organization results.

In the traditional, resource-oriented worldview, if you lift the lid off any business, the first level of detail you would see is the organization chart or

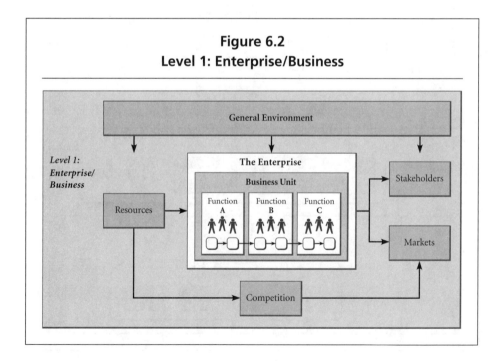

**Figure 6.2**
**Level 1: Enterprise/Business**

resource buckets. In applying the value dimension lens, we are departing from this view. You do see the resource dimension but in the context of the work to be performed. Determining exactly how to organize businesses around products, services, and markets (that is, determining a business model) is the first set of decisions regarding the organization of work. Those decisions are, in fact, all about how to organize the work of the enterprise so it can be performed effectively and efficiently, can be managed effectively, and offers the potential for establishing a sustainable competitive advantage. The decisions to be made impact both the design of work processes at a macro level and the design of work units.

## Level 2: Value Creation System

At Level 2 are the three processing sub-systems working together to create valued products and services, which constitute the Value Creation System (Figure 6.3). As we stated in Chapter 2, every business has some approximation of the Launched, Sold, and Delivered sub-systems as depicted in Level 2, usually largely invisible and not well managed.

As at Level 1, there are work design and resource choices to be made at Level 2. For example, how many Value Creation Systems should there be? It may seem as though it would always be just one system per business unit, but it's not always that simple. A business may have multiple products. Are they are designed, sold, manufactured, and delivered the same way? With the same resources? Or do we need to have different processes, different teams,

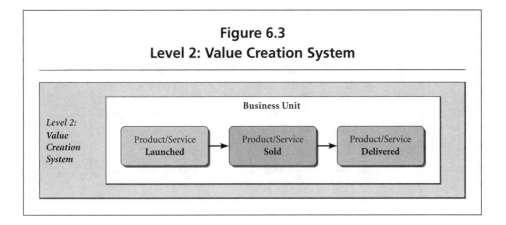

**Figure 6.3**
**Level 2: Value Creation System**

Business Unit

Level 2:
*Value*
*Creation*
*System*

Product/Service
**Launched**
→
Product/Service
**Sold**
→
Product/Service
**Delivered**

different sites, to deliver effectively and efficiently? This decision can affect business performance, manageability, and the potential for competitive advantage.

### Level 3: Processing Sub-Systems

The next level in the model is the processing sub-systems (Figure 6.4). Launched, Sold, and Delivered are each made up of work processes necessary to achieve their respective goals. The process goals and resources of the individual processes within each sub-system must be aligned with one another to accomplish overall goals.

### Level 4: Single Process

The next level of value-adding work is the single process (Figure 6.5). Once again it is essential that a given process not only achieve its own goals but be aligned to the goals of the sub-system in which it resides. And the same principles of design are applied in both designing the process and organizing the resources, namely: Can the process be effectively and efficiently performed? Can the process be effectively managed? Does the process design offer a competitive advantage? And, of course, the design challenges can be formidable even at this level because a single process can be very complex, cross-functional, variable, and hard to understand and manage from end to end.

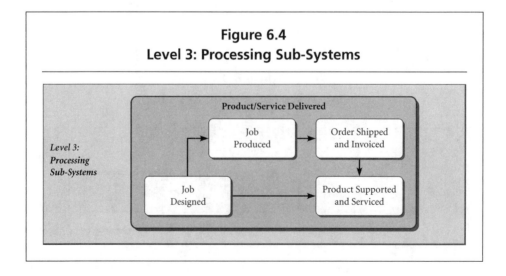

**Figure 6.4**
**Level 3: Processing Sub-Systems**

## Level 5: The Performer Level

The performer or sub-process level (Figure 6.6) is the link to the performer, through the structure of sub-processes, work tasks, and sub-tasks. This is the level at which the resource dimension is obvious, but the work design is still important. There are important tradeoffs to be made at this level between human and technology performers, balancing the intelligence and adaptability of the human against the consistency and control of technology.

The majority of process improvement work done in organizations today is at Level 5, buried within functions. The flaw with this approach is that when "improvement" work starts at this level, there is high risk of maximizing the

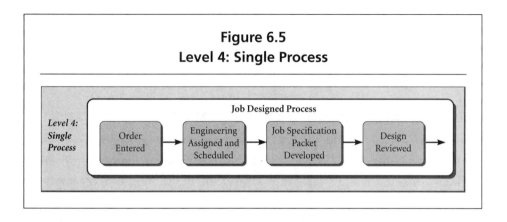

**Figure 6.5**
**Level 4: Single Process**

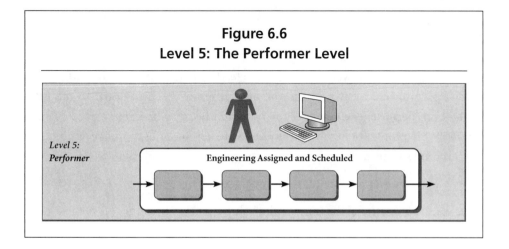

**Figure 6.6**
**Level 5: The Performer Level**

performance of one sub-process or function but sub-optimizing the performance of the organization. If the resource dimension is the prevailing view of an organization, there is a great bias to identifying processes (usually really sub-processes) as operating almost exclusively within functions. When looked at this way, there is no way to connect a functional silo's sub-process to organization results without a lot of accounting hocus-pocus.

The alternative view recognizes both the value and resource dimensions of a business. This view of an organization illustrates the reality that most processes (and even sub-processes) are cross-functional, linked to a processing sub-system, and must be analyzed and designed or improved as a whole.

Work and process definition should start at the top, with the business context. Each level of the processing system hierarchy provides the important, critical performance context for subsequent levels. At each level, you are making "organizing work" decisions to optimize performance at that level—but in the performance context provided by the preceding level.

## VALUE CREATION ARCHITECTURE DEFINITION

One way to start down the path to a management system that integrates the resource and value dimensions is to define the organization's key processes. The value dimension is generally not visible nor understood the same way by everyone in management, so defining the value dimension can be an important and necessary first step. The value creation architecture is a set of blueprints of how work is accomplished in the organization.

Development of a value creation architecture generally takes a dedicated group, composed of executives and key employees and headed by someone who knows how to define processes.

It is this view that Owens wants for the leaders and employees at Belding. He doesn't plan to build out a picture of the entire architecture down to the fifth level—both because it would take too long and because he doesn't need all that detail at this point. Right now he wants four key pictures to make visible the organization's value and resource dimensions:

1. A view of the Belding business super-system

2. A cross-functional diagram of the Value Creation System

3. A high-level picture of its key processes

4. A diagram of the distribution of current resources across the Value Creation System

These diagrams would be enough to help him educate his leadership team, something to point to and say, "*This* is the business we're running here. This is what we have to manage together, what we have to make decisions about, not back in our own little corners of the company but as a team that is responsible for the entire enterprise."

When Owens ran the "sensing" session, he was on the lookout for employees he judged as being natural leaders—people who appeared committed to the success of the organization, persuasive and effective with their peers and superiors, knowledgeable about the company, its problems, and its potential. He didn't care what part of the organization they came from or what their level of authority was—he just wanted a team of the willing and able.

Once he identified the people he wanted on the project team, he talked with their managers to clear the way, then convened the project team. To assist him, Owens brought in Sara, an experienced "Performance Architect" from Corporate. Sara helped educate the team about the three dimensions of an organization and the value of pictures of the business in this format. The team members went to work immediately. Part Three (Chapters 12 through 14) shows examples of the templates and tools referred to in the Belding case. That section is designed for people who want to apply our approach to the design of management systems. For those who prefer to stay with the highlights, the narrative case should be sufficient to show how the ideas in this book are put into action.

## Phase 1

The project team gathered pertinent data from appropriate functional areas and then developed an "is" business super-system map (Figure 12.1, in Part Three). The team then facilitated a review of the map with the executive team. The outcome of this session was that the executives reached agreement on the current reality of all critical components of the super-system (market, resources, competition, general environment) and their assumptions about trends over the next three years for each of the super-system components.

## Phase 2

The project team then gathered data on how the company currently develops, introduces, sells, and produces its products. Based on these data, the project team developed the other key pictures Owens wanted, including the following:

- Cross-Functional Value Creation System Map—This map (Figure 12.2) captures all the processes and functions that must work together to deliver valued products to customers. It is a critical management tool. The map was annotated to note where the company's product lines differed in the course of the Value Creation System.

- Business Process Framework—The framework map (Figure 12.3) is a high-level "roll-up" that shows all the significant processes (that is, value creation processes, management processes, and contributing processes) of Belding and their systemic interrelationships. The framework provides executives and employees with a common view of all the major processes of the business. The document is a concise summary of the value-adding work that must be performed and managed to provide value to customers. The picture is work-centric and does not reflect who does the work, so the primary focus of dialogue, troubleshooting, and decision making stays on the work and on creation and delivery of value.

- Value-Resource Detail Chart—This document (Figure 12.4) shows where the organization's resources (both human performers and technologies) are distributed across the Value Creation System. It is invaluable in revealing gaps in support for critical areas, and sometimes overlaps.

## Phase 3

Owens, with help from Sara and the project team, facilitated a two-day retreat with the extended leadership team (VPs and direct reports) to review and validate the maps. The agenda included a detailed walk-through and validation of the diagrams, identification of major disconnects in the current Value Creation System, prioritization of processes to be improved, and prioritization of processes for future documentation. Many of the disconnects had been touched on during the sensing session, but without the understanding of real root cause that these pictorial views of the business provided.

Most important to Owens was that he achieved his objective of introducing his executives to this way of viewing their organization.

One participant said, "We thought we had a coordinated sequence to get profitable products to market, but nobody really had a coherent view of it. Executives and managers only saw their individual functional silos."

To another participant, the most valuable insight was the need for aligned goals: "We've never had anything like total system-wide goals or aligned 'Launched-Sold-Delivered' goals. Our only goals are established within functions, never across functions."

The maps revealed the complexity of the business to some participants for the first time: "This really is a complicated cross-functional business—but manageable once you see all the parts." Said one executive, "Most every one of our current operating problems is cross-functional in nature and can't be adequately addressed by a single VP or function." Another pointed out, "I have to admit I never really 'got' this process stuff until now. But with these maps, I can see the entire business, and I can see that we really kind of missed the real notion of 'process.' It is not about the work flows within Production; it's about connecting that work to all the other work that has to come together in order to really deliver something of value. I see now how processes are woven into everything we do, not just in Production. It's an eye-opener."

After the meeting, the project team, at Owens' request, permanently pinned up all of the diagrams on the walls of the executive conference room for ready reference. (You can find these maps in Part Three of this book.)

Owens thought he had succeeded in guiding the executives through the first step of his agenda. Now he wanted to engage them in the actual work of rethinking a portion of the work system. During the executive meeting, the Order-to-Cash process was identified as the most critical to customer satisfaction, yet was suffering from major inefficiencies. To Owens, this was an opportunity. To get the executives to think and collaborate cross-functionally, he knew the best way was to stop talking and have them work on something together. The Order-to-Cash process was an ideal candidate.

Owens also knew that it was critical to convince his team that this was legitimate executive work. He was aware that most top executives at this point would say, "I have teams of people who do that stuff for me so my managers and I can do more important stuff." The result has been to relegate process to specialists at lower levels. Owens does not intend to just use this opportunity as a get-your-hands-dirty exercise. Design at this level is the job of executives. They are the only ones who can make the appropriate competitive advantage decisions and appropriate tradeoffs. Only executives can say, "We will go with a more expensive solution because it gives us competitive advantage" or "We want to go cheap here because it doesn't give us an advantage."

In the next chapter, Owens initiates a project that will help his executives and everyone in Belding learn in a concrete fashion how to understand and improve the value dimension.

# Demonstrating How

O wens wants his executives to learn about and buy into his notions about the Value Creation System, the need to understand the dimensions of value and resources, and the need to manage the organization as a system. He knows that these abstractions are learned most effectively by applying them rather than simply talking about them and delegating the details of design to underlings. And he wants to make the point as dramatically as possible to the entire company that this "process stuff" is not too low-level for executives—on the contrary, process work is strategic work if approached properly. And he knows there are precedents he can follow.

## THE EXECUTIVE PIP

When the Rummler methodology for process improvement was first invented in the 1980s, it was applied at Motorola with business management teams that ran the company's product divisions. In contrast, process improvement projects today rarely engage executives. Instead, such initiatives are conducted with project teams composed of staffers, technical specialists, and sometimes employees from line organizations. The teams tend to be headed by experts in process work (Six Sigma Black Belts, for example).

The problem with today's approach is that process improvement work is no longer viewed as management work—it has become the realm of specialists. Yet that early approach at Motorola was powerful.

The process addressed was always a critical value-adding one, usually at the very heart of the business, such as product development or order fulfillment. The head of the project team was the general manager (GM) of the business. The other team participants were the members of his or her executive staff. They were assisted by another group of mid-level managers, technical experts, and staffers who would do the project "grunt" work, such as gathering performance data, creating process maps, and organizing meetings (all the tasks that a process improvement team leader does today). But then the GM ran a series of meetings in which the executive team would review the "is" process, identify problem areas, come up with solutions, and agree on a plan of action for implementing the solutions. That is, they did the crucial analysis and design work that is today relegated to people typically several levels below them. The solutions belonged to those executives, so you can believe they were implemented. No stalling, no protracted "up-selling."

The executive process improvement project (or PIP) always got great attention from all employees because of who the participants were, and always achieved remarkable results. So at Motorola we used that approach whenever we entered a product division and did process improvement work for the first time. The executive team "modeled the way." After that, the division often sponsored training for its employees, followed by multiple process improvement projects on a smaller scale, all of them following the prescribed methodology that the executives had used and thus endorsed.

That approach was why Motorola was so successful in process improvement in the 1980s and 1990s. Unfortunately, when process improvement and management notions migrated to other companies, it was much harder getting executives to participate. In many of those companies, there was often a presumption that initiatives of any kind were "championed" by executives but executed by employees at lower levels. So steering teams and other techniques were used to get some temporary leadership of projects, and the notion of the Executive PIP gradually died away.

We highly recommend that you consider the Executive PIP as the best, fastest, and most powerful way to introduce a new way of managing to your organization. Even more important, designing or improving a company's value-creating processes is strategic work, and it should be led by executives, not delegated away to lower levels of the organization.

To execute an Executive PIP, you need several things:

1. *A critical business issue.* You need a powerful, overwhelming reason why improvement is needed. Process improvement work should not be done

just to do it, or just to "learn," but instead should be applied to real and important issues, such as a need to grow the business, to best a competitor, to grow revenues, or to contain costs. It must be an issue you can articulate and for which you can establish strong, quantitative goals.

2. *A process related to the critical business issue.* You need to single out the process, or set of processes, most closely related to the issue—a process that if improved would make a positive impact on the issue. It should be at level 2, 3, or 4 of the Value Creation Hierarchy, but not below. For help in defining the processes, see the previous chapter on value creation architecture and talk with your internal resources.

3. *An improvement methodology.* In our companion book, *White Space Revisited,* we describe the Rummler Process Methodology in great detail, and it is an approach easily adapted to the Executive PIP, since it has the same origins.[1]

4. *A project team.* As we described earlier, the project team at Motorola was typically two-tiered, with the GM and executives as the designers and decision-makers aided by a group of content experts from their organization who provide information and do a lot of the detail work. For Owens, his project team will function as the group of content experts.

5. *A follow-up strategy.* To capitalize on what is learned during the executive experience, there are decisions to be made about how to spread this approach to other parts of the organization (for example, documentation of the methodology and training).

There are four phases in an Executive PIP, each of which can be tailored to a company's situation:

- *Phase 1:* The content experts gather performance data, do interviews, and develop a map of the existing ("is") process (see Figure 7.1) and supporting information for the executives.

- *Phase 2:* The executive team reviews the "is" process guided by the content experts, identifies process deficiencies ("disconnects"), and prioritizes them.

- *Phase 3:* The executive team develops a set of solutions (or sometimes alternatives) to address process disconnects and creates a high-level implementation plan.

# Figure 7.1
## Cross-Functional Process Map

**Belding Order-to-Cash**

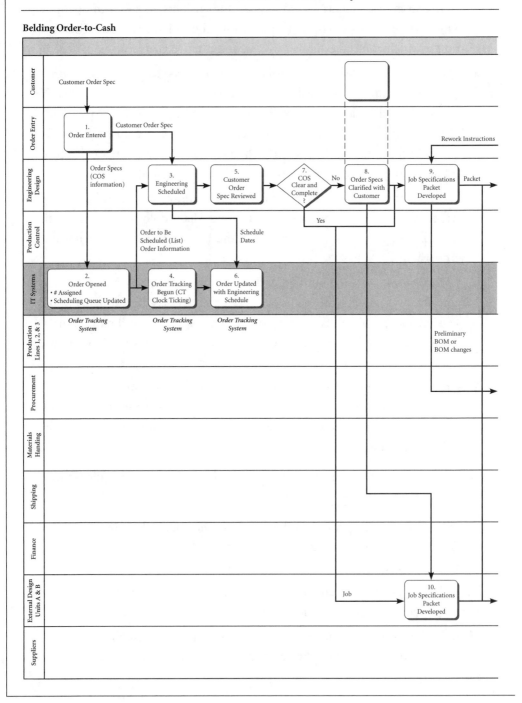

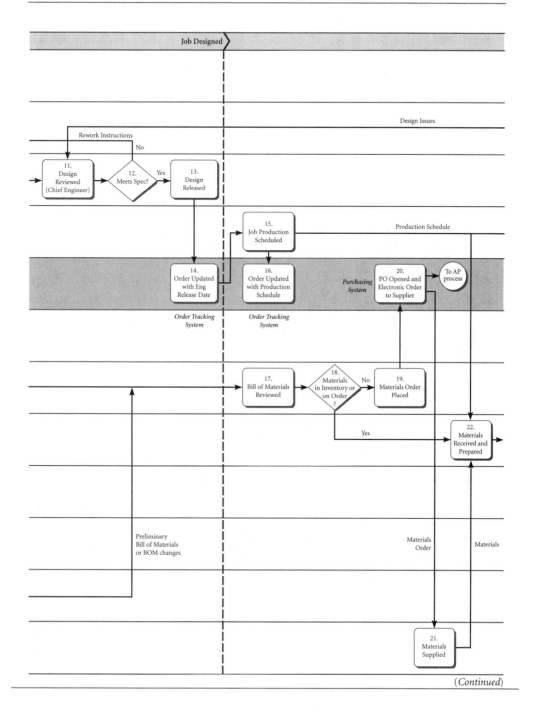

# Figure 7.1
## Cross-Functional Process Map (*Continued*)

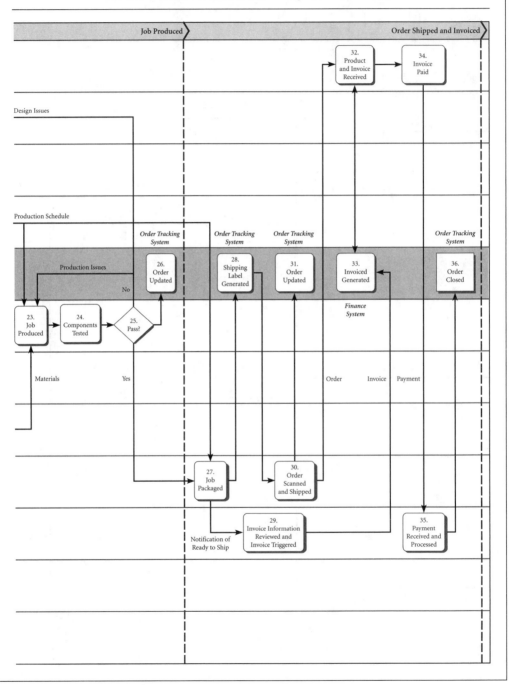

- *Phase 4:* The actions are handed off to others to execute, and the executives now function as a review body as the project continues to completion. But most important, they also use the process that has been redesigned as the basis for installing a process management model.[2]

Since its introduction by Geary Rummler and Alan Brache in 1990,[3] this cross-functional process map (or swimlane chart, as it is often called), shown in Figure 7.1, is the most widely adopted and effective tool for showing the relationship between work (the value dimension) and resources performing the work (human and technology).

So now let's return to Belding and see how Owens applied this notion of the Executive PIP.

## THE ORDER-TO-CASH PROCESS IMPROVEMENT PROJECT

One outcome of the value creation architecture effort was identification of the Order-to-Cash process (that is, work activities from the time the customer agrees to order a product until Belding receives payment for the order) as a key process that needed to be analyzed, redesigned, and managed.

For CEO Owens, it was an opportunity, but also a challenge, to demonstrate the power of two-dimension management. It might seem obvious that Order-to-Cash is an important cross-functional process that requires a cross-functional management system, but it is not easy to grasp for an organization unused to thinking in process terms. And it can seem threatening to impose a horizontal management system on the vertical resource management structure.

Owens first discussed the need to improve the Order-to-Cash process with the executive team. He identified the need for improvement as a "critical business issue" that spanned the whole organization and therefore required everyone's participation and cooperation. Then he announced to the executive team that he was going to lead them through an improvement of the process. He got some stalling and pushback, but he was resolute enough that the grumbling evaporated. He assigned Sara, the Performance Architect, and the project team to identify and interview key participants in the Order-to-Cash process, to gather more data on the goals and performance of the Order-to-Cash process, and to create a cross-functional map of the process as it was being currently performed (Figure 7.1).

A schedule was established that called for the executive team, abetted by the project team and other invited content experts, to participate in four half-day meetings over a two-week period to analyze and redesign the Order-to-Cash process.

## Meeting 1

In this meeting the focus was on the current process and its performance. A wall-sized print of the "is" process map was on the wall and became the chief vehicle for conducting the meeting. Owens established himself as team leader and final arbiter, Sara as the meeting facilitator, the executive team as the collective owners of the process, and the project team and other invited specialists as the experts on current performance.

Then Sara led a walk-through of the map on the wall, calling on various people to testify to the accuracy of the map and to the problems (or "disconnects") that hampered performance and resulted in unhappy customers. The content experts were only too happy to speak up about the deficiencies they experienced in the process and the frustrations of their own work groups in trying to do the right thing in an atmosphere of always-late, always-short, always-wrong. For some of the executives, the realization of how bad this process was in so many ways was astounding; some had never worked at this level of the organization and others had forgotten their own past experiences, but their empathy for the performers grew by the hour. For other executives, it was embarrassing to have the poor performance of their own areas uncovered, the only consolation being that by the time the review was completed, every area had had its uncomfortable revelations.

Owens, mostly watching and listening, saw the first glimmerings of real process ownership and real understanding that you can't fix a cross-functional process by tinkering here and there but that the thing has to be reconceived holistically. By the end of the meeting, he was satisfied that he had moved the stone of two-dimension management a little more.

## Meeting 2

In this session, the executives were led through an evaluation of the goals for this process and in establishing new ones down several levels. Then they came up with several deliberately sketchy ideas of how the process could be redesigned to meet or exceed those goals. This meeting ended with the executives pumped up about the potential they saw for making big improvements across the end-to-end process. At the end, Owens made the point, to the nodding of many heads, "Now you can see that two-dimension management means you own the whole thing, together, not just your own resources. It doesn't hold together if all you are accountable for is your own department. These goals you just set have to be achieved collectively."

## Meeting 3

The third meeting was devoted to redesigning the Order-to-Cash process. Sara led the executives in drawing a picture of the new, improved process, deriving some of the design from the sketchy ideas from the previous meeting but also engaging the executives and content experts in formulating ways to eliminate or reduce every single disconnect on their list. The resulting process design was high-level but with enough detail that the project team and others could flesh it out later.

## Meeting 4

The last meeting was to plan the next steps. Owens had been hanging back during the redesign work, not wanting to impose his ideas too much, but he came back front and center now to make it clear that this new process *would* be implemented and with everyone's active support. As the next steps were decided, he would turn to this executive or that and demand immediate commitment (as in, "Starting on Monday . . .").

The final step to go on the list was Owens' own addition. Owens pointed out that in his past experience he had seen well-intentioned process improvement efforts like this one die away because, while the work process was improved for a time, the corresponding management system didn't change. So Owens appointed an Order-to-Cash Process Management Team consisting of the VPs of Sales, Engineering, Procurement, Production, Shipping, and Operations (supported by functional managers as required).

The Process Management Team would be accountable for ensuring that the Order-to-Cash process met its goals and for aligning those process goals to functional department goals. This meant that the appointed functional VPs would be accountable for two sets of goals: the usual functional resource (budget) goals *and* the cross-functional Order-to-Cash process (value creation) goals.

To drive home the seriousness of this dual responsibility, Owens then announced that he would be establishing the following bonus compensation policy (already approved by Corporate):

- Quarterly bonuses (as had always been the policy).
- VPs' bonus compensation to be weighted (new).
  - 60 percent for Order-to-Cash process performance (value management)
  - 40 percent for achieving functional budget performance (resource management)
- Even if functional budget goals were met during a quarter, that bonus was not paid if the Order-to-Cash goals were not met (new).

Now Owens had everyone's attention (even if some had remained privately skeptical until now). The notion of two-dimension management had become real, concrete, and tied to the company's reward system.

Putting in the Process Management Team and altering the bonus policy so that the Order-to-Cash process could be effectively managed and supported amounted to a partial redesign of Belding's management system, but there was more to do. A broader redesign would be next on Owens' agenda.

# Evolution of a Management System

The approach to creating a management system we describe in this book is an evolutionary one. The reason is practicality. Just about every organization we know of and have worked with to install two-dimension management has succeeded after first gaining some practical experience in applying process improvement methodology and then building the beginnings of a management system on top of that redesigned process.

In organizations in which the decision from the outset has been to install a company-wide management system of the sort we describe here, success is still possible but harder to attain. In part, that is because, without some experience in process improvement first, the organization has not really learned the language or benefits of a process approach to business. Tackling the management system first keeps the concept of process in the theoretical realm, where it's harder for people to understand why they are creating this new approach to management. However, with a process improvement project already conducted, especially once it has yielded tangible results, it is much easier to convince people that the process approach is of great potential value.

The activities we described in the last two chapters give you a possible first step on the evolutionary path:

- The advantage of doing an Executive PIP is that people get a concrete, dramatic example of the power of process improvement and a strong commitment to continue down this path. But you have only focused on one process; you have stopped well short of defining and managing your entire value dimension.

- If you start by defining your value creation architecture, you have a clear understanding of the value dimension, with all of the key processes and how they relate to each other. But you have done nothing with them, and the architecture, while interesting, is kind of abstract to many people. You haven't had the learning that comes from doing a process improvement project.

Whether you start by conducting an Executive PIP or by defining the value creation architecture of your business, you are only partway. So however you started, do the reverse as your second step. That is, if you started with an Executive PIP, then do a value creation architecture definition. If you started by defining your value creation architecture, then choose a key process that needs improvement and do an Executive PIP (or at the very least, a standard process improvement project with a steering team and design team, as described in our companion book, *White Space Revisited*[1]).

Once these two steps are accomplished you are in position to install the management system that will govern both the value and the resource dimensions.

## MANAGEMENT SYSTEM, STAGE I

If you follow the Rummler Process Methodology, you will redesign a given work process and the corresponding process management system for that process at the same time. (That is what Owens is about to do at Belding.) The process management system is partial: it puts in place the goals, measures, performance trackers, management calendar, and management guides for that single process, but not for the entire value dimension. Yet it is a start at imposing horizontal value creation management on the vertical resource management structure of the business.

The usual way of going about this is to appoint a Process Management Team for the process that has been redesigned. The team members consist of the VPs of those functions that participate in the process, supported by other functional managers as required.

The Process Management Team is accountable for ensuring that the work process meets its established goals. This means that the appointed functional VPs are accountable for two sets of goals: their usual functional resource (budget) goals *and* the cross-functional work process (value creation) goals. To make this stick, it is wise to link the reward system to process results, as Owens did.

Using a cross-functional process map, the Process Management Team determines what performance they need from each participating function in order to meet the process goals set by the CEO. Each function's management team then assesses the impact of the process requirements on their "first approximation" budget. The Function Management Team negotiates budget versus performance tradeoffs with the Process Management Team. The result is some modification of goals, demands, or budgets between various functions to accommodate the requirements of the process.

Once the performance year begins, both the Process Management Team and Function Management Teams use the value creation architecture documents on the wall of the executive conference room to troubleshoot below-par performance and identify root causes for correction. The teams might be aided in their work by an assigned Performance Architect like Sara at Belding.

Their routines for managing the process and their contributing functions are shown in Table 8.1.

## PROS AND CONS OF THE STAGE I MANAGEMENT SYSTEM

This approach to process management does not result in a separate "bolt-on" management system. Performance of the process is treated as essential to business performance. Process management is an integral part of the larger management system. The management system designed for a single value creation process does achieve linkage between this Level 4 process and the business, where customer expectations and enterprise requirements are visible.

However, there is no mechanism to see that the Launched, Sold, and Delivered sub-systems are aligned. Because of the emphasis on a single (even if essential) process, the allocation of resources to the single redesigned process could negatively affect other important performance goals. Thus, the focus on one process could be contributing to the sub-optimization of the total business performance system. There is no good way to ascertain this without a broader approach to management.

The bottom line is, while it is beneficial to link one important process to enterprise goals and customer expectations, there are still so many unlinked activities and so many opportunities for sub-optimization that this achievement

## Table 8.1
## Performance Management Routine

| Component | Daily/Weekly | Monthly | Quarterly | Annually |
|---|---|---|---|---|
| | | ACTIVITIES PER TIME PERIOD | | |
| **Process Management Team (PMT)** | | • Review monthly process performance<br>• Review issues<br>• Ask questions<br>• Take/recommend action<br>• Update database | • Review quarterly process performance<br>• Review issues<br>• Ask questions<br>• Change goals and/or resource allocation as appropriate<br>• Update database | • Review annual process performance<br>• Set process improvement goals for next year<br>• Establish process goals and resource requirements for next year |
| **Process Performance and Management Database** | Database updated | Database updated | Database updated | Database updated |
| **Function Management Team (FMT)** | • Monitor process and job performance as appropriate<br>• Take action as necessary<br>• Raise issues with the PMT as appropriate<br>• Update database | • Implement changes as directed by the PMT | • Adjust goals and resource allocation as appropriate | • Recommend process improvement and resource requirements modifications to the PMT |
| **Process Architect** | • Monitor process performance<br>• Respond to requests for help<br>• Conduct research for improving process performance<br>• Make recommendations to the PMT as appropriate<br>• Update database | • Support implementation of changes recommended by the PMT | • Support implementation of changes recommended by the PMT | • Recommend process improvements to the PMT |

is far from the true goal of enterprise-wide performance management. In truth, there should be no such thing as "process management," just management. An effective enterprise performance management system would link all levels of the Value Creation System, thus ensuring that the work done at every level inside the organization results in production of the goods and services that customers want, at a cost and profit level that the organization desires.

## PROCESS MANAGEMENT, STAGE II

Eventually, the shortcomings of a management system focused on a single process become apparent enough to stir a desire to move to a broader application of two-dimension management. Based on an organization's success in managing value creation and resource allocation in concert for one process, it will become evident that the management notion should be extended to the entire company—a management system that will link all five levels, from enterprise to performer.

In the next two chapters, we elaborate on the management system model that was introduced in Chapter 4. Then we will watch as Owens installs a Stage I process management system for the Order-to-Cash process, and then a Stage II two-dimension management system for the entire enterprise.

# Performance Planned

$P$lanning is the starting point for aligning the value dimension to the resource dimension, ensuring that the key value-adding work of the organization is properly resourced and managed for results. This chapter describes in greater detail the Performance Planned portion of the performance management system that was introduced in Chapter 4. This description includes all of the elements and tools of a Stage II management system, even though at first Owens does not implement all of these things at Belding.

## PERFORMANCE PLANNING SYSTEM

The planning system is designed to make sure the organization's value delivery system is the driver for decision making (Table 9.1). It is intended to achieve the following:

- The goals of the primary, value-adding processing sub-systems (Launched, Sold, and Delivered) must be aligned horizontally across the organization's Value Creation System to achieve line-of-business or enterprise goals.

- The goals of the work processes within each primary processing sub-system must be aligned with the goals of the sub-system.

- Resource allocation and goals for all processes (primary and contributing) must be balanced to avoid sub-optimization of the total organization.

This means that the usual sequence of planning that happens in most organizations (that is, enterprise goals are cascaded down to the functional areas for execution) must be altered. Instead, the sequence is as shown in Table 9.1.

The major difference between this and the usual cascading of goals down inside an organization is that, before function and individual goals are

<table>
<tr><td colspan="2" align="center">**Table 9.1**<br>**Management Planning Sequence**</td></tr>
<tr><td>**Old Way**</td><td>**New Way**</td></tr>
<tr><td>Belding's CEO receives earnings guidelines and expectations from Corporate.</td><td>Belding's CEO receives earnings guidelines and expectations from Corporate.</td></tr>
<tr><td>The CEO and the Director of Finance meet individually with VPs to discuss operating and budget goals for each function for the next year.</td><td>Enterprise goals are set by the Leadership Team, based on customer requirements and financial stake-holder expectations.</td></tr>
<tr><td></td><td>Goals for the Value Creation System are set to achieve enterprise goals.</td></tr>
<tr><td></td><td>Primary processing sub-systems (i.e., Launched, Sold, Delivered) goals are set to support the Value Creation System goals.</td></tr>
<tr><td></td><td>Process goals are set to support the primary processing sub-system goals.</td></tr>
<tr><td>VPs and their functions prepare draft budgets for the next fiscal year (total and by month). These proposed budgets are sent to the Director of Finance, who consolidates them into a draft Belding budget.</td><td>Function goals are set to support individual processes and primary processing sub-system goals, and resources are allocated accordingly.</td></tr>
<tr><td>The CEO and Director of Finance then meet individually with each VP to bring each proposed budget "into line."</td><td></td></tr>
<tr><td>The Finance Department publishes the final Belding budget.</td><td>The Finance Department publishes the final Belding budget.</td></tr>
</table>

established, there first must be goals for the primary processing sub-systems and for all Level 4 processes. Process goals before silo goals—that's the key to breaking up the predominance of turf in resource decision making.

This approach is driven by the external expectations of customers and financial stakeholders. Those expectations are then converted into requirements for the internal Value Creation System. It is at this level where key decisions about resources and tradeoffs are made because there is still a clear view of customer and shareholder requirements, a view that is lost the further down you go into the functional areas.

The planning approach outlined here also gets the dimensions of value and resources in the right sequence: first figure out the important goals for the work (that is, the process goals) before distributing downward to the functions (that is, the function goals). To get this kind of planning approach in place, three things are needed:

- Definition of the roles of management in planning
- The planning sequence formalized into a management process
- A set of planning tools

## DEFINING THE ROLES OF MANAGEMENT

One of the major questions facing an organization that installs this approach to management is how far to go in defining management roles to manage both the vertical (resource) dimension and the horizontal (value) dimension.

One approach we can call "informal." It amounts to simply identifying various people and organizations as having both a vertical responsibility and horizontal responsibilities for a process, a sub-system, or an entire organization. For example, at Belding the leaders in charge of the functions that participate in the Order-to-Cash process (Production, Order Entry, Production Control, Procurement, Handling, Shipping, Finance, Operations, and several external companies) are already responsible for the performance of their respective organizations. Owens could just designate them as both individually responsible for the performance of their areas and collectively responsible for performance of the process as a whole. The potential drawback to this informality is that it doesn't necessarily change anything; it's a team of peers, with nobody in charge. Hoping that cross-functional collaboration will happen sometimes doesn't work out very well or for very long.

Owens could go a little further and designate one person (usually the head of the functional area with the greatest amount of contribution to the process, in this case, probably Operations) as the "process owner" and therefore informal leader of the heads of the functions participating in the process. The process owner then tries to lead the functions in any decisions that affect the overall design or performance of the process. This approach is largely based on the charisma and persuasive skills of the designated process owner rather than on real authority; sometimes that works well but not always.

The other approach—the one Owens took—is "formal." He defined a cross-functional team as collectively responsible for the process and linked substantial rewards to the performance of that process. He made it explicit that each member of the team has to wear two hats: one for his or her department or area and the other for the process as a whole. He is using the Ben Franklin dictum that the team members "must indeed all hang together, or most assuredly, [they] will all hang separately." He also assigns the Operations VP to be process owner, but the most powerful aspect of his formal two-dimension management approach is that it is backed up by consequences.

Which is better, informal or formal? It depends, of course, on the organization, but where there are strong silos with long histories, the more formal approach is probably most effective in breaking up the vertical mentality.

At Belding, in Stage I there is only one Process Management Team, which manages the Order-to-Cash process. The members are managers of functions that participate in that process.

The management structure put in place in Stage II for managing the total Value Creation System at Belding is an expansion of the structure established to manage a single process. In addition to the Order-to-Cash Process Management Team, the following additional horizontal management teams are eventually created:

- Teams to manage each of the major sub-systems of Belding's Value Creation System, which means a team for Launched, a team for Sold, and a team for Delivered. The members of these management teams come from the functions that participate in the sub-systems. For example, on the Sold sub-system management team there are managers from Sales, Marketing, and Public Relations; on the Launched sub-system management team are managers from Product Development, Research, and Marketing; on the Delivered sub-system management team are managers from Production, Shipping, Finance, Production Control, and Order Entry. The sub-system management teams are the key link to functions as regards performance planning and management.

- A team to bridge the white spaces between the three sub-systems. This team already existed; it is the senior executive team that reports directly to Owens and oversees the entire Belding enterprise. What Owens had to make clear to this team is that he holds them collectively accountable to achieve financial and operating goals together. When they are specifically engaged in reviewing or working on the Value Creation System as a whole, he refers to them as the Value Creation Management Team.

- Process Management Teams for sizable Level 4 cross-functional processes within Launched, Sold, or Delivered. For example, in addition to the Order-to-Cash process, the Product Development process within the Launched sub-system involves several functions to produce the necessary outputs, and thus would benefit from a Process Management Team.

How many cross-functional teams should be put in place for a given organization? A reasonable question, because you don't want to establish so many teams and other horizontal mechanisms that they cause confusion or get in the way of doing the work. At Belding, what we described above as the Stage II management system is an elaborate hierarchy of teams that parallel the Value Creation Hierarchy. But whether you need that much horizontal infrastructure is a question you should ask about your own organization. You'll want to avoid proliferating "process management" for every work process, thus creating an overly complex management structure.

For each of these teams, Owens (with Sara's assistance) spells out the roles and responsibilities. The format that Sara uses is shown in Figure 9.1, with a full example from Belding in Chapter 13 of this book. For each level of the hierarchy—starting with the entire enterprise, then descending to each sub-level of the Value Creation System, and finally linking to the functional areas and their management teams—the entire infrastructure of management is explicitly defined. The value of this tool is that it makes clear what each team is expected to accomplish in the management planning process, which can cause ambiguity when setting up multiple horizontal teams on top of an existing management system.

## Figure 9.1
## Management Domain Chart Format

| BELDING MANAGEMENT DOMAIN CHART | | | |
|---|---|---|---|
| Domain/Level | Position | Value Add | Performance Planned |
| Enterprise | CEO/Executive Team | | |
| Value Creation System | Value Creation Management Team | | |
| Processing Sub-System | Sub-System Management Team | | |
| Process | Process Management Team | | |
| Function | Functional Area Management Team | | |

## THE PLANNING PROCESS

In addition to role definition, it is very helpful to lay out a specific management process for planning, showing exactly when, where, and how certain planning activities happen and how they are interwoven with other managerial events. The tool we have found most useful to depict these activities is a management calendar (the format is in Figure 9.2, and a full example is shown in Figure 13.7 in Part Three). Because management teams tend to do their work of decision making and direction setting in regularly scheduled meetings, a calendar format is a good way to capture the majority of this activity. (There are, of course, many other individual activities a manager performs, but we are most interested in defining the moments when managers act in concert to make decisions that affect the value and resource dimensions.)

## FEATURES OF THIS PLANNING PROCESS

This approach to planning has some significant differences from the typical resource-oriented, functionally controlled annual planning event:

First, this planning process does not have functions independently submitting their goals and budgets, thereby competing for resources, with the final allocation of dollars being driven by the Finance department. Instead, the Value Creation Management Team sets priorities for the next level down (that is, the

# Figure 9.2
## Management Planning Calendar Format

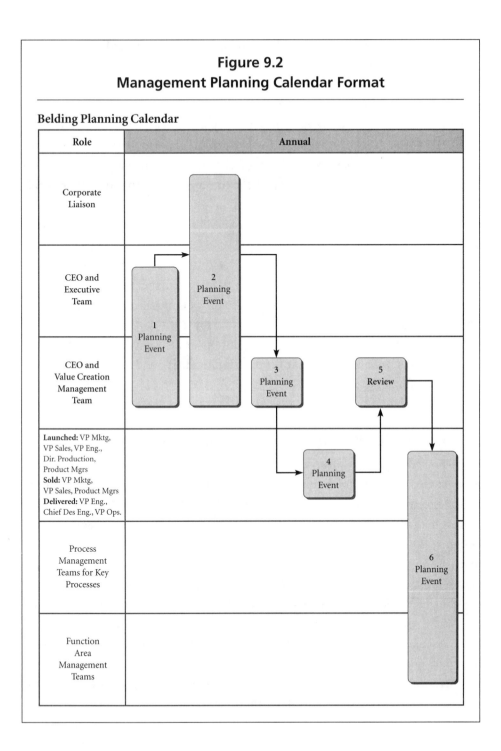

**Belding Planning Calendar**

| Role | Annual |
|---|---|
| Corporate Liaison | |
| CEO and Executive Team | 1 Planning Event    2 Planning Event |
| CEO and Value Creation Management Team | 3 Planning Event    5 Review |
| **Launched:** VP Mktg, VP Sales, VP Eng., Dir. Production, Product Mgrs  **Sold:** VP Mktg, VP Sales, Product Mgrs  **Delivered:** VP Eng., Chief Des Eng., VP Ops. | 4 Planning Event |
| Process Management Teams for Key Processes | 6 Planning Event |
| Function Area Management Teams | |

primary processing sub-systems of Launched, Sold, and Delivered) with the goal of *optimizing* the entire Value Creation System. With their Value Creation System hats on, the executives will reach consensus on how Belding's resource dollars are to be allocated to achieve business goals.

Each processing sub-system management team consists of a functional VP, who acts as the executive chair, and other senior management representatives of key functions that perform the processes that make up the processing sub-system in question. The team is jointly held accountable for the sub-system goals for the year. Joint accountability ensures that tradeoffs to optimize the whole process are being identified and made, thus avoiding the risks of sub-optimizing at the expense of the whole.

The Value Creation Management Team is assuming responsibility for optimization of the entire Value Creation System. It is systematically and strategically making realistic tradeoffs from a perspective of total organization performance. This is in contrast to traditional practice, whereby a VP on the executive operating committee argues for resources to benefit his or her own function, and there is no mechanism for ensuring that the decision made is good for the whole organization, customers, and stakeholders.

## A DIFFERENCE IN MANAGERIAL BEHAVIOR

What does this process mean in practical terms during the planning and goal-setting activities of a senior management team for a business? It means that the senior executives don't just agree on the goals for the year, but also test them against the cross-functional processes that carry out those goals and agree on the design and goals for those processes as well. This is a level of quality and detail that is rarely, if ever, reached during the typical goal-setting wrangles that happen in most companies. Goals might be agreed to, but then the senior executives are allowed to decide for themselves how they will achieve those goals inside their own parts of the organization. There is seldom any close questioning of how these goals can be met. It is, after all, what senior executives are supposed to be doing—deciding how they will task their subordinates to get the work done. It is heretical to suggest this conversation should take place at the executive team level, where everyone can see just how aligned they really are around these goals.

It can be amazing to watch the amount of misalignment that is allowed to exist in some organizations. An example: The owner of a software company was convinced that his business would grow and be more profitable if it offered services in addition to its suite of software products. There was a long history of complaints from customers who had trouble with some of the products after installation, and much of it was due to poor fit with the customers' specific needs. The owner formed a services division and staffed it with people who knew how to conduct a "front-door analysis" that would help the technical staff customize the product before it was installed. These services were put in place, but after several months virtually none were sold.

During a major "come to Jesus" meeting with the sales force, the owner discovered that the sales reps did not like the notion of having to sell "services." It was much more complex and took much longer than just selling a "box" of software products, and the longer sales cycle held up their commissions. So even though the VP of Sales had signed on to goals requiring the sale of services, her sales staff just stuck to what they knew. And while the owner yelled and screamed, he was stymied in trying to figure out how to make the sales reps change their behavior. So he let them get away with it. (Of course, executives who will not wear both hats should be replaced because the buck did indeed stop with the VP of Sales, who was winking at her sales reps as she handed out the service goals.) Without an adequate Performance Managed side of the management system, this owner did not have visibility into what was happening after goals were set.

## OWENS' FOCUS IN STAGE I

Owens knew he was not going to try to put in place an entire management system based just on the Order-to-Cash process. But he could implement some of the most important elements, such as defined managerial roles for managing the process, a set of process performance goals, and a set of performance measures (or metrics). He knew that he needed to demonstrate how to "plan differently," not just preach about it. The biggest challenge would be that, even though the new annual planning process called for setting process goals for the Order-to-Cash process, and there was a Process Management Team in place to do this goal setting, there was likely to be some ambiguity about what this team was supposed to do and what a process goal was. So with Sara's help, Owens had the team establish a set of goals and corresponding measures for the Order-to-Cash process, using a tool called a measures chain. (A sample measures chain can be found in Figure 13.4 in Part Three.) A measures chain helps you to figure out where you want to place metrics within a given process. It is like deciding where to insert the dipstick into the performance engine to see how things are operating.

Owens used the measures chain as a tool for coaching the Process Management Team in how to think about performance planning. After pointing out the need for having process goals, and thus metrics, he asked the team to start, not with the enterprise financial and operational goals already established for the year but with customer expectations. Because the Order-to-Cash process had recently been redesigned due to customer dissatisfaction, the management team already knew quite well what expectations customers had. Once they had identified key customer expectations for timeliness, quality, and price, the team aligned those expectations with the already established Belding financial and operational targets relevant to the Order-to-Cash process. For example, customers had become extremely unhappy about the large number of late deliveries of some Belding products. Yet no Belding goal had been set for on-time delivery. "So let's set one," Owens urged.

Then the team translated the customer expectations and business goals into measures for the Order-to-Cash process. Once measures for the whole process were agreed on, the team then distributed those measures at the appropriate places along the process. As you can see in the example in Figure 13.4, some of these measures (for orders not meeting spec and contributions per job) are cross-functional, which means that the functional areas are collectively accountable for achieving them, while other goals (for example, rework) are the responsibility of a single function (in the case of rework, Engineering). So for the first time, Belding had a set of horizontal goals—that is, goals that would require the effective performance of multiple functional areas to achieve them.

Then Owens had the management team consider the resource dimension in relation to the Order-to-Cash process. The questions he posed were, "Are any of the disconnects we have had with this process being caused by resource issues, for example, our poor record on delivery? Do we have enough resources? Do we have the right kind of people deployed along that process? Have they been trained? Do they know what they're doing?" These questions triggered a passionate discussion about the lack of resources in a couple areas where delays in order processing were common, and eventually a decision was made to shift some resources into Order Entry and Production Control while doing more hiring of people for those areas and backfilling where necessary.

At the end of this discussion, Owens pointed out, "This is the kind of resource allocation and budgeting discussion we should be having. We started by looking at the performance of the Order-to-Cash process and then asking where the resources should be in that process, instead of having the usual scenario where everybody is just jockeying to get as many resources for his area as possible. Understanding the requirements of the value dimension before we discuss resource tradeoffs makes for a rational conversation."

After that conversation, the Process Management Team agreed on when, where, and how they would meet in order to oversee the progress of implementing the redesigned Order-to-Cash process and how they would engage with line managers in managing the process on a day-to-day basis. These simple steps were the beginning of a new Performance Planned and Managed approach, which we will describe in more detail in Chapter 10.

## OWENS' APPROACH FOR STAGE II

Owens waited to implement Stage II until the altered Order-to-Cash planning process had been in place for over a year and Belding managers had twice conducted the annual planning events the new way, by setting goals for the Order-to-Cash process before cascading down to functional goals. In addition, the redesigned Order-to-Cash process, now being managed by the Process Management Team Owens had instituted, was producing impressive results. On-time deliveries now averaged over 97 percent; returns and warranty claims had dropped dramatically; and customer complaints tailed off significantly. These results were heavily promoted throughout Belding. The Process Management Team for the Order-to-Cash process was doing many a briefing on how the process was redesigned and how the improvements were being achieved, which began to convince many skeptics that this process stuff had practical benefits.

This "positive press" gave Owens a good basis for expanding the approach to the entire value creation architecture. He also knew from experience that the Belding management team had needed time to get used to planning and managing with one process before he tried to expand these concepts. He took the following steps to ready the organization for an expansion of two-dimension management:

1. He had the entire value creation architecture of Belding defined down to cross-functional Level 4 maps and some select definition at Level 5 based on need. This was accomplished by a small team of key managers guided by Sara. Over a six-week period, they defined the entire value creation architecture, mapping its key processes. The key tools are described in Part Three.

2. He established horizontal management teams to own and operate the expanded management system.

3. He expanded the annual Performance Planned approach to all Level 4 processes. (The full Performance Planned calendar is shown in Figure 13.7 in Part Three.)

4. Once the plans were put into place, the management side of the system could be enacted, with performance monitoring, performance support, and corrective action as key managerial accountabilities. Owens put in place all the elements of a two-dimension Performance Planned and Managed system. This is further described in the next chapter, with illustrations of the tools and models provided in Part Three.

# Performance Managed

The next items on Owens' agenda are "Measure and manage better" and "Support performance" (Figure 10.1). By installing elements of performance planning for the Order-to-Cash process, Owens has some of the means in place to begin managing that part of the business differently. But there are more elements of a complete performance management system to be installed, and, just as important, certain management practices to alter.

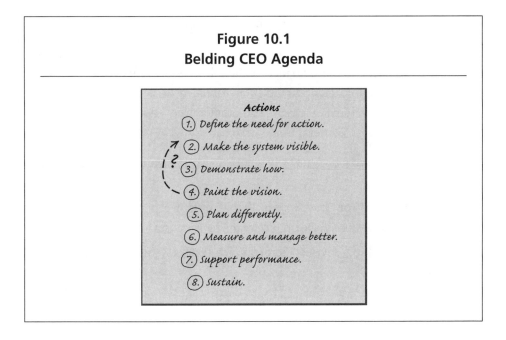

**Figure 10.1
Belding CEO Agenda**

*Actions*

1. Define the need for action.
2. Make the system visible.
3. Demonstrate how.
4. Paint the vision.
5. Plan differently.
6. Measure and manage better.
7. Support performance.
8. Sustain.

This chapter details the Performance Managed portion of the performance management system introduced in Chapter 4. (This description includes all of the elements of Stage II, Performance Managed, but Owens applies only some of these elements during Stage I.)

Performance Managed comprises those management tasks that must happen once plans have been approved and performers begin executing the plans. It includes monitoring performance against metrics, identifying any deviations from plans, determining what corrective actions must take place to get performance on track, and then taking those necessary actions. It also includes performance support tasks such as providing many forms of performance assistance (training, equipping, assigning, coaching, and so on) given to performers prior to and during their execution of work.

## PERFORMANCE MANAGED

In our performance management system, expectations and plans are set and cascaded down from the enterprise through the value creation and process levels to connect with function and job plans and goals. Performance Managed happens at all levels as plans are executed. As performance occurs, management activities consist of:

- Performance is monitored.
- Variations are identified and diagnosed.
- Corrective actions (corrective, preventive, sustaining) are taken as required.

Once process execution begins, monitoring happens, reversing the sequence that planning took, with performance at the job level being monitored by first-line supervision and on back up to the enterprise level.

To perform these actions in a manner that effectively addresses both the value and resource dimensions, several things are needed:

- Performance metrics for all levels of the organization's value creation architecture
- Instrument panels (or "dashboards")[1] that organize performance data in a way that helps diagnose performance and isolate causes
- A system of tracking devices (performance trackers) that links processes to the dashboard
- Assignment of performance monitoring and management responsibilities to appropriate managers or management teams

To be able to monitor performance against goals, managers need relevant metrics at every level of the value creation architecture. To create those metrics, we apply the measures chain tool to the business, sub-systems, and processes (Levels 1 to 4 and sometimes 5) in the organization's value creation architecture. The measures chains identify the critical dimensions of performance and associated measures for a given set of work and where performance data are required to monitor the work as it is performed.

When measures chains are created for the organization's value creation architecture, the management team has a powerful means of monitoring and controlling performance across the organization. The metrics at lower levels can be linked together, providing metrics for each of the processing sub-systems and up through the entire business. Together these metrics can be the basis for a management dashboard, providing a management team insight into performance across an enterprise (Figure 10.2).

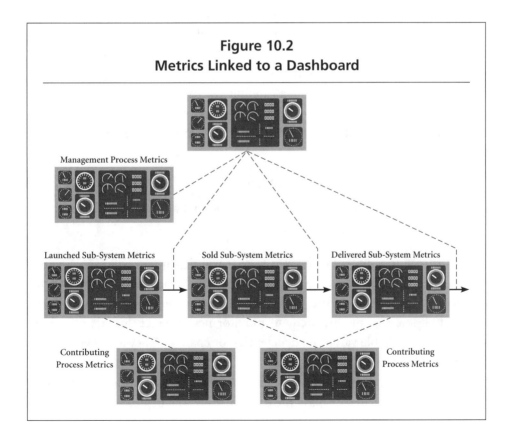

**Figure 10.2
Metrics Linked to a Dashboard**

Management Process Metrics

Launched Sub-System Metrics

Sold Sub-System Metrics

Delivered Sub-System Metrics

Contributing Process Metrics

Contributing Process Metrics

To enable Belding managers to collect and review all of these performance data, a formal tracking and reporting system is a must. Owens wants to develop a set of tracking reports that provide organized, logical, linked results on performance at all levels of the hierarchy, from the enterprise level . . .

- to the Value Creation System level
- to the processing sub-system level
- to the single process level
- to functions and performers

The trackers are linked together to populate a dashboard that will provide views of performance organized for the users of the data, which are the management teams listed in the management domain matrix. Figure 10.3 is an illustration of one dashboard for Belding. The dashboard provides the managers of value creation across the enterprise a view of both the value and the resource dimensions. The shaded trackers are those reports most relevant to this particular management team. The trackers provide data about a variety of performance indicators, all driven from results of the Value Creation System processes as well as from the functional areas and the contributing sub-systems and processes.

Tracking reports themselves are a carefully constructed data set that provides critical information on performance. The typical tracker contains plan versus actual data on interrelated variables over time. Some features of an effective tracker are

- No single measures (always correlations)
- No snapshots in time (always a period of time so that trends are discoverable)
- No data on one variable in isolation

The format and content of a given tracker will depend on what information is required and the best way to format the information. When combined with the management calendar, the trackers are a key set of tools for management teams at all levels of the hierarchy to monitor performance and act effectively to address undesirable variation, deficiencies, or changes. They are developed by looking at all of the variables in a process.

This concept can be taken down to each management job in the organization. For example, Figure 10.4 displays the dashboard for the Regional Sales Manager

## Figure 10.3
## Belding Tracker System

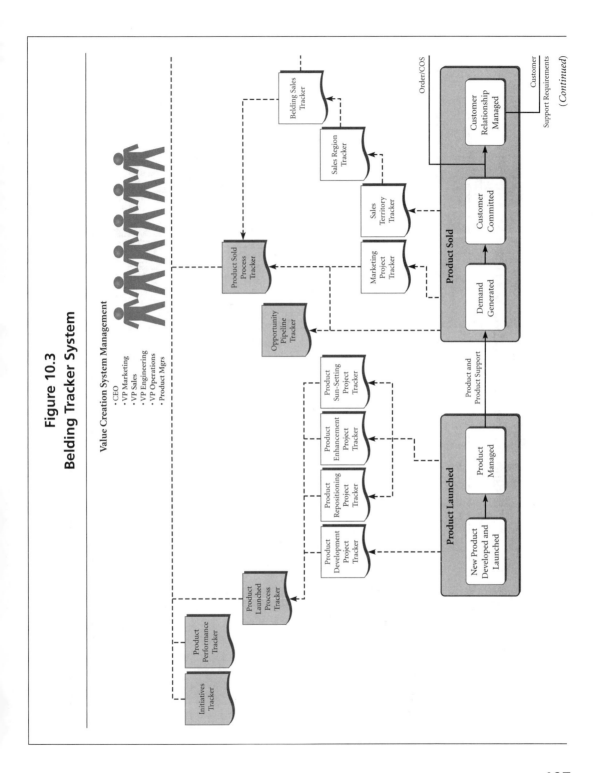

(*Continued*)

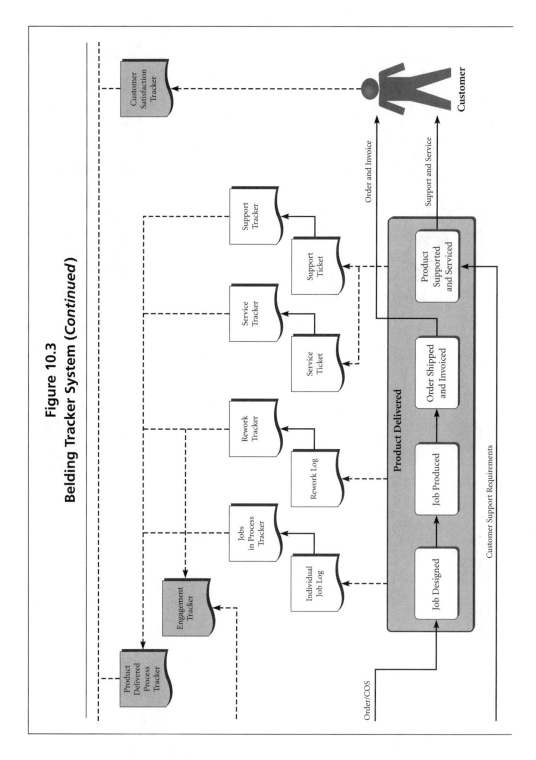

## Figure 10.3
## Belding Tracker System (Continued)

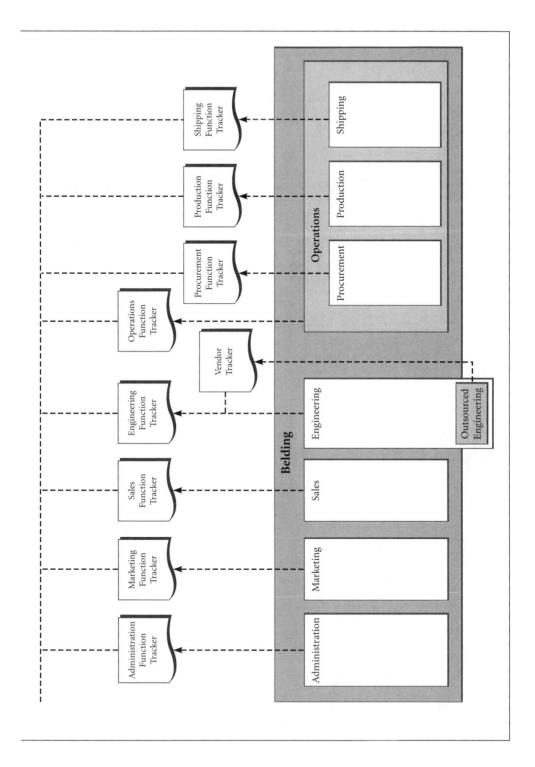

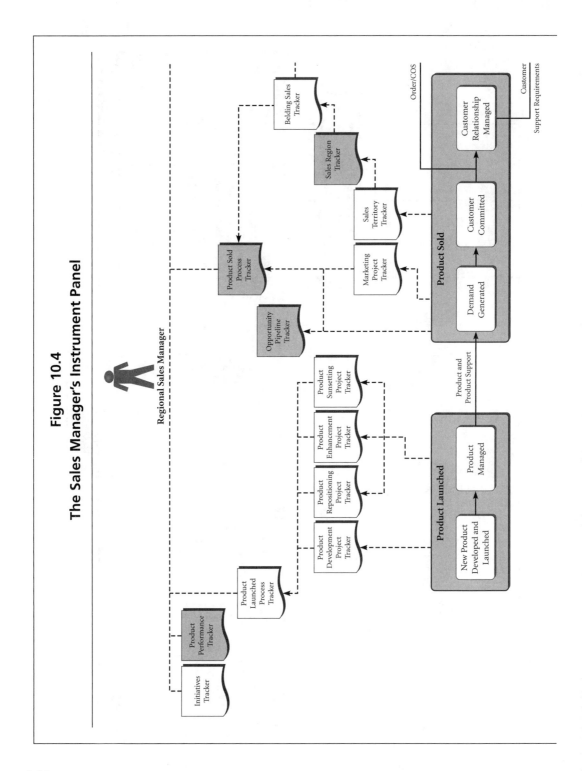

**Figure 10.4**
**The Sales Manager's Instrument Panel**

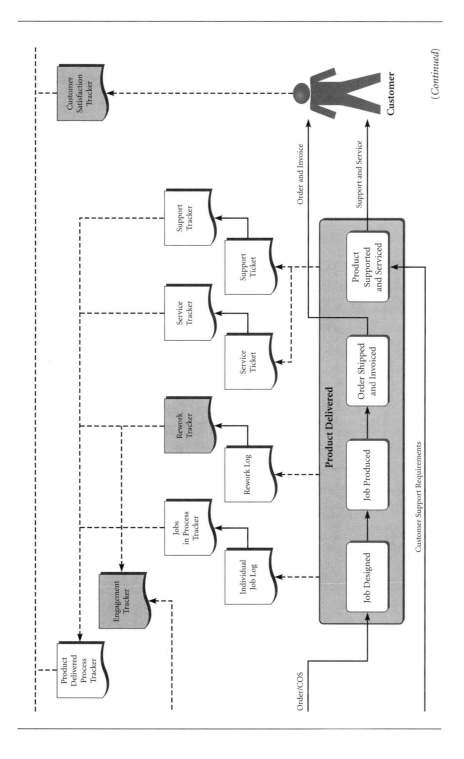

*(Continued)*

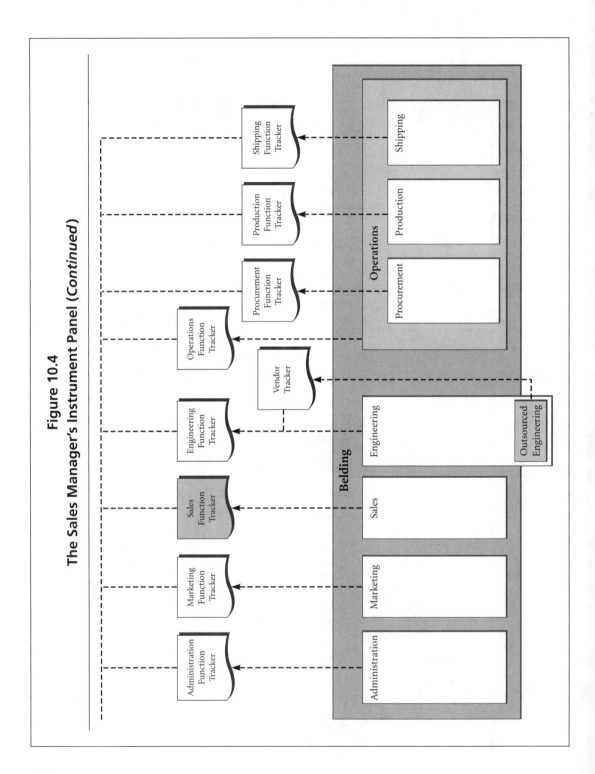

Figure 10.4
The Sales Manager's Instrument Panel (*Continued*)

job at Belding. The highlighted trackers are of special importance for monitoring the work that directly accomplishes sales goals, but some also provide data on other processes and functional areas that are especially important to Sales.

## THE MANAGEMENT PROCESS

The new Belding management calendar includes all the events required for the management teams to collectively make decisions and take actions to sustain and improve the Value Creation System. The format for the Performance Managed calendar is shown in Figure 10.5. (A detailed version of this calendar can be found in Figure 13.8 in Part Three.) The calendar is divided into time durations (quarterly, monthly, weekly to daily) in order to capture both the sequence and the schedule of events in which Belding managers collaborate in managing the two dimensions of the company. The calendar also has a "By Event" category because some management activities are triggered by certain circumstances rather than by time of year.

## FEATURES OF THIS MANAGEMENT PROCESS

The following observations track the numbered events on the Belding management calendar to be found in Figure 13.8 in Part Three:

*As part of the management process,* the individual functions and Process Management Teams propose plans to improve their respective performance, but these preliminary plans are reviewed by the Value Creation Management Team before any action takes place. This ensures that the Value Creation System is not being sub-optimized by the independent action of some function or Process Management Team. The Value Creation Management Team functions as the central intelligence of the business processing system that delivers value to customers and stakeholders.

*Even the management system is evaluated and continuously improved.* These opportunities may include technology upgrades or redesign of a management process to ensure timely management actions.

*Tactical adjustments are made monthly to stay on plan.* Changes in assumptions, goals, plans, and budgets are made quarterly to optimize the Value Creation System and continue to meet corporate and business goals.

In general, the Value Creation Management and Launched, Sold, and Delivered Management Teams, individual Process Management Teams, and product

# Figure 10.5
## Performance Managed Calendar Format

**Management Calendar Format**

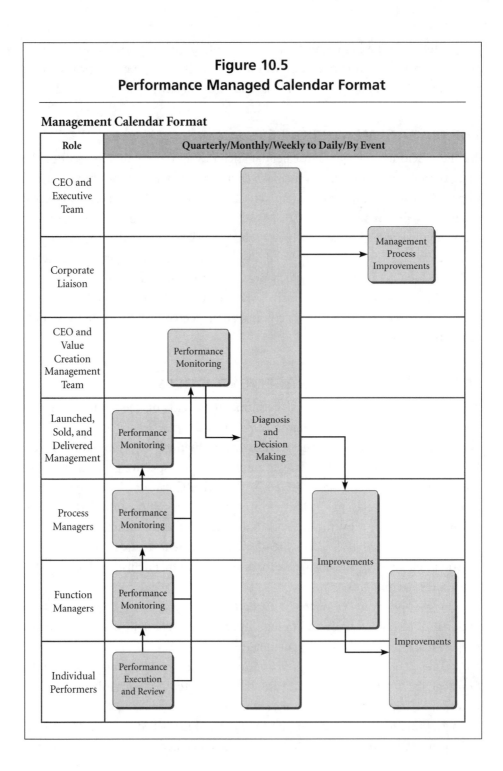

managers are noting trends, asking questions, and identifying potential actions to be discussed in appropriate monthly forums. By contrast, managers of functional areas are generally taking action immediately.

## PERFORMANCE SUPPORT

Our notion of performance support is not unique to two-dimension management. However, we are including this here because it is required for effective management.

If you review the management model in Figure 4.4, Chapter 4, you will notice that "performance support" is included in planning. In the second step of Performance Planned, managers at each level are supposed to determine what support is needed (that is, the performance requirements) at the next level down. In the third step, when plans are operationalized, provisioning of all necessary support is supposed to be included. However, you cannot tell just from the performance management model exactly what constitutes "support."

To answer the question of what performance support is, let us examine another model we use called the Human Performance System (HPS), shown in Figure 10.6. This model describes the situation in which every performer exists, for good or ill.

The model depicts the variables of the Human Performance System as they ideally should exist, namely that for any given performer there should be

- *Output definition:* The performer knows what outputs and outcomes are expected and what standards determine success.

- *Inputs:* All required supplies, materials, and so on, are available; a signal to begin is triggered; and the performer has all the necessary tools, equipment, funds, instructions, and so forth, in order to transform the inputs into outputs as expected.

- *Consequences:* What happens when the performer executes the job or task is sufficiently positive that the performer is likely to repeat the same behavior.

- *Feedback:* The performer frequently gets information that indicates how well he or she is performing or what the results of performance have been.

- *Knowledge, skills, capacity:* The performer has been adequately trained in the job requirements and has the necessary attributes or capabilities required.

The Human Performance System model describes all the important variables of performance support. When providing performance support, someone is providing one or more elements of this model—for example, providing

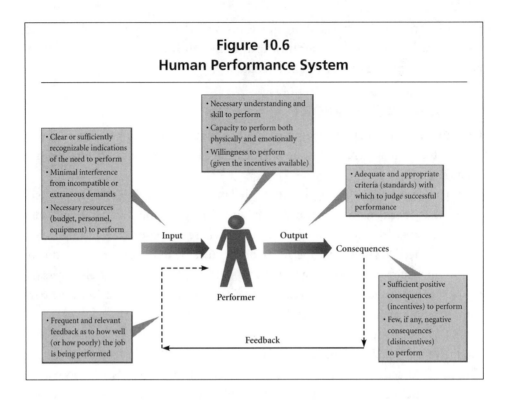

## Figure 10.6
## Human Performance System

- Clear or sufficiently recognizable indications of the need to perform
- Minimal interference from incompatible or extraneous demands
- Necessary resources (budget, personnel, equipment) to perform

- Necessary understanding and skill to perform
- Capacity to perform both physically and emotionally
- Willingness to perform (given the incentives available)

- Adequate and appropriate criteria (standards) with which to judge successful performance

Input

Output

Consequences

Performer

- Sufficient positive consequences (incentives) to perform
- Few, if any, negative consequences (disincentives) to perform

- Frequent and relevant feedback as to how well (or how poorly) the job is being performed

Feedback

training for all new performers, ensuring that all performers have the right equipment they need, making sure everyone doing the job understands what the daily output requirement is, monitoring the work as it is performed, or providing on-the-spot coaching and correction of technique. Everything in the Human Performance System model is an element of performance support, but only a couple of the variables (the inputs and possibly the feedback) are likely to be provided electronically.

So who is responsible for performance support as we have described it in the Human Performance System model? Who designs the Human Performance System for a job? Who provides the required instructions, training, equipment, coaching, feedback, and consequences? It's the manager, of course. In fact, it would not be too much to say that providing performance support is as critical as performance planning and management.

For each element in the Human Performance System model, there is a corresponding set of managerial tasks that together comprise performance support. Table 10.1 summarizes these managerial tasks.

# Table 10.1
## Human Performance System Variables vs. Managerial Tasks

| HPS Variable | Managerial Performance Support Tasks |
|---|---|
| Output requirements and standards | • Define exactly what outputs and outcomes are expected from a given job or process.<br>• Define the performance standards (quantity, quality, time, cost, etc.) for the outputs.<br>• Communicate these requirements clearly to the performers. |
| Inputs | • Determine exactly what resources are needed by performers.<br>• Provide the resources in sufficient quantities when needed.<br>• Ensure a continual re-supply of consumable inputs.<br>• Monitor the work environment and eliminate anything that hinders performance (e.g., inventory, poor work space, job interference, poor written instructions). |
| Consequences | • Design the job or task so that it can be performed without excessive difficulty by a well-prepared employee under most circumstances.<br>• Observe the job as it is being performed and make changes to eliminate causes of delay, irritation, ambiguity, overload, and other sources of poor performance. |
| Feedback | • Provide constructive coaching as the job is being performed.<br>• Provide understandable written and verbal information about the performance frequently.<br>• Provide frequent feedback about results (for example, customer comments, downstream comments, quantitative results). |
| Knowledge, skills, capacity | • Define the knowledge, skills, and capacity needed to do the job.<br>• Establish a learning system to provide both initial and ongoing formal training to provide knowledge and skills.<br>• Oversee actual performance and gauge whether formal training is providing appropriate and useful content.<br>• Provide job requirements to HR so that qualified candidates are hired. |

It is clear that to perform these managerial tasks, performance support is not a passive responsibility. "Overseeing actual performance," for example, is not an occasional look-see to find out whether all is well—it is an ongoing assessment of how well the work is going and anticipating the needs of performers before they run out of materials, time, patience, or something else. This is different from what we described as performance monitoring. The frequency of that kind of monitoring will be different by management level, but monitoring is reviewing results. By contrast, overseeing performance is being there and watching the job performance, if at all possible, while results are being produced. Sometimes the difference may be academic, and for some jobs, of course, close oversight may not be practical or necessary. But the difference we want to emphasize is after-the-fact monitoring of results versus the active oversight of work to support performers when they need help of some kind while doing their jobs.

Figure 10.7 shows in more detail what the manager does in designing and managing a Human Performance System. It starts with defining and designing the Human Performance System of each job, which includes specifying desired performance and designing the work, and then evolves into an ongoing role of performance optimization as performance is being executed. This model makes it clear that one of the major roles of a manager at any level is to both define and provide performance support.

Some kinds of performance support activities are needed infrequently, while others might be required constantly. For example, a line manager's activities

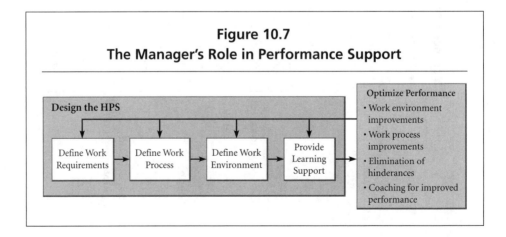

**Figure 10.7**
**The Manager's Role in Performance Support**

Design the HPS

Define Work Requirements → Define Work Process → Define Work Environment → Provide Learning Support

Optimize Performance
• Work environment improvements
• Work process improvements
• Elimination of hinderances
• Coaching for improved performance

typically include making sure that every employee receives basic training when newly hired (an infrequent responsibility), but also require providing frequent coaching on the line as employees execute their jobs. Management tasks such as expectation-setting are, of course, going to be different at different management levels. Typically, the CEO sets out performance expectations for the enterprise for the upcoming year and then monitors results on a quarterly and annual basis. At the line-manager level, performance expectations could conceivably change daily or even hourly and could be different by job, product line, or shift.

Accordingly, the scale of performance support also differs by management level. For example, the CEO has to be concerned with provisioning of learning for all performers in the organization, while the line manager has a much smaller scope. Yet the managerial tasks are largely the same: defining the output requirements, designing the performance, designing the work environment, overseeing performance execution, and providing coaching. The CEO, of course, is unlikely to be involved in many of the day-to-day activities such as coaching of employees other than direct reports, but he or she is still indirectly responsible for the quality of every HPS at every level of the company.

Table 10.2 lists the tasks that managers need to address in order to fully address the Human Performance System when implementing a work change and supporting the ongoing performance of the process. For each element in the HPS model, there is a corresponding set of design tasks and managerial tasks.

By explicitly designing the Human Performance System and aligning it to the corresponding management system, managers can deliver predictable and sustainable results. Failure to pay attention to systems that surround and influence an organization's performers will result in project failures that we have all seen, such as:

- Technology implementations that failed because they did not take into account the full users' context, resulting in expensive work-arounds and late-in-the-game development rework

- New job performance expectations that are initially met but suffer erosion over time because the balance of consequences doesn't support the performers meeting those expectations

- Process performance that declines after implementation because there is no feedback system for performers that allows them to adjust performance

## Table 10.2
## Implementing and Managing the Human Performance System

| HPS Variable | Work Design and Implementation Tasks | Ongoing Managerial Performance Support Tasks |
|---|---|---|
| Output requirements and standards | • Define exactly what outputs and outcomes are expected from a given organization, job, or process.<br><br>• Redefine the performance standards (quantity, quality, time, cost, etc.) for the outputs.<br><br>• Communicate these requirements clearly to the performers (human) and/or developers and maintainers of support tools/technology as a part of implementing the changes. | • Redefine the outputs and outcomes as the business environment and customer requirements change.<br><br>• Redefine the performance standards (quantity, quality, time, cost, etc.) for the outputs.<br><br>• Communicate these requirements clearly to the performers/maintainers on a continual basis. |
| Inputs/ resources | • Specify what resources are needed by performers.<br><br>• Ensure or add capability to the enabling systems that will supply the inputs/resources.<br><br>• Evaluate and adjust the work environment to eliminate anything that hinders performance (e.g., poor work space, job interference). | • Adjust resources requirements as the business environment and customer requirements change.<br><br>• Provide the resources in sufficient quantities when needed.<br><br>• Ensure a continual re-supply of consumable inputs.<br><br>• Monitor the work environment and eliminate anything that hinders performance (e.g., poor work space, job interference, contradictory instructions). |

| | | |
|---|---|---|
| Consequences | • Design the job or task so that it can be performed without excessive difficulty by a well-prepared employee under most circumstances. | • Observe the job as it is being performed and make changes to eliminate causes of delay, irritation, ambiguity, overload, and other negative consequences. |
| Feedback | • Design a feedback system to provide relevant and timely feedback to performers (human) and/or to maintaining functions (technology).<br>• Define the management and maintenance roles and responsibilities regarding monitoring, analysis, and corrective action. | • Provide constructive coaching as the job is being performed (human).<br>• Frequently provide understandable written and verbal information about the performance.<br>• Provide feedback about results (e.g., customer comments, downstream comments, quantitative results). |
| Knowledge, skills, capacity | • Define the additional knowledge, skills, and capacity needed to do the job (human).<br>• Specify and ensure the development and delivery of appropriate training as a part of implementation.<br>• Integrate training into the new hire/ongoing learning system.<br>• Define and communicate the technology capacity requirements to developers and maintenance functions. | • Maintain an inventory of the knowledge, skills and capacity needed to do the job.<br>• Establish a learning system to offer both initial and ongoing formal training to provide knowledge and skills.<br>• Monitor actual performance and gauge whether formal training is providing appropriate and useful content.<br>• Provide job requirements to HR so that qualified candidates are hired.<br>• Provide capacity requirements to maintaining functions. |

## THE CEO'S FOCUS IN STAGE I

Belding already had a management system in place, with some metrics in current use, a management calendar of sorts, and established management behaviors. Owens intends to insert a more robust set of tools and practices but wants to do so without too much upset or confusion. So his approach is incremental.

He appointed a management team for the Order-to-Cash process. The team had developed a measures chain, identified process goals and metrics, and begun to meet regularly to manage the process. Owens knew that this was a make-or-break moment. If the team members learned to work together and saw progress from their efforts to manage the process, they would become a success model for the broader application of process management; if they floundered, the effort could be quickly doomed.

So Owens participated in the weekly Process Management Team meetings and coached the team members on their roles. His primary attention was to the kinds of questions to ask. The meetings consisted mostly of having employees from the various functional areas come in to make reports on their progress toward goals. Owens noticed that the managers on the Process Management Team were quite comfortable asking questions and commenting on the performance of their own functional areas (Sales, Engineering, Finance, etc.), but they were far less sure of themselves when it came to understanding what the other departments were doing. So the meetings were conducted like typical staff meetings, with most team members paying little attention except when their own people were on stage and having to defend themselves. Owens had to change this mentality if he were ever going to break down the silos at Belding. So he mandated that each week only one functional area would give a report, and the focus of the entire Process Management Team would be on that area. During the reviews, he often led the questioning; when he did this, the management team would see that he was trying to understand not just what had happened but why and what could be done to fix any problems or deficiencies anywhere along the chain of activities in the process.

After several weeks of these meetings, the management team had become more adept and comfortable at probing for performance issues and at recognizing patterns. For example, they noticed that a decline in customer meetings in the upstream sales process would lead to a decline in orders several weeks later, so they became more and more interested in understanding the sales process and activities, even though that process was outside their official scope.

The Process Management Team became quite good at asking probing questions and diagnosing underlying performance problems in the process. Eventually, Owens asked Sara and her team to codify these questions in a document, and it became a guide for managers. (A copy of this guide is shown in Figure 13.10 in Part Three.)

The other outcome of these meetings was that the Process Management Team members found themselves asking for some of the same data repeatedly, which helped them understand the Order-to-Cash process. Sara and her team created several trackers containing these data and set up a performance dashboard for the management team. (See samples of the trackers in Figure 13.9 in Part Three.)

Owens also taught the Process Management Team to adjust its approach to performance support. One current practice was for each department to decide on its own what training support it needed and to contract with Training for delivery of courses. Having no other guidance, Training treated all requests as first come, first served, and it almost always had an overload of requests, with some departments waiting months for delivery. The Process Management Team decided to end this approach because it could see that training bottlenecks really hurt performance in some key areas, such as Engineering, more than others. It formalized a training request approach that became the basis for a company-wide support and initiative prioritization process. (There is a description of this process in Chapter 11.)

## THE CEO'S APPROACH IN STAGE II

Owens waited to launch a broader application of the Performance Management System until there was pent-up interest in doing so. As we described in Chapter 9, he waited about a year before applying the new planning approach to the entire business. He also sponsored the mapping out of Belding's entire value creation architecture and promoted the positive results being gained from the redesigned Order-to-Cash process.

But still Owens waited before initiating a full-scale initiative to apply all of the elements of the Performance Management System. He first wanted to see signs indicating that managers and employees were beginning to learn to operate effectively in a horizontal mode. Rather than initiating everything himself, he waited until there were managers asking whether it would make sense to install a horizontal management team to deal with the white-space issues between Launched and Delivered. He waited until a number of employees had raised significant white-space issues for the still-troubled New Product Development process. In this stage, Owens wanted to part ways with his "visionary dictatorship" leadership style and begin to broaden the leadership of this effort. He was well aware that if he did not do this and were to leave the company, the whole concept would soon fall apart.

Yet even when the positive signs appeared, Owens' approach was incremental. He did not immediately put in place all of the Process Management Teams described in Chapter 9. He focused on an area where there was existing interest—namely, the critical gaps between the Launched and Delivered sub-systems. Owens installed an analysis team and convened them to diagnose the current situation. There were major, well-known conflicts between the designers of new products and the manufacturing people who had to build them, the gist being that new products were often too expensive and complex to produce and ended up losing a lot of money. The analysis team's diagnosis resulted in a decision to conduct an Executive PIP on the New Product Development process, but the key difference between this and every previous improvement attempt was that the design team would include both product design engineers and Production staff.

Once the process was redesigned and metrics were established with a measures chain, the management team for Launched and Delivered met regularly to review progress and make decisions collaboratively. After several months, Owens changed the team structure, establishing a permanent horizontal team to manage across the processes within Launched, a similar team to manage across the Sold processes, and a third to manage across the Delivered processes. This immediately begged the question of who should deal with the white-space issues that spanned any of the major sub-systems (across Launched and Delivered, for example, which the problems in the New Product Development process did span). That question gave Owens the rationale for installing the Value Creation Management Team, whose mission was to oversee and address white-space problems across any of the sub-systems, including contributing sub-systems, and their impact on the Value Creation System.

The biggest problem Owens faced with the Value Creation Management Team was the potential confusion in their mission versus their existing roles. The members of that team were the top executives of Belding, Owens' direct reports. They could very well wonder how the Value Creation Management Team was going to be any different from the executive team, where they already saw themselves as collectively running the enterprise. Owens pointed out that in some respects this was true. "We already collectively manage the Value Creation System," he said, "or should. But very little of our dialogue, except during the annual planning exercise, is on the entire work system. We are all too busy representing our own areas. So a 'white-space' issue like the one we had between Launched and Delivered ends up being a protracted argument. This team's role will be to focus on those kind of issues, and there are, unfortunately, quite a few of them." Owens and his executives had seen lots of ineffective teams and committees in their careers. What is different here is that they used the domain matrix to make their mission, things to watch, questions to ask, and actions to take very, very clear. The emphasis was on outcomes.

The VP of Finance, Owens noted, was already very adept at "wearing two hats." When in his role of leading the Finance department, organizing it, getting work executed, and vying for resources, the Finance VP had his functional hat on. But when he was creating the Belding budget, he was trying to think, plan, and act on behalf of the entire enterprise in his role as overseer of the company's assets. "But not all of you," Owens said, "put on that enterprise hat."

As he did with the original Process Management Team for Order-to-Cash, Owens made the bonuses of managers on the sub-system teams and Value Creation Management Team partially dependent on their contributions to those horizontal teams.


## THE BOTTOM LINE

We now have a management framework that summarizes all the critical planning, managing, and supporting activities, from enterprise to individual, that take place over a calendar year. We have a management system that integrates the value and resource dimensions so that management decisions and actions are based on the potential effects on both dimensions, with the ultimate purpose of delivering value to customers and stakeholders.

The system we have set up is an excellent one for "matrix" organizations; it applies equally well to the standard functionally siloed company but with much greater clarity and commitment to the horizontal realm of management.

And finally, we have something that is not merely a bolt-on addition to the management system, as process management has so often wound up being. This *is* the new management system.

In the next chapter we will describe what Owens does to sustain the approach he has put in place.

# What It Will Take

The last item on Owens' agenda is "Sustain" (Figure 11.1). He now has in place what we will call the 3-D Enterprise, an organization in which the two dimensions of value and resources are kept in proper balance by the third dimension of management. Now that the full performance management system is operational and working effectively at Belding, what does he need to do over the long haul to ensure there is no backsliding to old practices and to make the company effective at adapting to the ever-changing business environment?

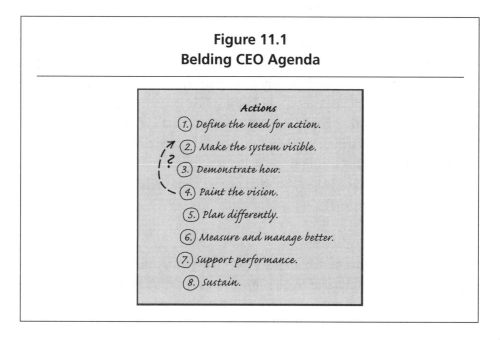

**Figure 11.1**
**Belding CEO Agenda**

*Actions*
1. Define the need for action.
2. Make the system visible.
3. Demonstrate how.
4. Paint the vision.
5. Plan differently.
6. Measure and manage better.
7. Support performance.
8. Sustain.

The unbalanced, near-exclusive focus on resource management that Owens found at Belding when he first joined the company is the management tradition in most organizations. It has become the standard culture, and its reinforcers are many. The focus on resource management is supported by corporate infrastructure: it is built into the chart of accounts, the HR performance management system, hiring and promotional practices, and organization design. Resource management is taught in B-schools, which themselves are often organized in powerful silos that mirror the functional areas found in the companies to which they send their graduates. All of that presents some pretty big barriers to making a permanent shift to a three-dimensional enterprise in which value and resource management are balanced. And the old culture will never completely go away, as Vamik Volkan argues.[1] Lurking in the background, the silo mentality presents an ongoing set of risks to sustaining the change. Success will require a combination of strong leadership and some systemic changes.

## WHAT THE LEADER MUST DO

The single most important element in sustaining the change will of course be what Owens himself does. He introduced this new direction; convinced, cajoled, and pressured others to follow him; cultivated allies and subdued resisters; allocated time, resources, and his own credibility to making two-dimensional management a reality at Belding. The effort succeeded because of him, and he now represents the greatest risk factor to its longevity. If, for example, in a few months he has read some management book and is eagerly flogging his staff to adopt this latest notion, they'll be onto him. The true believers will feel betrayed (and exhausted), while the cynics will feel justified in not being totally committed. It's not that another good idea will never come along nor that Owens can never adjust his approach or thinking, but sustaining the change will happen due in large measure to his continuity, his attention span, and the signals he gives about what is important to him. So what can he or any leader do to nurture and sustain the 3-D Enterprise?

### Be the Champion of Value

If you want your people to be attentive to the issue of value creation, you must hold them accountable to allocating much of their management time to the subject of creating and improving value and to ensuring that the company understands what customers value. If you build a management calendar like we describe in this book, you will have created the infrastructure for management discussions and decision making about the value dimension. But beyond that formal structure is the everyday use of the language and tools we have described—using the value creation architecture, for example, as managers and employees discuss issues and ideas and make decisions. What is the impact of a resource management decision (let's hire more people, let's downsize, let's reorganize, let's change the pay system) on the value dimension? What is the impact of a value decision (let's offer a new product, let's pursue a different market, let's change our competitive strategy) on the resource dimension?

Here are some examples of tradeoffs and decisions drawn from our own experiences, in which both the value and resource dimensions were affected but only one dimension might have been considered until leaders asked the right questions:

- "Let's start selling product X online." This was a value dimension decision, but how would it affect the resource dimension? (The company had a large staff of traditional sales people. Do they go away, or will there be two competing channels to market? Who gets the commissions for online sales? Who manages online selling? What is the process for online selling?)

- "Let's implement this ERP system." This is a resource decision (software being a resource), but with huge implications for the value dimension. ERP software has hardwired certain work processes so that they cannot be altered, at least not without expensive customization. It makes for efficient processing but can become handcuffs for companies that want to be nimble and capable of altering internal practices to meet changing customer requirements. Yet most buyers of ERP systems in the last decade did not pause to consider the future impact on value creation and work processes of what they considered to be work simplification.

- "Let's start a new line of business." Current business is stagnating but there are profits to be made if we get into this related line of work. So let's just add it to our offerings. A value dimension decision, but with huge impact on the resource dimension, especially if we just load all this new work onto the same people who are sustaining the existing business. (This was the phenomenon we saw at one company, which added a major new line of business but with little realization as to how it was straining the existing resources until it looked at its evolving Value Creation System.)

## Be the Guardian of Continuing Value

As top executive at Belding, Owens must help everyone in the organization continue to see the collective mission, to create and deliver value, no matter how complicated and fuzzy the organization's aims might become.

Over time all organizations evolve and become ever more complex. Even if you are leading a small start-up organization with a management team that has a good handle on how you create and deliver value, over time that clear view will become obscured. Complexity is increased with each new market segment, each new regulation, each new supplier base, each acquisition, and with every step change in volume or reach. The result is not a deliberately designed value creation machine, but an organically evolving collection of structures, processes, practices, and resources.

To peer across that complexity and continue to identify the organizational purpose of value creation is the great challenge of leadership, but it must be done. If you are somewhere in the middle of an organization and you don't hear the value message from the top, in time you just don't hear it anymore.

## Create a Culture of Proactive Value Improvement

Improvement in organizations is often leaderless. It may be happening all right, but with a lack of clear purpose, and may not add up to value improvement.

So much of the improvement effort we see is small-scale, largely aimed at making small positive adjustments to what is already in place, and the driver is very often just cost reduction. Seen from the view of the Value Creation Hierarchy, most of these efforts are down at the fourth or fifth levels, aimed at single processes or sub-processes or at the performer level. But while value certainly can be increased incrementally by continually finding ways to reduce the cost side of a business, there is often much more potential in increasing the value side of the equation by finding new ways to market, with innovative products and services, by transforming the entire organization in a different direction.

As the leader, you can ensure that little resource fixes are not sub-optimizing and are not mistaken for value improvement. You can demand both. In most organizations, there are very few people who can see distant opportunity outside. Most employees have their heads down, doing their jobs inside their siloed areas. It's often only the senior leadership who can recognize changes in the business environment that create value opportunities or dangers to the status quo.

A way to challenge your employees about value improvement versus small initiatives is to keep the value dimension visible. Those diagrams of the Value Creation System, the business process framework, the value resources chart, and the process maps are tools for asking whether the right things are being worked on, at the right level, and with the appropriate impact. Those pictures can help everyone understand the scope and scale of improvement and can also shorten the time to implement changes because it is easier to see where the implementation will take place.

### Make "Value Engineering" a Managerial Responsibility

To coin a phrase, let's call the work of designing, maintaining, and changing the value dimension of an organization "value engineering." As leader, you can make value engineering a primary part of the mission and agenda of your leadership team. With each trigger of change, you can require your organization's leaders to sit down together and adapt the Value Creation System. *They* do the redesign, not delegate the task.

With any large-scale change, you need to identify the new set of decisions and tradeoffs. What parts of the organization do we invest in for competitive advantage? What parts of the organization do we leverage for efficiency in this game-changing situation? The value dimension thus drives the resource dimension decisions—that is the essence of strategy. You need to guard against the natural tendency of the resource dimension to take over, to fix in place. None of the senior leaders should be allowed to sit out these decisions and simply elect to preserve their fiefdoms.

## SYSTEMIC CHANGES TO SUPPORT THE 3-D ENTERPRISE

The following are a number of suggestions to help in getting a 3-D Enterprise in place and in providing support as the changes gradually become institutionalized. These ideas are certainly not mandatory, but they come from our own experience in assisting and watching organizations as they progress from typical siloed management to a permanent improvement in the conduct of their business.

### Changes to Infrastructure

In most large organizations, there are pockets of problem-solving expertise scattered among the functional silos, many of them isolated from each other or, alternately, vying for the attention of senior management. This can result in competitive attitudes that lead to counterproductive sub-optimizing behaviors and wasteful projects. Our suspicion is that the dominant resource dimension viewpoint that leads to the optimization of functions (at the expense of the larger Value Creation System) is also the primary driver for sub-optimizing competitiveness among support functions, all of whom must scrabble for their scraps of funding separately and therefore tend to view each other as rivals instead of as allies.

What can be done to overcome this deeply imbedded tendency? A couple of things:

1. We would recommend a centralized approach to identifying, choosing, funding, and managing change initiatives—a change control management system that focuses on optimization of the enterprise-level Value Creation System. Such a system is described in our companion book on processes, *White Space Revisited*.[2] We will provide a quick description here.

2. The central figures in developing and implementing the change control management system are people we call Performance Architects.

**The Role of Performance Architects**   Performance Architects—whose membership could be drawn from multiple disciplines such as Six Sigma, Human Resources, Quality, Process Excellence, IT, and so on—could support the following kinds of work:

• Development and documentation of the organization's value creation architecture

• Analysis, design, redesign, and improvement of the organization's Value Creation System (all five levels)

• Analysis, design, redesign, and improvement of the organization's management system (all management levels)

In short, the role of Performance Architects is to provide design skills for the three dimensions of the enterprise (value, resources, and management). Their role would support the value creation architecture mapping and management system redesign efforts described in this book.

Their ongoing operational role could be the care and feeding of a formalized change control management system. In many organizations, as we saw at Belding, there is an endless stream of unmanaged changes under way that are un-prioritized, potentially redundant, insufficiently important, consuming incalculable amounts of staff time and energy, potentially counterproductive to one another, and most important of all, have the potential to sub-optimize the performance of the total Value Creation System. These change initiatives range from introducing Balanced Scorecards in Engineering to a Six Sigma project in Production to implementing a new CRM application in Sales. To be sure, in many organizations there are project management offices (PMOs), and project planning methodologies abound, but they are siloed. They exist in multiple places in big companies, and they don't "talk" to each other, the result being many different initiatives, sometimes at cross-purposes, all vying for resources.

An effective way to get a lasso around this is a single organizational change process. At Belding, this process was managed by the Value Creation Management Team, since they were accountable for the performance of the Value Creation System, and all these proposed changes ultimately affected its performance, positively or negatively. The objectives were to avoid inadvertent sub-optimization; properly prioritize needed changes; and manage the execution of change efforts. Supporting the management team in this effort is the Performance Architect group.

**The Change Control Management System**  The policy would be that performance improvement initiatives can happen in only one of two ways:

- As part of the annual planning process
- With approval of the Value Creation Management Team

All performance improvement initiatives, including IT projects, follow this process:

1. Every proposed performance improvement initiative is summarized in a one-page proposal.

2. If the initiative is input to the annual planning process, it will be reviewed by the Value Creation Management Team in that context. Otherwise, the proposal is sent to the Performance Architects, who log it into their database and conduct a brief feasibility and impact check to determine whether the initiative:

   - Is redundant
   - Is likely to produce the desired result for the proposed cost

- Is to be carried out at an appropriate point and with the necessary scope to be effective
- Could/should be modified to make it more effective
- Will sub-optimize Value Creation System performance
- Fits with longer-term strategic goals

3. The Performance Architects develop a preliminary project plan, identifying the resources required to achieve the desired improvement in performance. (For example, the project might include the resources necessary to survey customers, redesign an internal process, customize an IT application, or impart new skills via training.)

4. The Performance Architects forward the proposal and a recommendation to the Value Creation Management Team for review at their next monthly meeting.

5. The Value Creation Management Team considers the recommendation and makes their decision.

6. If the initiative is approved, the Value Creation Management Team appoints a member as sponsor of the project, regardless of size. The Performance Architect group then:
   - Finalizes the project plan, selects a project leader, and assembles a project team
   - Enters the project into their tracking system
   - Adds the project to the Change Initiative Tracking Map in the Management Bridge Room, which shows the location of all initiatives on the business process framework map
   - Monitors the progress of all change initiatives in the pipeline

7. The Value Creation Management Team reviews the progress of all initiatives quarterly.

For Belding, the benefits of having a Performance Architect group which runs a centralized change control management system included:

- The reduction of the number of initiatives floating around the organization by about two-thirds

- An almost complete stop to the knee-jerk, quick-fix, "do something" responses to ill-defined symptoms of poor performance
- Prioritization of projects at the Value Creation System level
- Performance "problems" no longer initiated deep in some functional silo and addressed with some narrow, incomplete, or inappropriate "solution"
- Management visibility into all projects
- An overall reduction in project cycle time, due to a robust front end that clarifies priorities and ongoing management of the required resources
- Value Creation Management Team accountability for the ultimate effectiveness of change efforts

The result is a single change initiative portfolio management system that focuses everyone on value throughout the phases of project definition, prioritization, execution, and results assessment.

**Improvement Methodology**   What can greatly facilitate the effectiveness of the two preceding infrastructure concepts (Performance Architects and a single change process) is a single improvement methodology. Earlier in this book we described the Executive PIP and Belding's improvement effort to redesign the Order-to-Cash process. Belding employed our process improvement methodology called the Rummler Process Methodology (RPM), which is described in detail in our companion book, *White Space Revisited: Creating Value Through Process.* But whether it is this methodology or another, the great advantage of having a single, formal improvement methodology is to cancel out the in-fighting that tends to occur when internal improvement groups each choose their own. It may not be evident from a senior leader's vantage point, but the amount of time and money that can be wasted on bitter internecine battles over tools and methods by specialists inside a company can be enormous. Meanwhile, things aren't being improved, or the efforts stall over methods and tools.

So choose a method, and then bestow on it the status of formal approval. Don't be sidetracked by arguments that someone's favorite technique doesn't fit. A robust improvement methodology becomes an umbrella for tools and techniques.

But also be careful. Choose a true methodology, which—stated as simply as possible—is a step-by-step process for doing improvement work. You can see the exact steps, understand the roles, understand the deliverables, and recognize the outcome. It is repeatable, teachable, and straightforward. Don't be fooled by things that masquerade as methodologies—for example, philosophies or concepts. *Kaizen*, the Japanese word for continuous improvement, is a valuable notion, an admirable goal. But if you decide that your organization should pursue kaizen, you haven't given the means for achieving it. The means is a teachable methodology. Many, many books and consultants out there offer visions, philosophies, and concepts, but relatively few ever tell you how to get there, so beware what you adopt from outside.

## Changes to the Prevailing Consequence System

In Chapter 10 we outlined a model called the Human Performance System, which posits that there is a finite set of variables that influence the choices and behaviors of people in organizations. The variables were expectations, resources, consequences, feedback, and the competencies and innate capacity of the performer. Of these, consequences are the governor of both short- and long-term behavior; indeed, some would argue that consequences are the most important of the variables.

Consequences are what happen to a performer, both positive and negative, short-term and long-term. Short-term consequences might be receiving thanks from a customer or boss, being assigned an interesting task, being yelled at, getting off work early, and so on. Long-term consequences may be receiving a raise, promotion, demotion, transfer, or termination.

The consequence system determines what happens to people when they do their jobs. It is potentially the strongest lever for performance change. In fact, we would argue the prevailing consequence system is organizational culture. Culture is often described as "how things are done around here" or "what's important here." The notion of consequences captures both parts of that definition—both behavior (what is done) and why (because it's viewed as important).

So the best way to make a change permanent, to "change the culture," is to harness the change to the consequence system—to alter, or add to, the consequence system so that it is aligned to the change you want. This is what Owens was doing (back in Chapter 7) when he altered the bonus system at Belding to reward collaborative results for the management team of the Order-to-Cash process.

The opposite is also true: Fail to link a change to the consequence system and it is unlikely to take hold, to become permanent. The kind of organization we have described in this book is one with a value-oriented culture. To both create and sustain it, one must clarify what is important and then reward the right behaviors—that is, reward those who stop looking at the world through resource-tinted glasses and who embrace the new lens of value.

Long-term, what would be required to sustain a 3-D Enterprise are changes to the compensation system so that part of compensation is for meeting value goals, not just resource goals such as staying within budget. Changes to promotion criteria and succession planning to put merit on value management would also be necessary. In addition to altering the formal reward systems, there is great leverage in simple acts of recognition. Identify those people, call attention to them, reward them publicly and generously.

Now none of this is news to most managers. Everyone who has been in a managerial role soon recognizes that a quick and reasonably effective way to get immediate attention to something (if not actual change) is to link it to the formal reward system—to pay systems, bonus plans, and promotions. In fact, what we've seen is that executives who want to engineer a big change often immediately jump to this tactic. But they don't always have the patience (or sometimes the insight) to alter the daily management practices inside their organizations, so they don't change short-term consequences, and these are the ones that govern day-to-day behavior.

Sometimes it is even harder to stop rewarding the wrong things. Suboptimization is often rewarded in organizations—like the bonus system we described in Chapter 3, where managers kept on building products that weren't selling because the bonus system paid them for production rather than revenue or profitability. Or the rewarding of heroics: When an extraordinary, heroic effort occurs, do thank the hero, but then immediately ask your people to find out why it took heroics to accomplish something. A well-designed, balanced, capable organization shouldn't need heroics; it needs performers who know what they're doing and know that the organization will support them in their roles. Dismantling part of the consequence system may be required, but you can expect that once a reward has been in place a while, it hardens into an expectation and becomes very difficult to replace or discard. It can be done, though, especially if balanced with new rewards but ones aligned to value creation.

## MANAGEMENT SUPPORT

What we have described requires a lot of changes to the management system, and thus to the roles of managers. The transition can be enhanced by providing managers with some aids. The following are two kinds of assistance to consider:

### 1. Job Aids for Managers

Until managing the value dimension becomes second nature, managers can benefit from tools that help them become versed. There are several tools in Chapter 13 that can be helpful:

- Sets of questions for managers to ask about performance of the value dimension. These questions are keyed to the levels of the Value Creation Hierarchy, so the questions differ depending on whether the scope of inquiry is the whole business, the entire Value Creation System, a processing sub-system, or a single process.
- Troubleshooting guides for understanding the new metrics that measure process performance.
- Meeting agendas that allocate time for reviewing value creation and process results before diving into resource dimension discussions.

### 2. Facilitation and Coaches

At first it can be awkward and confusing to run a management meeting that focuses attention on the Value Creation System, so just as Owen coached his first Process Management Team through their first meetings about the Order-to-Cash process, you may want to facilitate the new management meetings or find someone to help.

The other form of help can be coaches who work with individual managers to help them become comfortable with their new roles.

## TOWARD 2-D MANAGEMENT

The current state of management systems in most organizations favors the dominance of the resource dimension over the value dimension. This imbalance tends to cause dysfunctional behaviors of non-collaboration, building of personal fiefdoms, and focusing on sub-optimal goals and personal gain. The greatest driver of this imbalance is organizational complexity, which over time obscures an organization's primary purpose of creating and delivering value to customers. It would be wonderful if organizations could somehow keep themselves lean and focused on their core missions even as they grow. Many organizations have strived to do so, but the erosion of understanding about value creation seems pretty inevitable.

Making work processes leaner, simpler, and more effective is one means to restore clarity of organizational purpose, and that is the focus of our *White Space Revisited* book. The second way is to revise the management system, which is the focus of this book. These are not alternatives, however. Both are needed.

To be sure, major barriers to a 3-D Enterprise exist along the way, but a reorientation to value versus resources can help a company achieve far-reaching objectives. All the lofty notions that organizations strive for—innovation, agility, greatness, operational excellence, and so forth—are more tangible and actionable when the leaders focus on value.

It was certainly the case for S.K. Owens and his executives as their journey led Belding to great benefits and also positioned them strategically, agile and ready for whatever came next.

While this journey is tough, it is worth it.

# PART THREE

# A Closer Look at Belding

In Part Three we provide a closer look at the templates and tools we use to develop management systems for organizations. To illustrate how the various charts and tools look when filled out, we continue to follow the Belding case.

Our purpose here is to provide plenty of concrete examples for people who want to apply our approach to the design of management systems. For those who prefer to stay with the highlights, Chapters 1 through 11 are sufficient, but this section contains the nuts and bolts for those managers and practitioners who want to put the ideas in this book into action.

This section is constructed to match the previous chapters. First we look at the tools that are described as being used in Stage I of the revitalization of Belding. Then we delve into the tools and techniques Owens chooses in Stage II. And then we revisit Belding and look again at the seven scenarios first described in Chapter 4, but this time we walk through how they would be managed differently with an effectively designed management system in place.

# Belding Case Tools, Stage I chapter<br>**TWELVE**

**D**uring Stage I, Owens installed some elements of a balanced management system. Parts of Performance Planned were put in place but dealt with only one process (Order-to-Cash). He also put in place elements of Performance Managed, but once again largely related to the Order-to-Cash process.

Owens' first step in Stage I was to make the two dimensions of the Belding business visible. He accomplished this by having four pictures of the business developed, each of which provided certain details of the value or resource dimensions and how they were functioning currently.

## SUPER-SYSTEM MAP

The first tool was a super-system map. This tool depicts the environment in which a given organization exists, and it is a great device for testing the overall design of the internal organization against its ultimate reality: the external world. Because Owens was not sure all of his executives at Belding even understood the nature of the business the same way, he wanted to start with this from-the-outside view.

A super-system map typically shows the external factors affecting the organization:

- The consumer marketplace
- The capital marketplace
- Competition

- Resources/supply chain
- The general business environment of economy, culture, natural environment, government, and geo-political

Such a map can be used to identify current facts about a business (for example, market share, revenues, competitors, regulatory agencies) as well as trends (for example, growing competition, price pressure, emerging government regulations, economic predictions). Where helpful, you can show the customer's customers, tracing the value chain all the way to the final consumer. Sometimes this becomes highly complex, such as when an organization has developed multiple paths to the marketplace. The utility of diagramming all of this complexity can help a management team see what they are trying to manage and aid them in testing their assumptions and decisions.

A super-system map can also be used to develop or test an organization's strategy and internal design, which is why Owens wanted one developed during Stage I. Rather than rely on a rather arbitrary "threat/opportunity" exercise, he can conduct an annual super-system review to align the executive leadership team on a common view of the next three years. A template for drawing a super-system map is in Figure 12.1 at the end of this chapter.

## CROSS-FUNCTIONAL VALUE CREATION SYSTEM MAP

This type of map depicts the processes that constitute an organization's Value Creation System. It uses a cross-functional "swimlane" format, with the departments and key players participating in the system on the vertical axis and all of the major activities in the swimlanes. For Owens, this is the picture he can point to and say, "This is the core of our business. If we do not understand how this works and don't manage it for the optimum benefit of customers and stakeholders, we cannot succeed as a business."

The processes are organized into the major sub-systems of Launched, Sold, and Delivered. With such a map it is easy to tell how well these processes have been organized and linked together to deliver sustained value to the marketplace. The format for this map is shown in Figure 12.2 at the end of this chapter.

## BUSINESS PROCESS FRAMEWORK

The previous tool identified those work processes that create, sell, and deliver valued goods and services to customers. But there are many more processes that exist in any complex organization, and the business process framework serves to identify and organize all of them.

The processes on a business process framework chart are categorized as management processes, value-creating processes (the same ones that appeared in the cross-functional Value Creation System map), and contributing processes. This tool helps in distinguishing these types of processes, which are sometimes confused and as a result can be poorly designed, improperly resourced, and of questionable value. The framework provides a selection for doing process design, improvement, or management, which is why Owens wanted this picture developed during Stage I. The format for a business process framework is shown in Figure 12.3 at the end of the chapter.

## VALUE-RESOURCE DETAIL CHART

This tool aids in understanding the resource dimension and the value dimension in concert. It displays all of the major resources (human and technology in the example in Figure 12.4) and where they are deployed in support of the Value Creation System. It is a visually compelling depiction of how well resources are actually aligned in support of the value creation processes. Often it uncovers gaps in coverage or illogical allocation of resources—too much for some areas and too little for others. Owens wanted this tool during Stage I because he suspected that one of Belding's major flaws was illogical resource allocation, and this tool could help him prove his case.

Once developed, the chart can be very useful to those departments that supply resources (HR, IT, etc.). They can use it to do planning of resource acquisition and allocation in a way that clearly supports the organization's core processes. The format for a Value-Resource Detail Chart is shown in Figure 12.4. Instead of dots to show the allocation of resources to the processes, actual numbers can be used.

# Figure 12.1
## Belding Super-System Map

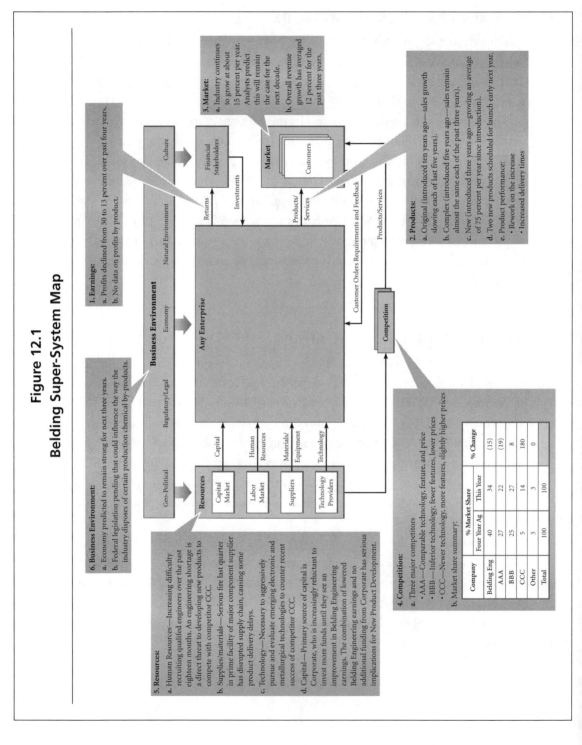

# Figure 12.2
## Cross-Functional Value Creation System Map

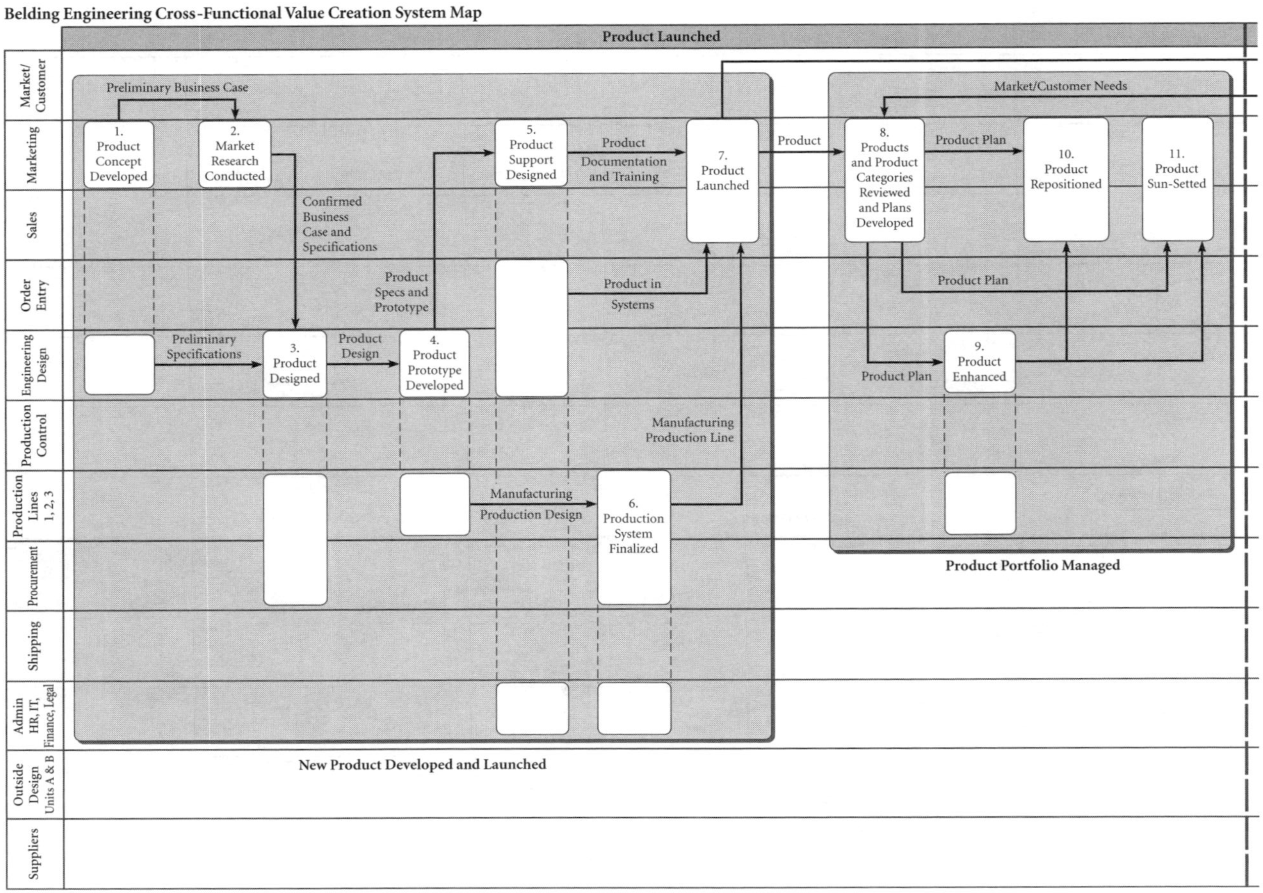

(*Continued*)

# Figure 12.2
## Cross-Functional Value Creation System Map (*Continued*)

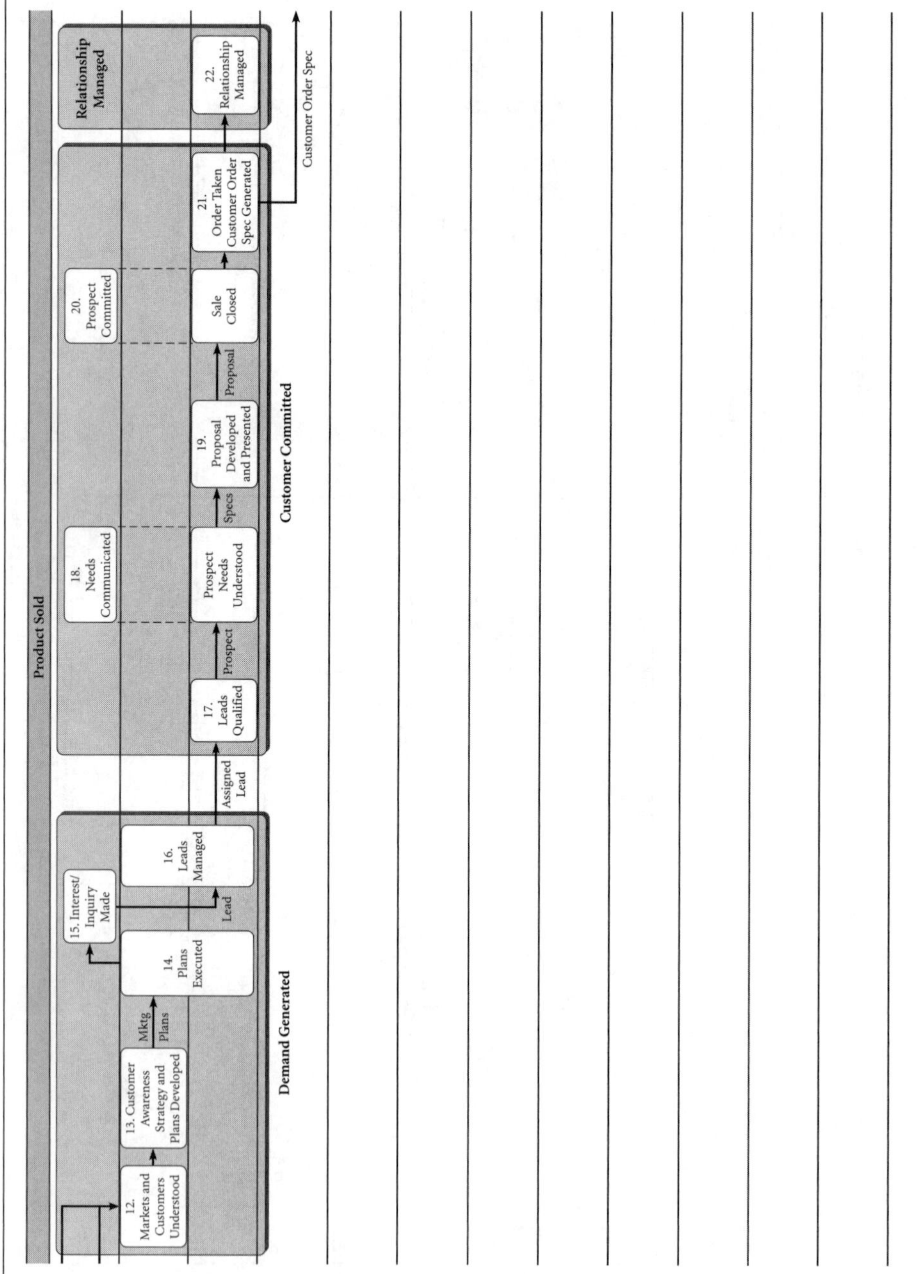

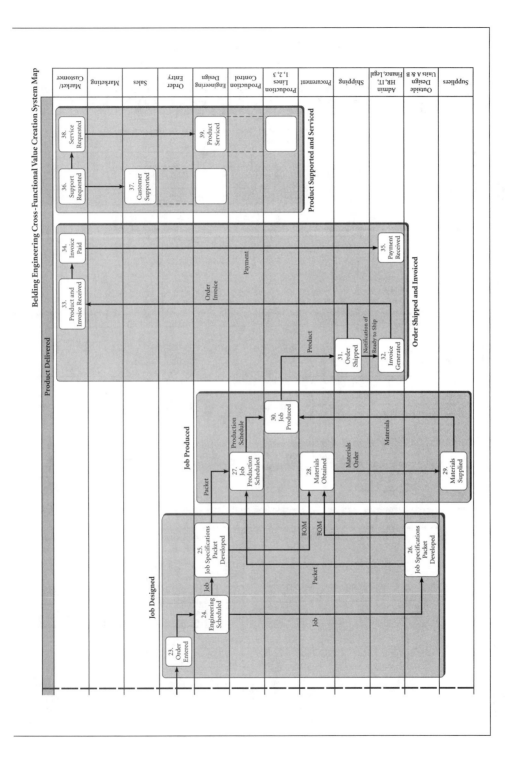

Belding Engineering Cross-Functional Value Creation System Map

# Figure 12.3
## Business Process Framework

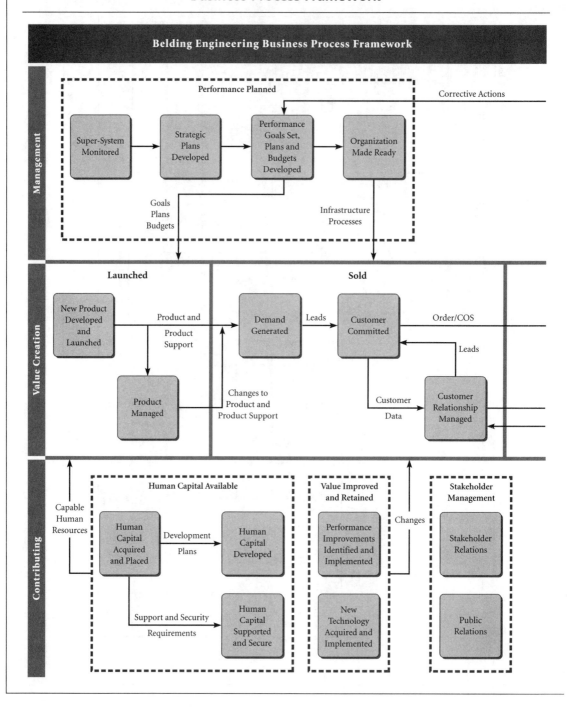

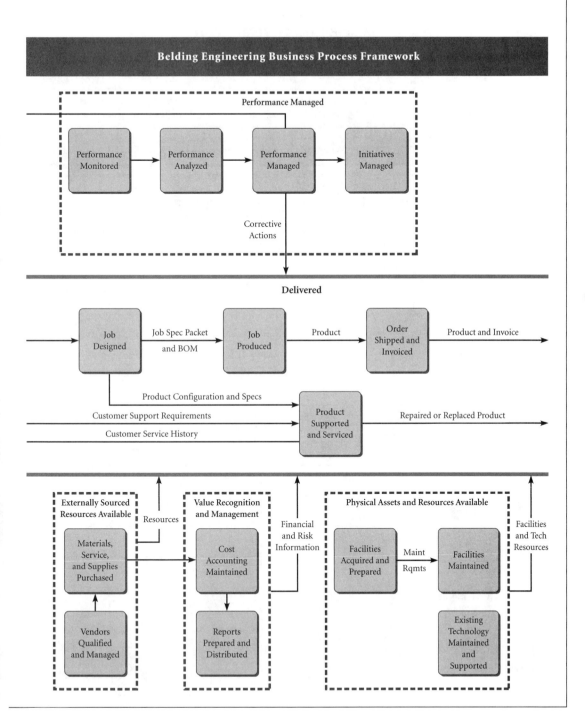

**Belding Engineering Business Process Framework**

Performance Managed

| Performance Monitored | Performance Analyzed | Performance Managed | Initiatives Managed |

Corrective Actions

**Delivered**

| Job Designed | Job Spec Packet and BOM | Job Produced | Product | Order Shipped and Invoiced | Product and Invoice |

Product Configuration and Specs

Customer Support Requirements

Customer Service History

Product Supported and Serviced

Repaired or Replaced Product

**Externally Sourced Resources Available**

Resources

Materials, Service, and Supplies Purchased

Vendors Qualified and Managed

**Value Recognition and Management**

Financial and Risk Information

Cost Accounting Maintained

Reports Prepared and Distributed

**Physical Assets and Resources Available**

Facilities and Tech Resources

Facilities Acquired and Prepared

Maint Rqmts

Facilities Maintained

Existing Technology Maintained and Supported

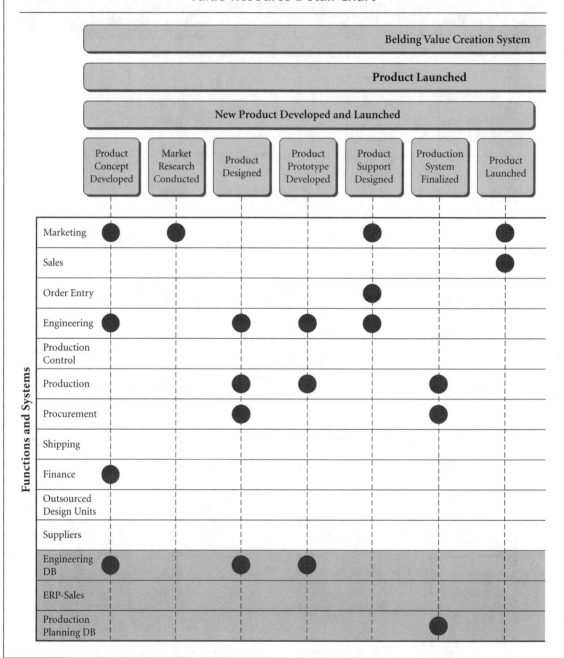

**Figure 12.4**
**Value-Resource Detail Chart**

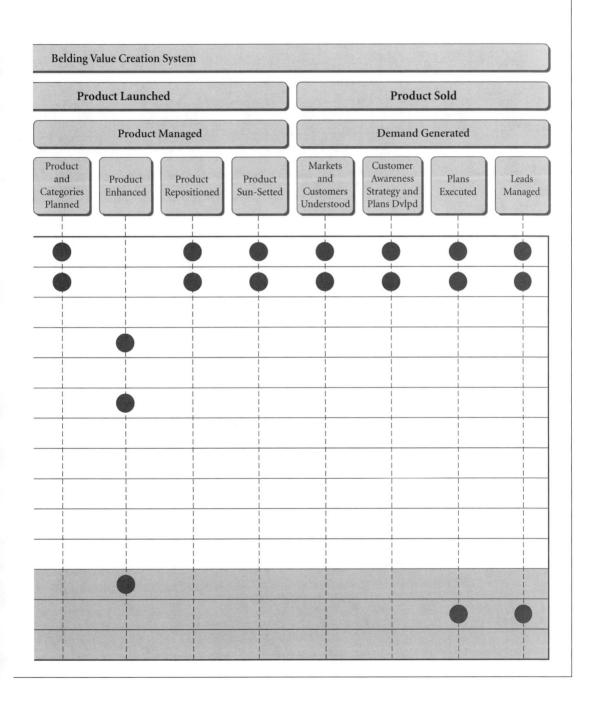

# Belding Case Tools, Stage II

D uring Stage II, Owens installed the remaining elements of the Belding management system. He completed the pieces of the value creation architecture that were not done in Stage I. Some of these helped in initiating the Executive PIP for the New Product Development process. To complete all of this documentation, he again called upon Sara, who led a small team of managers and others in creating this collection of diagrams. (See the samples at the end of this chapter.)

## VALUE CREATION ARCHITECTURE MAPS

### Belding Value-Resource Map

This diagram was a simple but powerful way of diagnosing the participation of key functions in Belding's Value Creation System. Shown in Figure 13.1 at the end of the chapter, the picture verified that the Product Launched sub-system was not supported by several key departments (that is, Sales and Production), which helped to explain why Belding had developed such a poor record for new product launches.

The format for this diagram is simple: it shows on one page the three major components (Launched, Sold, and Delivered) of the Value Creation System for the business and which departments, regions, or areas were involved in those components. The map provides a bird's-eye view of both the value and resource dimensions and can be the first indicator that a given organization has distributed its resources illogically.

## Cross-Functional Processing Sub-System Map

This tool was applied as "drill-downs" of the three processing sub-systems of Launched, Sold, and Delivered. The format is the same cross-functional "swim-lane" format used for single process mapping and provides a lot of detail about the steps in the sub-system and who is accountable for executing them. An example is shown in Figure 13.2 at the end of the chapter.

## Cross-Functional Process Maps

To complete the architecture in Stage II, Owens also had swimlane maps developed down to Level 4 for all those primary and contributing processes identified on the business process framework and some definition at Level 5 where needed. The documenters also provided a list of disconnects and preliminary recommendations for improvement for each process mapped. An example from the maps is shown in Figure 13.3 at the end of the chapter.

## Measures Chains

For each cross-functional process map, Sara and her team also developed a measures chain. Figure 13.4 shows the measures chain created for the Job Designed process. For the other cross-functional process maps created in Stage II, Sara and her team developed measures chains with the same format. Each one starts by defining the performance dimensions (such as quality, timeliness, cost, and so forth) important to the customer for that process and the possible measures (external end-of-process measures) for those dimensions. Compatible metrics are then defined for the entire process (internal end-of-process measures) and each of the sub-processes (sub-process measures).

## PERFORMANCE PLANNED AND MANAGED

In Stage II, Owens built a complete management system of Performance Planned and Managed for each level of the managerial hierarchy of Belding. Figure 13.5 at the end of the chapter shows how the management system links each management role to a level of the Value Creation Hierarchy. Performance planning cascades from enterprise level all the way down to the performers who are executing their jobs inside work processes; conversely, as performance is executed, managers are monitoring and reporting performance results upward. Diagnostics and corrections are taken when results do not match expectations.

Owens expanded the management of the value dimension by establishing management teams for the Launched, Sold, and Delivered sub-systems and designated process owners for certain important processes, such as New Product Development. He enlarged the management calendar to include planning at all levels of the Value Creation Hierarchy and for all processes. He had metrics, dashboards, and trackers created for all the key processes. And finally, to help current and future managers to understand and operate the two-dimension management system, he had a set of management guides developed.

The tools that comprise the management system are displayed in Figure 13.6 at the end of the chapter. The purpose of each of these tools is described in the following pages. Note that the essentials for the management system are identifying the processes and mapping the value creation architecture. Then measures chains were created to determine the metrics for each identified process.

## Management Domain Matrix

To complete the picture of what various managers do in Performance Planned and Managed, Owens had the management domain matrix finalized so that it showed the actions of managers at each level of the organization in their roles of performance planning, performance monitoring, diagnosing deviations, and taking corrective actions. In Table 13.1 at the end of the chapter is the full domain chart for Belding, with all the horizontal management roles in place down to the functional level.

The Domain column in Table 13.1 lists management roles and their "domain" (scope and level) of responsibility. The domains are listed in descending scope. The first domain, for example, is responsible for the performance of the entire enterprise; the next one is responsible for the Value Creation System inside the enterprise, and so on. The role and membership of each team are also listed. In many cases, the same individuals are on more than one team, but their specific responsibilities are different. The Sales VP shows up at every level: first as a member of the executive team in charge of the whole enterprise, then as a member of the Value Creation Management Team, as head of the team that oversees the Sold processing sub-system, as process owner of the Customer Committed Team, and finally as head of the Sales function. This is the "multiple hats" effect: a single executive or manager can have multiple roles to carry out when value management is explicitly defined and overlaid on the existing organization chart.

The second column on the chart describes the overall mission and objectives of each team. In the Performance Planned column are the specific planning activities the team or individual is expected to accomplish. The scope of planning narrows according to role as you move from top to bottom on the chart. In parallel are the Performance Monitoring activities expected for each role.

The last two columns are an expansion on performance monitoring, included because when value management is added to the responsibilities of managers, they sometimes are not certain just what they are supposed to be monitoring or what to do when they do spot a negative trend or potential issue.

## Management Calendar

In Stage I, Owens chartered a Process Management Team for the Order-to-Cash process and had them develop goals and metrics for the process. In Stage II he established a formal management calendar to include all the planning and managing activities of the entire enterprise. Included in the calendar were all of the teams and roles listed in the management domain chart, as well as all of the planning and management of the functional areas and contributing processes. Figure 13.7 shows the Performance Planned portion of the calendar. Performance Managed (organized into events that happen quarterly, monthly, weekly to daily) is in Figure 13.8. Both figures are at the end of this chapter.

## Performance Trackers

Performance trackers were developed to populate the Belding tracking system described in Chapter 10. In Figure 13.9 at the end of the chapter are some sample formats for performance trackers at Belding. Each tracker is designed to provide insight into actual performance against the goals established during Performance Planned. While the formats of trackers can vary depending on the type and amount of data, they all have certain features in common:

- They track trends over time rather than providing single data points, which are usually not very helpful in understanding what may be affecting performance.

- They correlate multiple variables to provide insight into what may be affecting what. When correlations are combined with trends over time, the manager has a powerful way of understanding gradual deterioration in performance instead of being surprised by what seem to be sudden changes.

- The correlations often measure variables that are controlled by quite different parts of the organization: for example, tooling costs, which are managed by Engineering, versus product defect rates, which are managed by Production. This kind of data can help to encourage collaboration across functional silos to address performance issues.

Once the tracking system is in place, it can be associated with the management calendar so that one can see at a glance who is looking at what trackers and when they should be doing so. In Figure 13.10, Belding's management calendar is lined up with the trackers to show when each tracker is supposed to be reviewed.

The new measurement system for Belding can be summarized by tallying up the performance indicators across the Value Creation System of Launched, Sold, and Delivered and across the functional areas. In the first row of Figure 13.11 (at the end of this chapter), you see the old Belding performance measures versus the new ones, which are far more complete and provide true coverage to both the vertical resource organization and the horizontal work system.

## Management Guides

For managers who may need assistance in monitoring performance and making decisions about appropriate actions (think of managers new to the job or to a particular area), additional assistance was developed.

Figure 13.12 shows a performance tracker for discounts and a user's guide for interpreting the information on the performance tracker. The guide is organized according to typical problem scenarios that the manager might see on the discounts tracker. The guide provides what scenarios to look for, possible causes of the problem, and possible actions for resolving the issue.

Table 13.2 provides another example of a management guide, in this case questions that managers at Belding could ask to elicit more performance information, including possible causes of issues and sources for data (which in many cases are the trackers that compose the Belding performance tracking system).

## Troubleshooting Logic Diagrams

Much of the management work required to manage the organization as a system is diagnosing and acting on performance feedback with the appropriate corrective action, which might be to provide coaching, better training or feedback, different tools or methods, and so on. Troubleshooting tools such as the one in

Figure 13.13 at the end of the chapter are intended to help managers assess data, draw the right conclusions, and choose the right actions.

## Meeting Agendas

In most organizations, the best arena for managing the organization as a system is in regular meetings in which management teams plan and make decisions. The management calendar is typically built according to the schedule of management meetings. The final tool we present here is a sample meeting agenda (Figure 13.14) that aids Belding's management teams in organizing their meetings to ensure that content and decision making include both the value and the resource dimensions.

The collective purpose of these management system design tools is to help management teams optimize performance without falling into functional turf problems.

For example, the management calendar in our illustrations includes a monthly Performance Managed meeting to emphasize that functions exist to support the value creation processes, which in turn meet customer and organization requirements. It works like this:

- The executive team of the president and all vice presidents meets every month for a review of operations and performance against goals. It is usually a four-hour meeting, chaired by the president.

- The first thirty minutes of the meeting focus on a quick briefing on performance against corporate goals for the month and year-to-date, including financials, sales performance, and customer satisfaction data.

- The next segment of the meeting, usually an hour and a half, is a review of process performance against goals. The Process Management Team Chair (also a functional VP on the executive team) for each value creation process reports on how his or her process has performed against the goals for the period. The Chair/VP is also expected to comment on any issues regarding sub-optimization of the process by any function.

- On a rotational basis, each month the performance of one of the contributing processes is reviewed in a similar manner. The president is a big advocate of "functions exist to support processes" and listens carefully during this segment of the meeting for indications that this is not the case.

- In the final hour-and-a-half segment of the meeting, the focus shifts to a review of each major function in the company. Each VP gives a brief summary of his or her function's performance against monthly goals and raises any issues he or she is having or anticipates having in supporting any of the value creation processes.

- The CEO is quick to ask questions if he senses a function is failing to support one of the processes as required. If such a problem is identified, the president leads a positive "problem-solving" discussion of why the problem exists and what must be done (by all VPs, not just that function VP) to correct the problem, prevent the problem from happening again, and recover from the problem.

A company may have thousands of individuals in hundreds of jobs performing more or less related activities aimed at meeting ever-changing customer requirements or expectations. It is a major management challenge to provide direction for such a complex organism. The alternative is to view the company as a processing system that delivers valued products to customers through a handful of critical processes—basically three value creation subsystems and several contributing processes. With this processing system view of organizations, the primary management task for executives and managers becomes two-fold:

- First, ensure that the internal processing system is aligned with the external "super-system" requirements and reality. For example, if customers expect to receive their orders in five days (because that is what your competition does), then you need to be sure that "five days" is the standard for delivery of the Order Fulfillment process. Likewise with expectations for New Product Development, Customer Service, and so on.

- Second, ensure that the internal processing system is efficient and effective in meeting organization goals and customer requirements. That is, if you set an order fulfillment standard of five days, your job as a management team is to see that the order fulfillment process can meet that standard. You must see that the process is appropriately designed and resourced to consistently meet that customer-driven performance goal.

The whole idea of the management system is to make complex organizations more manageable.

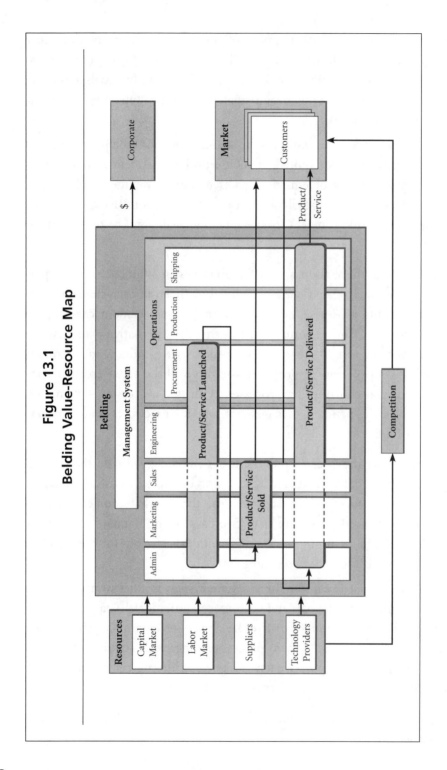

## Figure 13.1
## Belding Value-Resource Map

# Figure 13.2
## "Launched" Processing Sub-System Map

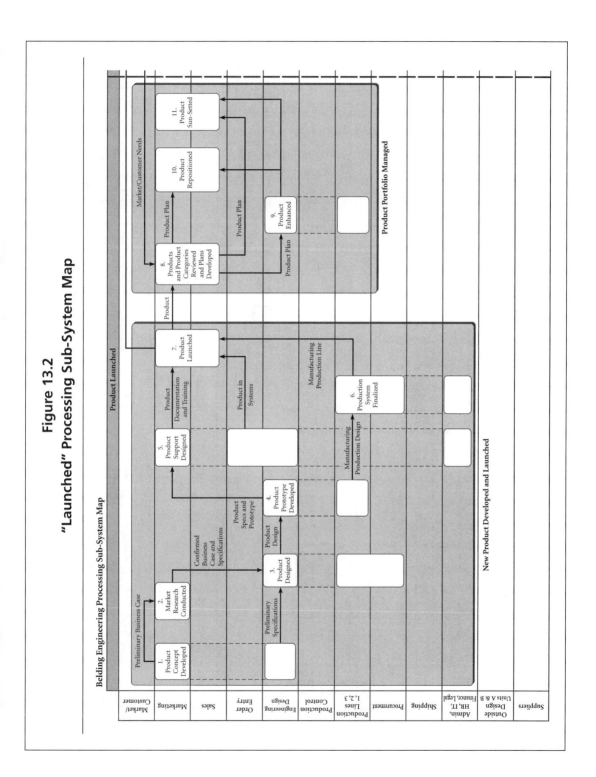

# Figure 13.3
## "Job Designed" Process

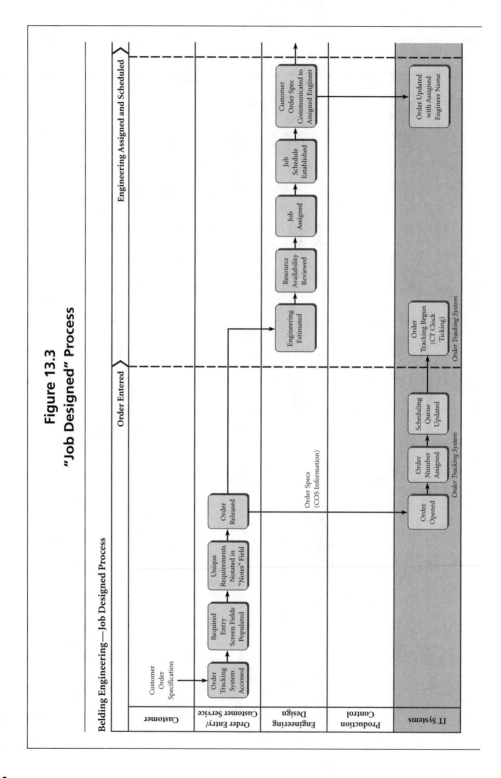

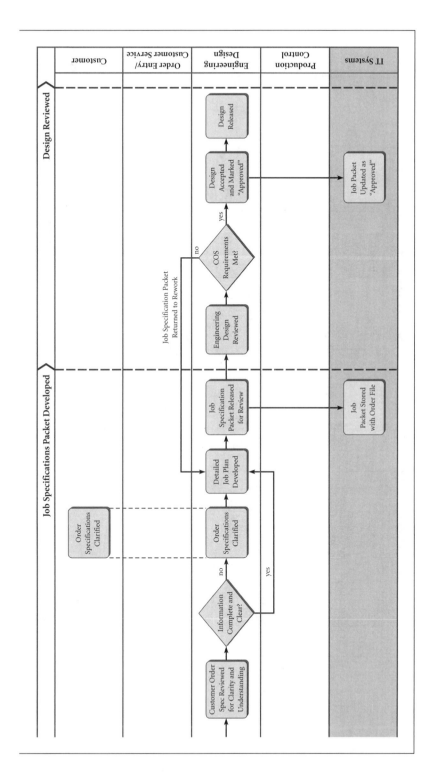

## Figure 13.4
## Measures Chain for Belding's Job Designed Process

| Input Metrics | Sub-Process Metrics Order Entered | Sub-Process Metrics Engineering Assigned and Scheduled | Sub-Process Metrics Job Specifications Packet Developed | Sub-Process Metrics Design Reviewed | Internal End-of-Process Metrics | External End-of-Process Metrics | Related Enterprise Metrics |
|---|---|---|---|---|---|---|---|
| Inputs | Sub-Process Outputs | Sub-Process Outputs | Sub-Process Outputs | Sub-Process Outputs | Process Outputs | | |
| • Customer Order | • Actionable Order | • Engineering Assignment<br>• Updated Order<br>• Engineering Schedule | • Job Packet including:<br>  • Engineering Drawing<br>  • Bill of Materials | • Approved Job Packet<br>• Released Design<br>• Released BOM | • Approved Job Packet<br>• Released Design<br>• Released BOM | | |
| **TIMELINESS METRICS** | | | | | | | |
| | • Cycle time order processed | • Cycle time to schedule confirmed | • Cycle time to packet completed<br>• Percent of design reuse | • Cycle time packet approved<br>• Backlog | • Cycle time order to release | • Late orders | • Customer satisfaction<br>• Market share<br>• Cost of goods sold |

**QUALITY METRICS**

| | | | | | | |
|---|---|---|---|---|---|---|
| • Customer orders by buyer type | • Order entry errors<br>• Number of orders requiring clarification with customer | • Design errors by type (caught in review, past review)<br>• BOM errors | • Jobs with rework due to design error<br>• Jobs with BOM errors | • Jobs with rework due to design error<br>• Jobs delayed due to BOM errors | • Orders not meeting spec | • Customer satisfaction<br>• Market share |

**ECONOMIC METRICS**

| | | | | | | |
|---|---|---|---|---|---|---|
| • Percent outside eng assignments | | • Design cost per job<br>• Materials cost per job<br>• Eng utilization<br>• Percent design reuse | • Number of jobs designed (by vendor)<br>• Design cost per job (by vendor)<br>• Materials cost per job<br>• Contribution per job | | | • Revenue<br>• Cost of goods sold |

# Figure 13.5
# Performance Planned and Managed Hierarchy

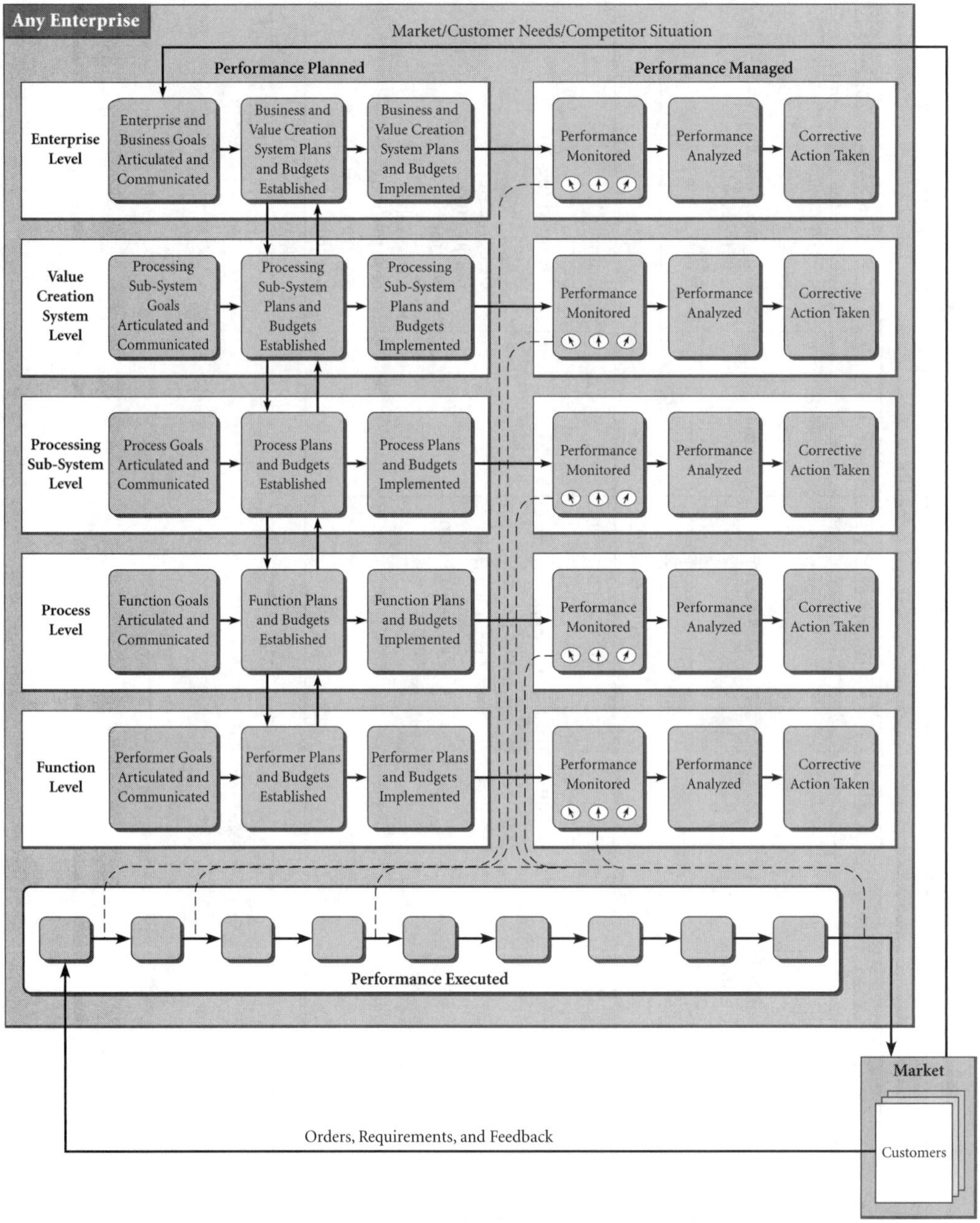

**Any Enterprise**

Market/Customer Needs/Competitor Situation

**Performance Planned**

**Performance Managed**

**Enterprise Level**

| Enterprise and Business Goals Articulated and Communicated | Business and Value Creation System Plans and Budgets Established | Business and Value Creation System Plans and Budgets Implemented | Performance Monitored | Performance Analyzed | Corrective Action Taken |

**Value Creation System Level**

| Processing Sub-System Goals Articulated and Communicated | Processing Sub-System Plans and Budgets Established | Processing Sub-System Plans and Budgets Implemented | Performance Monitored | Performance Analyzed | Corrective Action Taken |

**Processing Sub-System Level**

| Process Goals Articulated and Communicated | Process Plans and Budgets Established | Process Plans and Budgets Implemented | Performance Monitored | Performance Analyzed | Corrective Action Taken |

**Process Level**

| Function Goals Articulated and Communicated | Function Plans and Budgets Established | Function Plans and Budgets Implemented | Performance Monitored | Performance Analyzed | Corrective Action Taken |

**Function Level**

| Performer Goals Articulated and Communicated | Performer Plans and Budgets Established | Performer Plans and Budgets Implemented | Performance Monitored | Performance Analyzed | Corrective Action Taken |

**Performance Executed**

**Market**

Customers

Orders, Requirements, and Feedback

# Figure 13.6
## Belding Management System Tools

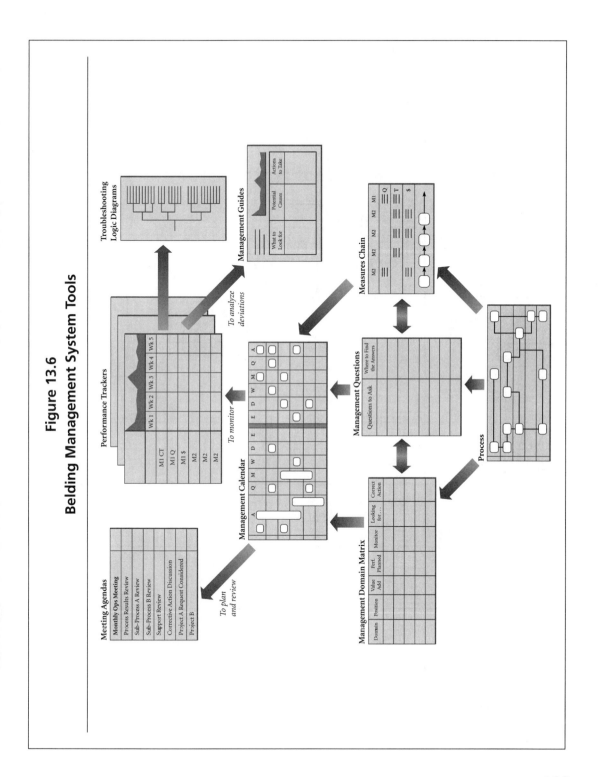

# Figure 13.7
## Belding Performance Planned Calendar

**Belding Engineering Planning Calendar**

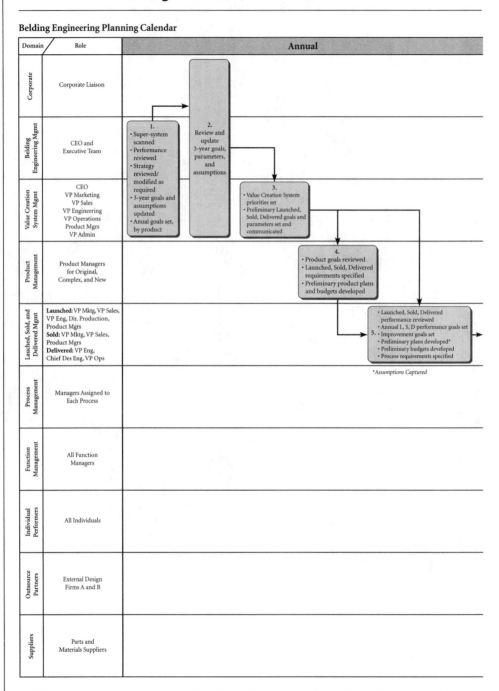

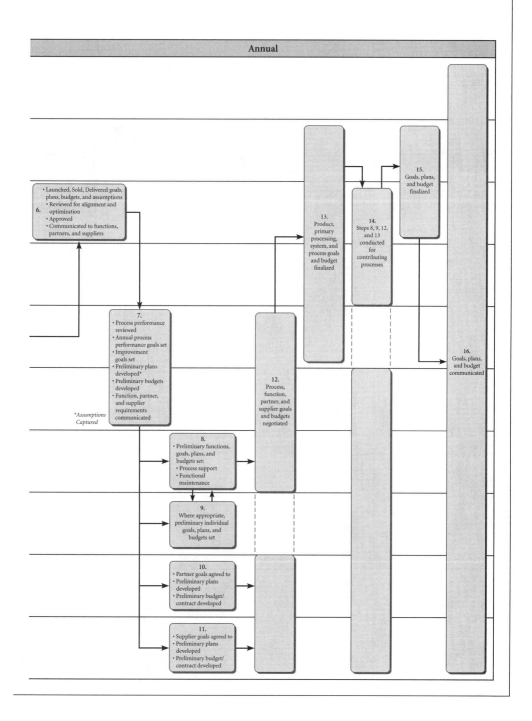

Annual

6.
- Launched, Sold, Delivered goals, plans, budgets, and assumptions
- Reviewed for alignment and optimization
- Approved
- Communicated to functions, partners, and suppliers

7.
- Process performance reviewed
- Annual process performance goals set
- Improvement goals set
- Preliminary plans developed*
- Preliminary budgets developed
- Function, partner, and supplier requirements communicated

*Assumptions Captured

8.
- Preliminary functions, goals, plans, and budgets set:
  - Process support
  - Functional maintenance

9.
Where appropriate, preliminary individual goals, plans, and budgets set

10.
- Partner goals agreed to
- Preliminary plans developed
- Preliminary budget/contract developed

11.
- Supplier goals agreed to
- Preliminary plans developed
- Preliminary budget/contract developed

12.
Process, function, partner, and supplier goals and budgets negotiated

13.
Product, primary processing, system, and process goals and budget finalized

14.
Steps 8, 9, 12, and 13 conducted for contributing processes

15.
Goals, plans, and budget finalized

16.
Goals, plans, and budget communicated

# Figure 13.8
## Belding Performance Managed Calendar

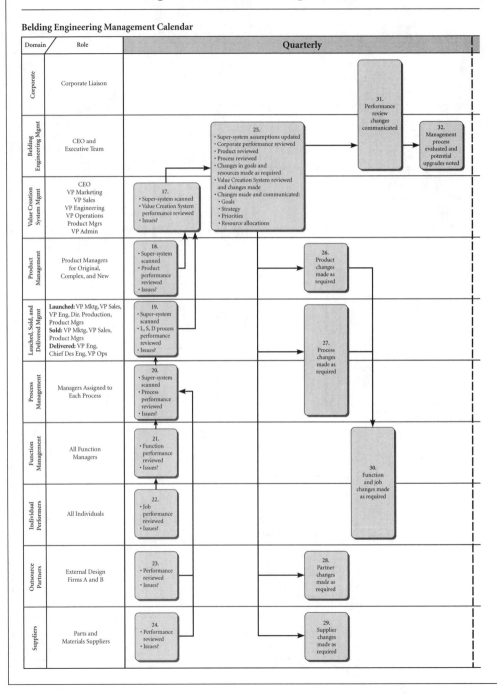

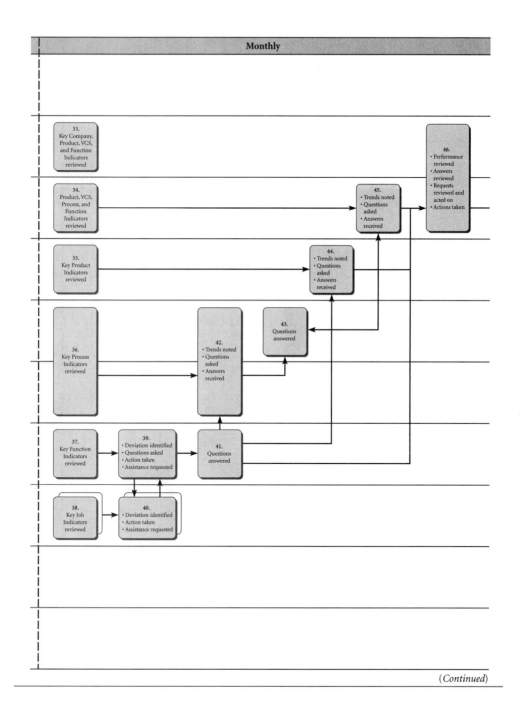

**Monthly**

33.
Key Company,
Product, VCS,
and Function
Indicators
reviewed

34.
Product, VCS,
Process, and
Function
Indicators
reviewed

35.
Key Product
Indicators
reviewed

36.
Key Process
Indicators
reviewed

37.
Key Function
Indicators
reviewed

38.
Key Job
Indicators
reviewed

39.
• Deviation identified
• Questions asked
• Action taken
• Assistance requested

40.
• Deviation identified
• Action taken
• Assistance requested

41.
Questions
answered

42.
• Trends noted
• Questions
  asked
• Answers
  received

43.
Questions
answered

44.
• Trends noted
• Questions
  asked
• Answers
  received

45.
• Trends noted
• Questions
  asked
• Answers
  received

46.
• Performance
  reviewed
• Answers
  reviewed
• Requests
  reviewed and
  acted on
• Actions taken

*(Continued)*

# Figure 13.8
## Belding Performance Managed Calendar (*Continued*)

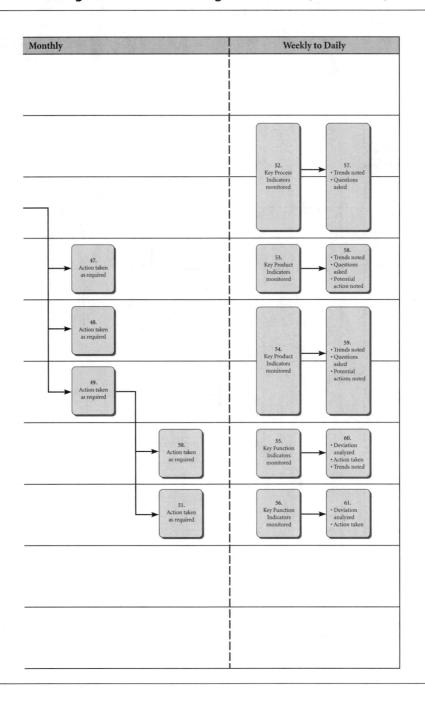

# Figure 13.9
## Sample Performance Trackers at Belding

**Rework Tracker**

| Rework | January | February | March | Quarter 1 |
|---|---|---|---|---|
| Total # Jobs Reworked | 10 | 7 | 9 | 25 |
| Total $ Cost of Reworked Jobs | $4,400,000 | $2,700,000 | $4,230,000 | $11,330,000 |
| Average Cost per Reworked Job | $440,000 | $385,714 | $470,000 | $435,769 |
| # Product A Jobs Reworked | 4 | 2 | 4 | 10 |
| $ of Product A (Original) Jobs Reworked | $2,600,000 | $1,250,000 | $2,680,000 | $6,530,000 |
| Average Cost per Reworked Product A Job | $650,000 | $625,000 | $670,000 | $653,000 |
| # Product B (Complex) Jobs Reworked | 0 | 0 | 0 | 0 |
| $ of Product B Jobs Reworked | 0 | 0 | 0 | 0 |
| Average Cost per Reworked Product B Job | 0 | 0 | 0 | 0 |
| # Product C (New) Jobs Reworked | 6 | 5 | 5 | 16 |
| $ of Product C Jobs Reworked | $3,200,000 | $1,830,000 | $2,990,000 | $8,020,000 |
| Average Cost per Reworked Product C Job | $300,000 | $290,000 | $310,000 | $300,000 |
| SALES Region (I) # Jobs Reworked | 6 | 4 | 5 | 15 |
| $ Jobs Reworked | $3,200,000 | $1,830,000 | $2,990,000 | $8,020,000 |
| SALES Region (II) # Jobs Reworked | 1 | 1 | 2 | 4 |
| $ Jobs Reworked | $300,000 | $290,000 | $620,000 | $1,210,000 |
| SALES Region (III) # Jobs Reworked | 3 | 2 | 2 | 7 |
| $ Jobs Reworked | $5,000,000 | $590,000 | $620,000 | $2,100,000 |
| Int. Design # Jobs Reworked | 1 | 0 | 0 | 1 |
| $ Jobs Reworked | $650,000 | $0 | $0 | $650,000 |
| External Design Unit (A) # Jobs Reworked | 8 | 6 | 7 | |
| $ Jobs Reworked | $3,100,000 | | | |
| External Design Unit (B) # Jobs Reworked | 1 | | | |
| $ Jobs Reworked | $550,000 | | | |

**Region One Sales Tracker**

| PERFORMANCE INDICATOR | | M1 Units | M1 Revenue | M2 Units | M2 Revenue | M3 Units | M3 Revenue |
|---|---|---|---|---|---|---|---|
| Sales—Total Units | Plan | 17 | $14,000,000 | 17 | $14,000,000 | 17 | $14,000,000 |
| | Actual | 23 | $10,125,000 | 23 | $9,500,000 | 27 | $11,250,000 |
| | Gap | 6 | ($3,875,000) | 6 | ($4,500,000) | 10 | ($2,750,000) |
| | Cum Gap | 6 | ($3,875,000) | 12 | ($8,375,000) | 22 | ($11,125,000) |
| Sales—Product A (Original) | Plan | 6 | $6,000,000 | 6 | $6,000,000 | 6 | $6,000,000 |
| | Actual | 6 | $6,000,000 | 5 | $5,000,000 | 6 | $6,000,000 |
| | Gap | 0 | 0 | (1) | ($1,000,000) | 0 | 0 |
| | Cum Gap | 0 | 0 | (1) | ($1,000,000) | (1) | ($1,000,000) |
| Sales—Product B (Complex) | Plan | 3 | $6,000,000 | 3 | $6,000,000 | 3 | $6,000,000 |
| | Actual | 0 | 0 | 0 | 0 | 0 | 0 |
| | Gap | (3) | ($6,000,000) | (3) | ($6,000,000) | (3) | ($6,000,000) |
| | Cum Gap | (3) | ($6,000,000) | (6) | ($12,000,000) | (9) | ($18,000,000) |
| Sales—Product B (New) | Plan | 8 | $2,000,000 | 8 | $2,000,000 | 8 | $2,000,000 |
| | Actual | 17 | $4,125,000 | 18 | $4,500,000 | 21 | $5,250,000 |
| | Gap | 9 | $2,125,000 | 10 | $2,500,000 | 11 | $3,250,000 |
| | Cum Gap | 9 | $2,125,000 | 19 | $4,625,000 | 30 | $7,875,000 |
| Average % Contribution—Total | Plan | 50% | | 50% | | 50% | |
| | Actual | 30% | | 38% | | 36% | |
| | Gap | (20%) | | (12%) | | (14%) | |
| Average % Contribution—Product A | Plan | 50% | | 50% | | 50% | |
| | Actual | 42% | | 36% | | 38% | |
| | Gap | (8%) | | (14%) | | (12%) | |
| Average % Contribution—Product B | Plan | 50% | | 50% | | 50% | |
| | Actual | – | | – | | – | |

**Belding Vendor Tracker—External Design Firm A**

| EXTERNAL DESIGN A | | Month 1 | Month 2 | Month 3 | Quarter |
|---|---|---|---|---|---|
| # New Jobs Assigned | Plan | 20 | 20 | 20 | 60 |
| | Actual | 20 | 21 | 20 | 61 |
| | Gap | 0 | 1 | 0 | 1 |
| # Jobs in Process | | 6 | 5 | 3 | 3 |
| # Jobs Completed | | 21 | 23 | 20 | 64 |
| % on Cycle Time | | 98 | 95 | 100 | 97 |
| % on Elapsed Time | | 97 | 98 | 99 | 98 |
| % on Labor Plan | | 85 | 90 | 95 | 90 |
| Reworked Jobs Attributable (Faulty Design) | # | 4 | 6 | 5 | 15 |
| | Cum # | 4 | 10 | 15 | 15 |
| | $ | $1,550,000 | $2,075,000 | $2,270,000 | $5,895,000 |
| | Cum $ | $1,550,000 | $3,625,000 | $5,895,000 | $5,895,000 |
| Average Contribution of Jobs | | 34% | 40% | 36% | 37% |
| Hours Invoiced | | 6300 | 6900 | 6000 | 19,200 |
| Fees Invoiced | | $1,260,000 | $1,380,000 | $1,200,000 | $3,840,000 |

*(Continued)*

# Figure 13.9
## Sample Performance Trackers at Belding (*Continued*)

**Belding Product Tracker (Product: Original)**

| PERFORMANCE INDICATOR | | M1 | M2 | M3 |
|---|---|---|---|---|
| Revenue | Plan | $19,000,000 | $19,000,000 | $19,000,000 |
| | Actual | $17,540,000 | $15,010,000 | $20,500,000 |
| | Gap | | | |
| | Cum Gap | | | |
| Jobs Sold | Plan | 19 | 19 | 19 |
| | Actual | 18 | 14 | 21 |
| | Gap | 1 | 5 | -2 |
| | Cum Gap | 1 | 6 | 4 |
| Active Leads | Plan | 50 | 50 | 50 |
| | Actual | 40 | 50 | 25 |
| Contribution | Plan | 50% | 50% | 50% |
| | Actual | 36% | 32% | 41% |
| Product Costs as % of Rev | Plan | 50% | 50% | 50% |
| | Actual | 64% | 66% | 59% |
| Materials Costs as % of Rev | Plan | 30% | 30% | 30% |
| | Actual | 40% | 42% | 36% |
| Design Labor Costs as % of Rev | Plan | 6% | 6% | 6% |
| | Actual | 5% | 6% | 6% |
| Production Labor Costs as % of Rev | Plan | 14% | 14% | 14% |
| | Actual | 19% | 18% | 17% |
| Total Jobs Produced | | 14 | 13 | 16 |
| # Jobs Reworked | | 4 | 2 | 4 |
| Rework Costs | | $2,600,000 | $1,250,000 | $2,680,000 |
| Warranty Costs | | $60,000 | $40,000 | $20,000 |
| # Warranty Repairs | | 3 | 2 | 1 |
| Customer Complaints—Total | | 12 | 7 | 10 |
| Late Delivery | | 5 | 6 | 5 |
| Not as Spec'd | | 3 | 1 | 3 |
| Service Complaint | | 1 | 0 | 0 |
| Spec'd Incorrectly | | 3 | 0 | 2 |

**Opportunity Pipeline Tracker**

| | Estimated Units | Estimated Revenue |
|---|---|---|
| **Opportunities—Total** | 236 | $198,875,000 |
| Opportunities—Total Stage One | 100 | $100,000,000 |
| Opportunities—Total Stage Two | 57 | $41,000,000 |
| Opportunities—Total Stage Three | 44 | $32,375,000 |
| Opportunities—Total Stage Four | 35 | $25,500,000 |
| **Product A (Original)—Total** | 48 | $48,000,000 |
| Product A (Original)—Stage Two | 21 | $21,000,000 |
| Product A (Original)—Stage Three | 15 | $15,000,000 |
| Product A (Original)—Stage Four | 12 | $12,000,000 |
| **Product B (Original)—Total** | 11 | $22,000,000 |
| Product B (Original)—Stage Two | 4 | $8,000,000 |
| Product B (Original)—Stage Three | 4 | $8,000,000 |
| Product B (Original)—Stage Four | 3 | $6,000,000 |
| **Product C (Original)—Total** | 77 | $28,875,000 |
| Product C (Original)—Stage Two | 32 | $12,000,000 |
| Product C (Original)—Stage Three | 25 | $9,375,000 |
| Product C (Original)—Stage Four | 20 | $7,500,000 |

Opportunity Mix Trend

Stage 3 Opportunities Mix Trend

# Figure 13.10
## Tracker System and Management Calendar

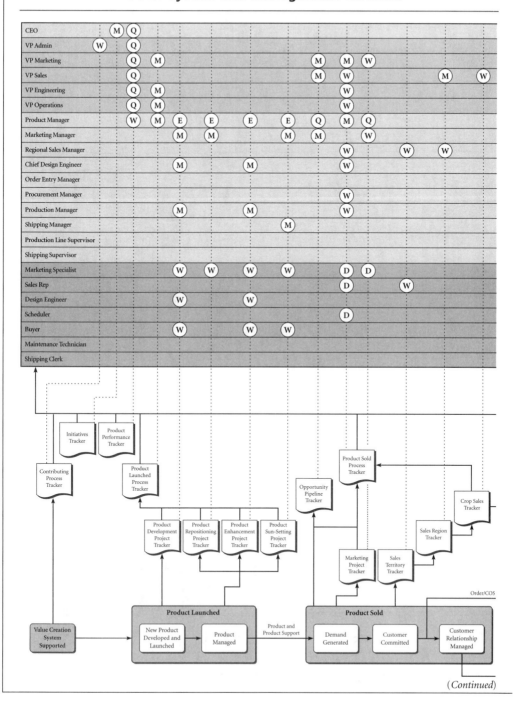

(*Continued*)

# Figure 13.10
## Tracker System and Management Calendar (*Continued*)

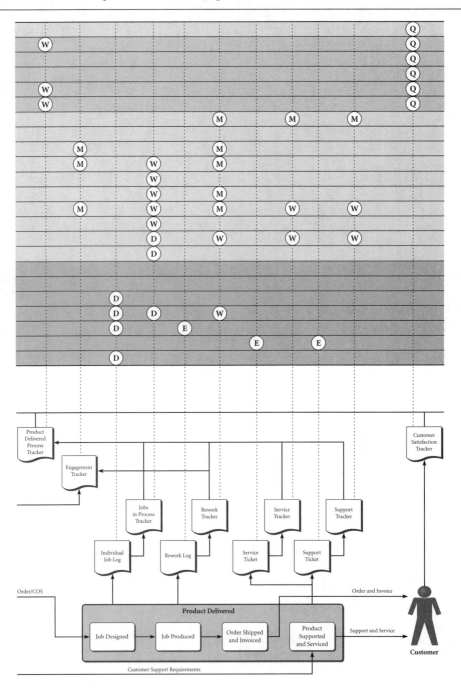

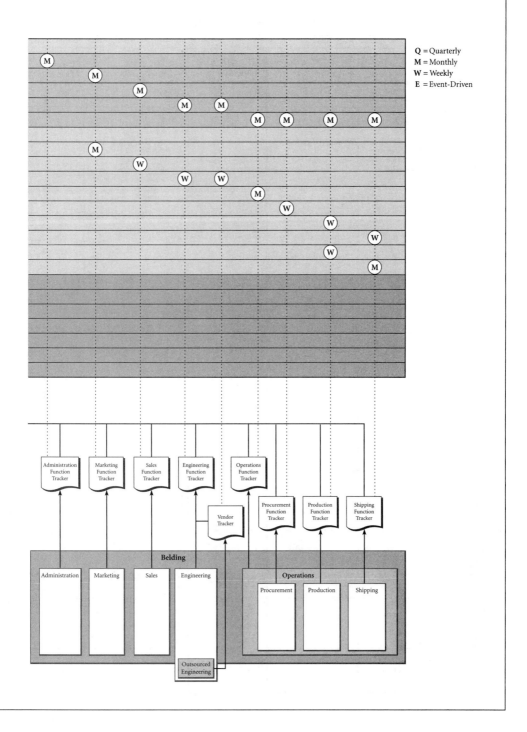

Q = Quarterly
M = Monthly
W = Weekly
E = Event-Driven

# Figure 13.11
## New Measurement System

| | | | | | |
|---|---|---|---|---|---|
| **VP Measures (Old Belding Engineering)** | • Admin Budget (Plan/Actual) | • Mktg Budget (Plan/Actual) | • Revenues (Plan/Actual) <br> • Sales Budget (Plan/Actual) | • Engineering Budget (Plan/Actual) <br> • NPD Projects (Plan/Actual) | • Operations Budget (Plan/Actual) <br> • Units Shipped (Plan/Actual) <br> • Cost per Unit Shipped (Plan/Actual) |
| **Function Indicators for Product Launched — New Product Developed and Launched** | • Systems Capability (to Support New Product) Available on Time | • Business Case Accuracy <br> • Research Project Budgets (Plan/Actual) <br> • Research Project Plans (Plan/Actual) <br> • Product Support Effectiveness <br> • Product Support Costs <br> • Product Support on Time <br> • Product Launch Budget (Plan/Actual) | • Sale Rep Product Training Completed on Time | • Product Performance— Failures <br> • Product Performance— Sustaining Eng Costs in 1st Year <br> • % Technology Reuse <br> • % Materials Reuse <br> • % Mfg Process Reuse <br> • Design Costs for New Product <br> • Design Project Plan (Plan/Actual) <br> • Spec Pkge Accuracy | |
| **Function Indicators for Product Launched — Product Portfolio Managed** | | • Product Analysis Quality <br> • Product Support Costs (Existing Products) <br> • Product Support Effectiveness (Existing Products) | • % Install Base Transitioned | • Sustaining Eng Costs <br> • Design Project Plan (Plan/Actual) <br> • Materials Cost Reductions Realized <br> • Mfg Cost Reductions Realized | |
| **Function Indicators for Product Sold — Demand Generated** | | • Lead Quality (% Qualified, % Closed) <br> • # Leads by Source <br> • Cost per Lead <br> • Rev Value of Qualified Leads | | | |
| **Function Indicators for Product Sold — Customer Committed** | | | • Orders—Revenue (Plan/Actual) <br> • Orders—Units (Plan/Actual) <br> • Cost per Sale <br> • Close Ratio <br> • Proposals Submitted <br> • COS Accuracy— Rework Due to COS Errors and Omissions | | |
| **Function Indicators for Product Sold — Customer Relationship Managed** | | | • Additional Sales <br> • Referrals <br> • Account Plans (Plan/Actual) | | |
| **Function Indicators for Product Delivered — Job Designed** | | | | • Design meets Spec <br> • Rework Due to Design <br> • Failures Due to Design <br> • Jobs Designed on Time <br> • Design Costs <br> • Job Costs | |
| **Function Indicators for Product Delivered — Job Produced** | | | | | |
| **Function Indicators for Product Delivered — Order Shipped and Invoiced** | • Invoice Timeliness <br> • Invoice Accuracy <br> • CT Invoice-to-Cash <br> • Late Payments Due to Errors | | | | |
| **Function Indicators for Product Delivered — Product Supported and Serviced** | • CT to Issue Resolution | | | • Customer Service Costs <br> • Warranty Costs <br> • CT to Issue Resolution | • On-Time Service |

| | Procurement Budget (Plan/Actual) • Materials Costs per Unit Shipped (Plan/Actual) | Production Budget (Plan/Actual) • Production Cost per Unit Shipped (Plan/Actual) | Shipping Budget (Plan/Actual) • Shipping Cost per Unit Shipped (Plan/Actual) | L, S, D Measures | VCS Measures |
|---|---|---|---|---|---|
| | • Prototype Materials Available on Time | • Prototypes Production on Time<br>• Prototype 1st Pass Yield<br>• Prototype Labor Costs<br>• Mfg Process Design Available on Time<br>• Mfg Capacity Available on Time<br>• Service Capacity Available on Time<br><br>• Mfg Cost Reductions Realized | | • Market Share (Projections/Actual)<br>• Product Performance<br>• Failures<br>• Warranties<br>• Margins<br>• Sustaining Costs<br>• Product Developed and Launched on Time and CT<br>• Product Developed and Launched Costs (Plan/Actual) | • Customer Satisfaction<br>• Product Met Spec<br>• Returns for Specs not Met<br>• Rework for Specs not Met<br>• Complaints for Specs not Met<br>• On-Time Delivery<br>• On-Time Service<br>• Product Failures<br>• Invoice Errors<br><br>• Rev—Product Shipped and Invoiced<br>• # Units—Product Shipped and Invoiced |
| | | | | • COS Errors<br>• Product Meets Customer Needs<br>• Returns for Wrong Product Specified<br>• Orders—Revenue<br>• Orders—Units<br>• Cost of Sales | • Product Margin<br><br>• Market Share |
| | • Materials Available on Time<br>• Inventory | • Product Meets Spec<br>• Rework Due to Production<br>• Failures Due to Production<br>• 1st Pass Yield<br>• Jobs Produced on Time<br>• Production Costs<br>• Job Costs | | • Production Errors<br>• Failures Due to Production<br>• Failures Due to Design<br>• Invoice Errors<br>• Products Shipped on Time<br>• COS to Ship CT<br>• On-Time Service/Replacement<br>• CT to Completed Service/Replacement<br>• CT to Issue Resolution<br>• Job Costs<br>• Warranty Costs<br>• Service Costs<br>• Customer Service Costs | |
| | | | • Jobs Shipped on Time<br>• Shipping Costs | | |
| | • Service Costs—Materials | • Service Costs—Labor<br>• On-Time Service or Replacement<br>• CT to Completed Service or Replacement | | | |

## Figure 13.12
## Sample Tracker with User's Guide

Discounts—August

| Order # | Product | Discount Price | Delta from Standard Price | Discount Reason Code | Sales Rep |
|---|---|---|---|---|---|
| 103-1245-88 | New—med | 495,000 | 5,000 | Comp bid | 021 |
| 103-1479-45 | Comlex—lge | 999,975,000 | 25,000 | Rework | 014 |
| 102-2848-56 | Complex—lge | 999,956,500 | 43,500 | Rework | 014 |
| 192-2374-25 | Original—med | 999,992,000 | 8,000 | Service comp | 003 |
| 107-7338-89 | Complex—lge | 999,976,500 | 23,500 | Rework | 012 |
| 113-1479-63 | Original—lge | 999,950,000 | 50,000 | Rework | 023 |
| 102-2848-57 | Original—med | 999,990,000 | 10,000 | Comp bid | 002 |
| 192-2374-26 | Original—med | 999,990,000 | 10,000 | Comp bid | 003 |
| 103-1245-90 | Complex—lge | 999,975,000 | 25,000 | Rework | 014 |
| 103-3567-47 | New—med | 493,000 | 7,000 | Comp bid | 014 |
| 102-8849-58 | New—med | 482,000 | 18,000 | Service comp | 014 |
| 192-2358-27 | Complex—med | 999,975,000 | 25,000 | Rework | 021 |
| 103-9475-91 | New—med | 490,000 | 10,000 | Comp bid | 003 |
| 103-1779-48 | Original—med | 999,985,000 | 15,000 | Rework | 025 |
| 102-5268-59 | Complex—lge | 999,985,000 | 15,000 | Rework | 014 |
| | | | 290,000 | | |

*Discounts Tracker User's Guide*

**Purpose:** To identify anomalies and/or trends in discounts

**Who uses this report:** Regional sales managers, sales reps (as feedback on their own performance)

**Review calendar:** Monthly or in order to review a specific sales/promotional period. Also used as a part of the sales reps review quarterly.

| What to look for: | Potential causes: | Actions to take: |
|---|---|---|
| *Scenario 1:* Unusually large number of discounts—evenly distributed over all/most reps | • Reps are having trouble in one area (look for reason tend). <br> • Reps are extending inappropriate discounts. <br> • A flaw in corporately designed products or policies is the root cause of the adjustments (check for a trend across all territories and regions). | 1. Look to see if there is also a trend in reasons. For example, a high number of wrong price adjustments would suggest that we may have a pricing issue. Items could be mislabeled or the pricing in ISIS could be incorrect. Go to scenario 4. <br> 2. If there are no discernable trends in reasons or reps, but the sum total of adjustments seems unreasonably high, review price adjustment policies and guidelines with all reps. Monitor more frequently for improvement. <br> 3. Check with Corporate to see if adjustments are up across all territories. |
| *Scenario 2:* Unusually large number of discounts—by one rep | • The sales rep is having trouble in a particular area (look for reason trend). <br> • The sales rep is extending inappropriate discounts. | 1. Look to see if there is also a trend in reasons for this rep's adjustments. For example, a high number of remake/rework adjustments would suggest that this sales rep may be having trouble with specifying the products. Go to scenario 5. <br> 2. If there are no discernable trends in reasons, but the sum total of adjustments seems unreasonably high, review price adjustment policies and guidelines with this rep. Monitor more frequently until there is improvement. |

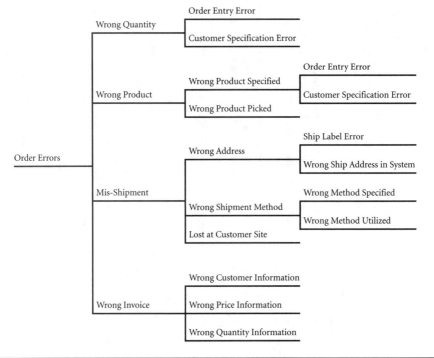

## Figure 13.13
## Troubleshooting Logic Diagram

Order Errors

- Wrong Quantity
  - Order Entry Error
  - Customer Specification Error
- Wrong Product
  - Wrong Product Specified
    - Order Entry Error
    - Customer Specification Error
  - Wrong Product Picked
- Mis-Shipment
  - Wrong Address
    - Ship Label Error
    - Wrong Ship Address in System
  - Wrong Shipment Method
    - Wrong Method Specified
    - Wrong Method Utilized
  - Lost at Customer Site
- Wrong Invoice
  - Wrong Customer Information
  - Wrong Price Information
  - Wrong Quantity Information

## Figure 13.14
## Sample Meeting Agenda

| Time | Agenda Item | Leader |
|------|-------------|--------|
| 8:00 | End-of-Process Metrics and Performance Reviewed | PL |
| 8:15 | Sub-Process C Performance Reviewed | DW |
| 8:25 | Sub-Process B Performance Reviewed | HO |
| 8:35 | Sub-Process A Performance Reviewed | PL |
| 8:45 | Support Process Performance Reviewed | FG & ML |
| 9:00 | Functions Contribution Reviewed | DW, HO, PL |
| 9:15 | Improvement Project A Reviewed | RA |
| 9:30 | Improvement Project B Reviewed | GR |
| 9:45 | Other Initiatives Reviewed | MC |
| 10:00 | Planning Assumptions Reviewed and Adjusted | PL |

## Table 13.1
## Belding Management Domain Matrix (Excerpt)

| Domain | Mission/ Value Add | Performance Planned | Performance Monitored | Looking for . . . | Corrective Actions |
|---|---|---|---|---|---|
| **Domain:** Enterprise<br><br>**Role:** Executive team<br><br>**Members:**<br>• CEO<br>• All VPs | • Optimize the enterprise<br>• Set direction and strategy: which markets, which offering, what competitive advantage<br>• Determine business model<br>• Determine the optimal organization structure<br>• Determine markets to abandon, lines of business to abandon | • Lines-of-business goals: revenues, margin contribution<br>• Allocate resources and asset base to lines of business<br>• Strategic Initiatives<br>• Plans for acquisition/ divestiture of assets<br>• Plans for acquisition/ divestiture of lines of business<br>• Major capital expenditures for business infrastructure | • Belding performance plan to actual<br>• Line-of-business and value chain system performance plan to actual—original, complex, and new<br>• Function performance plan to actual<br>• Super-system trends<br>• Strategic initiatives performance plan to actual (milestones and results) | • Trends across lines of business, functions that indicate a systemic issue/ misalignment<br>• Super-system trends that signal the need for the organization to adapt<br>• Initiatives and projects that are off plan—leading indicators of future performance of the organization | • Abandon lines of business (divest, sun-set)<br>• Initiate development of new lines of business<br>• Adjust lines of business and function goals and plans<br>• Adjust resource and asset allocation across lines of business, functions, and strategic initiatives<br>• Divest assets<br>• Build/acquire new assets<br>• Acquire additional capital<br>• Restructure the business |

(*Continued*)

## Table 13.1
## Belding Management Domain Matrix (Excerpt *Continued*)

| Domain | Mission/ Value Add | Performance Planned | Performance Monitored | Looking for . . . | Corrective Actions |
|---|---|---|---|---|---|
| **Domain:** Value Creation System | • Optimize the lines of business<br>• Manage the portfolio of products/services | • Lines-of-business goals: revenues, margin contribution<br>• Specify the resource levels required to meet lines-of-business goals | • Belding performance plan to actual<br>• Lines-of-business (Value Creation System) performance plan to actual: Product Launched, Product Sold, Product Delivered | • Trends across lines of business, primary processing sub-systems, functions that indicate a systemic issue or misalignment<br>• Super-system trends that signal the need for the organization to adapt | • Initiate process improvements<br>• Reallocate resources across the projects<br>• Abandon lines of business (divest, sun-set)<br>• Initiate development of new lines of business |
| **Role:** Value Creation Management Team | • Arbitration of corporate leverage opportunities (efficiencies of scale— i.e., one process, one facility, one flavor, etc.) and unique value creation opportunities (effectiveness in market/for customer— best, only, easiest, fastest, customized). | • Set sales, revenue, expense, and delivery goals for each line of business<br>• Specify changes to the lines-of-business portfolio<br>• Initiate New Product Development<br>• Initiate product enhancements | • Function performance plan to actual<br>• Contributing process performance plan to actual<br>• Super-system trends | • Initiatives and projects that are off plan—leading indicators of future performance of the organization | • Adjust lines of business and function goals and plans<br>• Adjust resource and asset allocation across lines of business, functions, and strategic initiatives<br>• Divest assets<br>• Build/acquire new assets |
| **Members:**<br>• VP Marketing<br>• VP Sales<br>• VP Engineering<br>• VP Ops | | | | | |

| Domain: Primary processing sub-system (Launched, Sold, or Delivered)<br><br>Role: Management team for Sold processing sub-system<br><br>Members:<br>• VP Marketing<br>• VP Sales<br>• VP IT<br>• VP HR | • Optimize the Product Sold primary processing sub-system<br>• Identify and propose leverage opportunities for Product Sold primary processing sub-system across the lines of business<br>• Monitor for misalignments with Product Launched and Product Delivered | • Product Sold plan<br>• Product Sold process improvement plan<br>• Process goals for Demand Generated, Customer Committed, and Customer Relationship Maintained processes<br>• Contributing process requirements to support Product Sold | • Product Sold performance plan to actual (# units, revenue, and contribution) (M) (W)<br>  • Sales by region<br>  • Sales by product type<br>• Sales pipeline (# and value of opportunities at each stage of process) (W)<br>• Customer satisfaction<br>• Super-system trends (Q)<br>• Portfolio performance (Q)<br>• Process improvement projects plan to actual (M) | • Trends across products and/or regions—indications that the "is" process is not capable of meeting the goals<br>• Sales pipeline trends—indications that the "is" process is not capable of meeting the goals<br>• Improvement project issues—roadblocks or resource issues<br>• Trends that indicate product design or support issues—indicators that Product Launched inputs are deficient | • Adjust resource and asset allocation across lines of business, functions, and strategic initiatives<br>• Initiate Value Creation System improvements<br>• Initiate portfolio changes<br>• Initiate process improvements<br>• Reallocate resources across the projects<br>• Request that Product Launch improve performance<br>• Initiate process improvements<br>• Reallocate resources across the projects |

(Continued)

Table 13.1

## Belding Management Domain Matrix (Excerpt *Continued*)

| Domain | Mission/Value Add | Performance Planned | Performance Monitored | Looking for . . . | Corrective Actions |
|---|---|---|---|---|---|
| **Domain:** Process<br><br>**Role:** Process owner of Customer Committed process<br><br>**Members:** VP Sales Process Team | • Optimize the Customer Committed process<br>• Identify or develop and integrate sales tools and practices across the lines of business and regions<br>• Identify leverage opportunities across the regional sales organization<br>• Identify and propose leverage opportunities for Customer Committed process across the lines of business | • Customer Committed process plan<br>• Customer Committed process improvement plan<br>• Function support requirements/goals<br>• Contributing process requirements to support the Customer Committed process | • Customer Committed performance plan to actual (# units, revenue and contribution) (M) (W)<br>• Sales by region<br>• Sales by product type<br>• Sales pipeline (# and value of opportunities at each stage of process) (W)<br>• Customer satisfaction<br>• Super-system trends (Q)<br>• Process improvement projects plan to actual (M) | • Trends across products and/or regions—indications that the "is" process is not capable of meeting the goals<br>• Sales pipeline trends—indications that the "is" process is not capable of meeting the goals<br>• Improvement project issues—roadblocks or resource issues | • Reallocate resources across the projects<br>• Reallocate resources across sales activities<br>• Initiate function improvements<br>• Abandon lines of business (divest, sun-set)<br>• Initiate development of new lines of business<br>• Adjust lines of business and function goals and plans<br>• Adjust resource and asset allocation across lines of business, functions, and strategic initiatives<br>• Divest assets<br>• Build/acquire new assets<br>• Acquire additional capital |

| Domain: Functional Area<br><br>Role: Function manager<br><br>Members:<br>• VP Sales (as functional manager)<br>• Regional Sales Directors | • Build and maintain capacity and functional excellence in the Sales and Sales Management disciplines<br>• Identify leverage opportunities across the regional Sales organization<br>• Identify and propose leverage opportunities for Product Sold process across the lines of business<br>• Manage development plan milestones of the Regional Sales Directors | • Sales plan and Sales expense budget<br>• Regional Sales goals<br>• Functional initiative plans<br>• Enabling process requirements to support Sales<br>• Development plans for Regional Sales Directors | • Sales function performance plan to actual<br>• Regional Sales performance plan to actual<br>• Sales pipeline<br>• Product Sold—Customer Committed and Relationship Maintained process performance plan to actual<br>• Super-system trends<br>• Region Manager performance (M)<br>• Region Manager development plans plan to actual (M)<br>• Function improvement projects plan to actual | • Indications that Sales function is not meeting or will not meet its process commitments for Product Sold<br>• Trends across products and/or regions<br>• Sales pipeline trends<br>• Function execution issues, resource issues, HPS issues<br>• Improvement project issues—roadblocks or resource issues | • Initiate process improvements<br>• Reallocate resources across the projects<br>• Request that Product Launch improve performance |
| --- | --- | --- | --- | --- | --- |

**Table 13.2**

**Sample Management Guide with Questions to Ask (Excerpt)**

| Domain | Performance Monitored | Looking for . . . | Corrective Actions | Questions to Ask | Where to Find Answers |
|---|---|---|---|---|---|
| **Domain:** Value Creation System<br><br>**Role:** Value Creation Management Team<br><br>**Members:**<br>• VP Marketing<br>• VP Sales<br>• VP Engineering<br>• VP Ops | • Belding performance plan to actual<br>• Lines-of-business (Value Creation System) performance plan to actual—Product Launched, Product Sold, Product Delivered<br>• Function performance plan to actual<br>• Contributing process performance plan to actual<br>• Super-system trends<br>• Strategic initiatives performance plan to actual (milestones and results) | • Trends across lines of business, primary processing sub-systems, functions that indicate a systemic issue or misalignment<br>• Super-system trends that signal the need for the organization to adapt<br>• Initiatives and projects that are off plan—leading indicators of future performance of the organization<br>• Trends in the pipelines—leading indicators of revenue and profitability | • Initiate process improvements<br>• Reallocate resources across the projects<br>• Abandon lines of business (divest, sun-set)<br>• Initiate development of new lines of business<br>• Adjust lines of business and function goals and plans<br>• Adjust resource and asset allocation across lines of business, functions, and strategic initiatives | **VALUE CREATION SYSTEM RESULTS**<br><br>1. Did we meet total portfolio contribution expectations for this period? What is the trend?<br><br>2. Did we meet portfolio revenue expectations for this period? What is the trend?<br><br>3. Did we meet product profit/contribution expectations for this period? What is the trend?<br><br>4. Did we meet product revenue expectations for this period? What is the trend?<br><br>5. Did we meet unit sales expectations for this period? What is the trend? | Product Performance Tracker<br><br>Product Performance Tracker<br><br>Product Performance Tracker<br><br>Product Performance Tracker<br><br>Product Performance Tracker |

# Return to Belding Engineering

When we first described Belding back in Chapter 4, the company suffered a series of crises handled so poorly the CEO was finally ousted. Belding was then put in different hands with CEO S.K. Owens, who applied an alternative approach to managing the organization.

Even though reality, unlike video games, does not allow replays, that's just what we will do. We will walk back through our seven scenarios introduced in Chapter 4 and see how those situations would turn out when Belding is operating as a 3-D Enterprise.

## SCENARIO 1

Remember that in this scenario, the management team receives bad news about "skyrocketing" late deliveries and decides to initiate a variety of actions, including a materials task force to investigate the cause of escalating materials costs, a quality awareness campaign, a stop to overtime, and limits on monthly shipping charges (Figure 14.1). All of these actions backfired, causing even worse problems and complaints. Our diagnosis was that the actions were all focused on the resource dimension, were badly organized, and lacked clear purpose.

How is this situation handled with the new management system in place?

The management team members for the Product Delivered processing sub-system are reviewing and analyzing the Product Delivered sub-system tracker, and they note the spike in late deliveries, shipping costs, and overtime. Drilling down on related trackers, they also note the increase in rework, which could help explain all of the other increases (Figure 14.2).

Analysis of the rework data points to two potential sources of the increase: jobs designed by external Design Unit A (a process performance issue) and faulty customer order specifications coming from the Product Sold–Customer Committed process (an input issue). Two actions were taken immediately:

1. The Design Unit A issue was assigned to the Engineering Manager to investigate and resolve.

2. The customer specs input issue was forwarded to the Customer Committed process owner.

Meanwhile the management team intends to continue monitoring rework closely.

1. The design issue was handled as follows: Using the rework and vendor trackers, the Engineering Manager shows the performance data to the owner of Design Unit A and they discuss actions to address the problem. The Engineering Manager makes it clear that Belding will continue to monitor performance closely and that Design Unit A is at risk of losing the Belding account if matters don't improve quickly. After this meeting, the Engineering Manager investigates alternative sources for engineering design services, just to be on the safe side.

2. The faulty customer specs problem was handled as follows: Using the Product Sold and regional sales trackers, the process owner of the Customer Committed process is able to isolate Region One as the primary source of the faulty customer order specs (see Figure 14.3). He investigates the problem orders further and finds out that when the buyer is a non-engineering employee, the customer order often has flawed or incomplete specs. It turns out that Region One sales reps have less technical expertise than sales reps in the other regions. The issue is given to the Region One manager to resolve.

Region One's manager arranges to have the order specs reviewed by Engineering on all orders to non-technical buyers for the next quarter. He also begins to consider how to bring in more technical expertise to the Sales team— by hiring, providing more training, or swapping reps with other regions.

## Long-Term Actions and Results

The Product Delivered management team has continued to monitor rework closely and to follow the actions taken by Engineering and Sales for Region One.

After two months, there has been marked improvement in the performance of Design Unit A, but Engineering now has its list of alternative vendors if the problems resurface.

The process owner of the Customer Committed process continues to monitor the sales rep issue. Region One management has coached the reps on customer order specs and provided some on-the-spot Engineering advisory teams. The process owner has also interviewed several qualified technical sales candidates who would enable him to move the order specs reviews back from Engineering to his own unit in the next few weeks.

Meanwhile, if these efforts in Sales do not resolve the customer order specs issue, the Product Delivered management team will escalate the issue to the Value Creation Management Team.

## Our Diagnosis

There are several key differences in the way this scenario was handled versus the original management reaction:

- First, the team that reacted to the late delivery crisis in the old scenario was the senior management team. Apparently, nobody else raised a flag or reacted to this growing crisis until it reached the senior staff, a typical, "Don't look at me!" behavior in the siloed organization. By contrast, this time the problem is noticed by a team watching over a portion of the Value Creation System and it took prompt steps to find out what was going on rather than waiting for the bad news to drift up to top management.

- In the original scenario the senior management team took action after its quarterly meeting, which means its response was lagging behind the flare-up of the problem by up to three months. Having no system in place for early detection of and reaction to performance problems is also a sign of the siloed organization, and it only makes the problems worse through inattention.

- In the revised scenario, resolution of the problems is assigned to the appropriate parties at the right level in the organization where the causes can be determined and quick action can take place. Despite what may look like a bureaucratic structure of management teams, what Belding has put in place is an interlocking set of teams to monitor performance and act on variation rather than wait for someone else to respond.

- There was widespread use of the information from the performance trackers to spot performance issues and to diagnose possible causes. Of course, performance problems can sometimes be so complex or difficult to diagnose that a special study is required to find out root causes; however, it is not that mystifying if you have data to make comparisons (in this scenario, the performance of the two external design companies and the sales reps in Region One versus other regions) to determine why variation is happening.

## SCENARIO 2

In this scenario, illustrated in Figure 14.4, Belding's Procurement Manager tries to reduce materials costs by adjusting the forecast order volume downward for long-lead-time parts, triggering shipment delays, revenue losses, and increased costs for procurement expediting as orders piled up. The Procurement Manager had no real clue as to how variables affected each other and took a seemingly rational cost-cutting step that created a disaster.

### Short-Term Actions and Results

In the new Scenario 2, the Product Delivered management team once again spots the trend of materials cost increases on the Product Delivered sub-system tracker (Figure 14.5).

But it turns out that Procurement has already been investigating the issue and has order data for the past six months that show a definite trend away from the sales forecast mix. In order to determine whether the trend will continue, the management team looks at the data from the opportunity pipeline tracker and finds that the shift has continued (Figure 14.6). Procurement has a plan ready to go. The Product Delivered management team alerts the Value Creation Management Team about the issue and proposed action immediately.

Procurement makes the appropriate adjustments to future materials orders to more closely match the mix in the pipeline. They also expedite the orders of parts needed to get Production back on track with existing orders.

Made aware of the misalignment between Product Sold and Product Delivered, the Value Creation Management Team asks the Product Sold team to determine whether the shift in the mix of sales is due to external market and competitive factors or if there is an internal cause. The Value Creation Management Team also looks at what adjustments may be needed in process and value creation plans and goals if this shift becomes permanent.

The Product Sold management team looked at the Belding sales tracker to see whether the shift in mix was evident in all regions or localized (Figure 14.7). The trend was evident in all regions.

Discussions with regional managers and several reps revealed that there are issues with one of the products—it was losing share to a competitor's new product because it lacks some key features. Armed with this analysis from Sales, the product manager for this product proposes to enhance the product by adding several of the features that the competition is touting. She discusses the proposal with the Launched management team and it is approved.

The Product Sold management team decides to put in place some special customer incentives to help with sales of the product until it can be enhanced to be more competitive.

## Long-Term Actions and Results

Given the important product issue that was uncovered, the Value Creation Management Team takes a major role in overseeing progress. The team takes the following actions over the next months:

- Monitors progress of the product enhancement project
- Monitors impact of the sales incentive
- Monitors effectiveness of the adjustments in materials orders by Procurement

Meanwhile, Procurement keeps a close watch on actual mix in the pipeline to see whether adjustments are right.

## Our Diagnosis

In the original scenario, the Procurement Manager was nailed with the responsibility to do something about materials costs. The subsequent actions were taken with inadequate information and faulty logic, but there was nobody to check the manager's thinking until after the fact. As it turned out, there were multiple causes of the problem, and not all of them could be addressed by the Procurement Manager working in his isolated silo. The alternative scenario showed an organization in which teamwork produced much better data, a more accurate cause analysis, and multiple actions to close the gap.

## SCENARIO 3

This scenario had the CEO attempting to engineer faster cycle time for the New Product Development process by negotiating separate goals with each participating function. The result was a lot of missed goals and overall worsened performance because the functional areas did not support each other (Figure 14.8).

In the revised scenario, the Value Creation Management Team recognizes the Product Development cycle time problem during the annual planning cycle. They bring in the Product Launched management team to determine how long it should take to bring a new product to market and regain competitiveness. Instead of the current eighteen to twenty-four months, the goal is set at twelve months. (Remember, this is the same goal that the CEO set in the original Scenario 3; the difference is in how the goal is pursued.)

### Long-Term Actions and Results

The Product Launched management team commissions a cross-functional design team to analyze the disconnects in the current New Product Development process and to come up with a process design that can achieve the twelve-month goal (Figure 14.9).

Once this design has been reviewed and approved, the product manager in charge of a product development project currently under way migrates the project effort to the new process. She then initiates the next product development project using the entire new process design.

The first new product launched using the new process design is out the door in fifteen months. Subsequent projects are consistently completed in twelve months or under. The New Product Development process design is supported and employed by all participating functions and becomes a model for product development in the corporation.

## Our Diagnosis

The key difference in this revised scenario is that instead of negotiating separate deals with each function and thereby guaranteeing a lack of cooperation, the Value Creation Management Team uses a cross-functional improvement effort that involves all relevant parties in diagnosing how the current process works and engaging them in a redesign that everyone commits to. A breakthrough like this is the typical result of conducting a cross-functional process improvement effort, but it's a new experience for Belding.

## SCENARIO 4

Scenario 4 was the classic resource-fixated approach to trimming the fat, by cutting 10 percent in all areas regardless of relative importance or contribution to value creation (Figure 14.10). The consequences were negative in all functional areas and, on a cumulative basis, Belding ended up less competent to serve customer needs and provide quality products.

In the revised scenario, the Value Creation Management Team is using the Sales pipeline tracker to track performance for the first two months of the year. In Month 3, they become convinced that assumptions about the market were overly optimistic. In order to achieve the year's business goals, it would be necessary to cut expenses by 10 percent for the remainder of the year. The first set of decisions they made were to reset priorities for the Value Creation System and processing sub-systems, as shown in Figure 14.11.

Given these budget reallocations, the management teams for Launched, Sold, and Delivered reset their priorities and budgets for each participating budget, as shown in Figure 14.12.

The third-level decisions were made by the functional areas, which adjusted their budgets for the remainder of the year as shown in Figure 14.13.

## Our Diagnosis

The Value Creation Management Team was adamant that cuts should not be made in the Launched processes because the company's turnaround depended on developing new products that would be more competitive. An across-the-board "shared pain" budget cut would be disastrous. Instead, the management teams acted in concert to make the appropriate cuts, working their way down from the priorities set at the Value Creation System level.

## SCENARIO 5

In the original scenario (Figure 14.14), the VP of Administration presented an argument for getting control over the endless number of initiatives within Belding, all sucking up resources and distracting from running the business, but to no avail. Without any particular rationale in place to choose the best projects or to stop ineffective ones, projects take on a life of their own.

In the revised scenario, the Value Creation Management Team establishes a formal process for identifying, selecting, funding, and overseeing improvement projects throughout Belding. This process becomes a "feeder" to the annual Performance Planned cycle. Any kind of improvement effort must go through this approval, or funding is not authorized, even by an individual functional manager, because it is recognized that all of these small individual "initiatives" add up to a large chunk of employee time unless they are carefully selected and closely monitored.

To manage the improvement project portfolio, Belding CEO Owens integrates numerous staff functions (including Training, OD, Quality, and IT) into a single team of Performance Architects. Owens tasks this team with owning the improvement portfolio and running the project selection process for the organization. Given their backgrounds in improvement, the Performance Architects also lead the improvement projects that are authorized each year.

## Our Diagnosis

The key to managing the initiatives differently is recognizing that they need some amount of centralized management or they will eat insidiously at organizational effectiveness. Belding integrates the planning and management of this kind of work with the running of the business, recognizing that both forms of endeavor require resources and therefore should be carefully assessed, funded only if real benefits are achievable, and managed to success or stopped early.

## SCENARIO 6

This scenario dealt with the biggest improvement initiative, a transformation of computer systems that went off the rails because a too-trusting management let itself be led by vendors down an expensive dead end (Figure 14.16).

In the revised scenario (Figure 14.17), the transformation effort is evaluated just like all other potential projects for its cost versus benefits, likelihood of success, and manageability. It is recognized that to keep this project within firm boundaries, it must be treated first and foremost as a *business* improvement project, not a technology project, with business leaders in charge. To make that feasible, several members of the Value Creation Management Team take the time to learn about technology from a management viewpoint, spending time with their own IT experts to learn how to run a big technology project effectively. The focus is on what the business wants to accomplish, with technology rightly treated as an enabler instead of the main reason for the initiative. First, a steering team is established to oversee this major undertaking. Then, the affected processes are analyzed and redesigned to meet business requirements, and the technology (or functional) requirements are derived.

When a technology vendor is hired, it is only after the process redesign work has been accomplished. And instead of being "in charge" of the project, the vendor is required to report to the Value Creation Management Team and to IT simultaneously. The implementation plan is created by the steering team instead of the vendor. The plan calls for weekly progress checks with tangible monthly deliverables, with the contract requiring an immediate halt if any deliverables are unsatisfactory.

### Our Diagnosis

In the original scenario, the entire project was technology-driven. There was little if any understanding of the business needs down at the level where technology is actually deployed—namely, down at the process level. The vision for what was needed came entirely from outside the company.

Once the project started, there was no management of the vendor; the project was treated as special and mysterious, until it became clear that things were not going well. While there are no guarantees of success, a much more forceful management of the project from the start can make a huge difference in the likelihood that goals will be achieved. The project plan is also more carefully constructed so that Belding gets value for its investment earlier, instead of spending a lot of money and then being surprised by a mediocre deliverable.

## THE FINAL SCENARIO

This final scenario shouldn't happen if all the others are managed differently, as we described. In the original, Corporate has become so dissatisfied with Belding's consistent inability to meet earnings projections that it results in the CEO being ousted (Figure 14.18).

But let's just say there is still an issue with accuracy of revenue and earnings projections at Belding. What would Owens do differently?

In the new scenario, the Value Creation Management Team follows the revenue and earnings tracker religiously. This tool (shown in Figure 14.19) makes it possible for Belding executives to more accurately project quarterly earnings and revenues and manage by identifying and acting on leading performance indicators. The indicators displayed in the tracker make it possible for the team to make adjustments in Value Creation System components that will close emerging gaps between planned and actual revenues and earnings.[1]

The leading indicators are metrics linked to the super-system and to the Launched, Sold, and Delivered processes. By keeping close tabs on these metrics, the Value Creation Management Team can see well in advance the impacts on revenues and earnings of current events and can take preventive action inside those processes before the situation worsens. In Figure 14.20 the leading indicators are arrayed across the super-system and Value Creation System processes.

## THE BOTTOM LINE

So the day is saved. Belding not only survives but thrives with this new management system, regaining its customer base, becoming competitive again with dynamic new products, and regaining the trust of its corporate stakeholders.

An exaggeration? Okay, maybe a little. But then so were the original scenarios, although not far from the reality of many companies. What the Belding case shows is that it *is* possible to operate differently, to manage both the value and resource dimensions proactively and for long-term value.

# Figure 14.1
## Scenario 1: Before

**Management Scenario 1:**

At the quarterly management offsite:
- Sales reported that customer complaints requiring late deliveries have "skyrocketed"
- The VP Operations reported:
  - Shipping costs have gotten "out of control"
  - An alarming jump in materials costs and labor overtime

**Management Action**

Alarmed at this news (and with no data at hand), the following transpired:
- By the end of the meeting:
  ➤ A Materials Costs Task Force was initiated to look in the cause of the escalating materials costs.
  ➤ A Quality Awareness Task Force was initiated to determine the best way to convey a sense of responsibility for quality in the Belding workforce.
- The VP Operations subsequently held a "come to Jesus" meeting with his managers and
  ➤ Ordered a stop to all overtime unless he personally approved it
  ➤ Set a limit on monthly shipping charges, using same period last year as the "benchmark"

| Action | Consequences of Action |
| --- | --- |
| Materials Task Force initiated | • "Time-burner" and distraction<br>• Without good data, unable to pinpoint cause of current problem<br>• After three-months, a report was generated,<br>  1. Outlining all the areas where materials costs are, or potentially could be, an issue<br>  2. Recommending a number of general "should-oughta" actions for controlling materials costs |
| Quality Awareness Task Force initiated | • "Time-burner" and distraction.<br>• Decided that training was necessary, since few members of management and the workforce were aware of the principle that "you can't inspect quality into the product" and that there were a number of Japanese quality improvement tools available.<br>• Spent two months interviewing possible Quality Awareness and Improvement training vendors. Selected a vendor and made a proposal to the GM to start the program.<br>• The GM tabled the proposal because of lack of funds. |
| VP Operations stops all overtime | • Production jobs begin to back up because labor demand exceeds supply.<br>• An "expeditor" system had to be put in place to see that the jobs of key customers got to the "'head of the line."<br>• Late deliveries "skyrocketed" and customer complaints increased even more. |
| VP Operations sets limits on shipping charges | • Late deliveries increase dramatically.<br>• Customer complaints and pressure from the Sales organization are so great that the VP reverses his decision after five weeks. |

## Figure 14.2
## Rework Tracker

| Rework | | January | February | March | Quarter 1 |
|---|---|---|---|---|---|
| Total # Jobs Reworked | | 10 | 7 | 9 | 26 |
| Total $ Cost of Reworked Jobs | | $4,400,000 | $2,700,000 | $4,230,000 | $11,330,000 |
| Average Cost per Reworked Job | | $440,000 | $385,714 | $470,000 | $435,769 |
| # Product A Jobs Reworked | | 4 | 2 | 4 | 10 |
| $ of Product A (Original) Jobs Reworked | | $2,600,000 | $1,250,000 | $2,680,000 | $6,530,000 |
| Average Cost per Reworked Product A Job | | $650,000 | $625,000 | $670,000 | $653,000 |
| # Product B (Complex) Jobs Reworked | | 0 | 0 | 0 | 0 |
| $ of Product B Jobs Reworked | | 0 | 0 | 0 | 0 |
| Average Cost per Reworked Product B Job | | 0 | 0 | 0 | 0 |
| # Product C (New) Jobs Reworked | | 6 | 5 | 5 | 16 |
| $ of Product C Jobs Reworked | | $3,200,000 | $1,830,000 | $2,990,000 | $8,020,000 |
| Average Cost per Reworked Product C Job | | $300,000 | $290,000 | $310,000 | $300,000 |
| SALES Region (I) | # Jobs Reworked | 6 | 4 | 5 | 15 |
| | $ Jobs Reworked | $3,200,000 | $1,830,000 | $2,990,000 | $8,020,000 |
| SALES Region (II) | # Jobs Reworked | 1 | 1 | 2 | 4 |
| | $ Jobs Reworked | $300,000 | $290,000 | $620,000 | $1,210,000 |
| SALES Region (III) | # Jobs Reworked | 3 | 2 | 2 | 7 |
| | $ Jobs Reworked | $5,000,000 | $590,000 | $620,000 | $2,100,000 |
| Int. Design | # Jobs Reworked | 1 | 0 | 0 | 1 |
| | $ Jobs Reworked | $650,000 | $0 | $0 | $650,000 |
| External Design Unit (A) | # Jobs Reworked | 8 | 6 | 7 | 21 |
| | $ Jobs Reworked | $3,100,000 | $2,075,000 | $2,890,000 | $8,065,000 |
| External Design Unit (B) | # Jobs Reworked | 1 | 1 | 2 | 4 |
| | $ Jobs Reworked | $550,000 | $625,000 | $1,340,000 | $2,615,000 |
| Product Line A | # Jobs Reworked | 2 | 1 | 3 | 6 |
| | $ Jobs Reworked | $560,000 | $525,000 | $1,650,000 | $3,225,000 |
| Product Line B | # Jobs Reworked | 2 | 2 | 1 | 5 |
| | $ Jobs Reworked | $1,300,000 | $915,000 | $670,000 | $2,885,000 |
| Product Line C | # Jobs Reworked | 6 | 4 | 5 | 15 |
| | $ Jobs Reworked | $2,150,000 | $1,160,000 | $1,910,000 | $5,220,000 |

# Figure 14.3
## Region One Sales Tracker

| PERFORAMNCE INDICATOR | | M1 | | M2 | | M3 | |
|---|---|---|---|---|---|---|---|
| | | Units | Revenue | Units | Revenue | Units | Revenue |
| Sales—Total Units | Plan | 17 | $14,000,000 | 17 | $14,000,000 | 17 | $14,000,000 |
| | Actual | 23 | $10,125,000 | 23 | $9,500,000 | 27 | $11,250,000 |
| | Gap | 6 | ($3,875,000) | 6 | ($4,500,000) | 10 | ($2,750,000) |
| | Cum Gap | 6 | ($3,875,000) | 12 | ($8,375,000) | 22 | ($11,125,000) |
| Sales—Product A (Original) | Plan | 6 | $6,000,000 | 6 | $6,000,000 | 6 | $6,000,000 |
| | Actual | 6 | $6,000,000 | 5 | $5,000,000 | 6 | $6,000,000 |
| | Gap | 0 | 0 | (1) | ($1,000,000) | 0 | 0 |
| | Cum Gap | 0 | 0 | (1) | ($1,000,000) | (1) | ($1,000,000) |
| Sales—Product B (Complex) | Plan | 3 | $6,000,000 | 3 | $6,000,000 | 3 | $6,000,000 |
| | Actual | 0 | 0 | 0 | 0 | 0 | 0 |
| | Gap | (3) | ($6,000,000) | (3) | ($6,000,000) | (3) | ($6,000,000) |
| | Cum Gap | (3) | ($6,000,000) | (6) | ($12,000,000) | (9) | ($18,000,000) |
| Sales—Product B (New) | Plan | 8 | $2,000,000 | 8 | $2,000,000 | 8 | $2,000,000 |
| | Actual | 17 | $4,125,000 | 18 | $4,500,000 | 21 | $5,250,000 |
| | Gap | 9 | $2,125,000 | 10 | $2,500,000 | 11 | $3,250,000 |
| | Cum Gap | 9 | $2,125,000 | 19 | $4,625,000 | 30 | $7,875,000 |
| | | M1 | | M2 | | M3 | |
| Average % Contribution—Total | Plan | 50% | | 50% | | 50% | |
| | Actual | 30% | | 38% | | 36% | |
| | Gap | (20%) | | (12%) | | (14%) | |

*(Continued)*

## Figure 14.3
## Region One Sales Tracker (*Continued*)

| | | | | |
|---|---|---|---|---|
| Average % Contribution—Product A | Plan | 50% | 50% | 50% |
| | Actual | 42% | 36% | 38% |
| | Gap | (8%) | (14%) | (12%) |
| Average % Contribution—Product B | Plan | 50% | 50% | 50% |
| | Actual | – | – | – |
| | Gap | – | – | – |
| Average % Contribution—Product C (New) | Plan | 50% | 50% | 50% |
| | Actual | 15% | 40% | 23% |
| | Gap | (35%) | (10%) | (27%) |
| Average Customer Satisfaction Rating—Total | | 65 | 61 | 53 |
| Average CS Rating—Product A | | 70 | 62 | 45 |
| Average CS Rating—Product B | | – | – | – |
| Average CS Rating—Product C | | 60 | 60 | 60 |
| Customer Complaints | | 8 | 12 | 15 |
| Jobs Spec'd Incorrectly—Product A | | 3 | 2 | 3 |
| Jobs Spec'd Incorrectly—Product B | | 0 | 0 | 0 |
| Jobs Spec'd Incorrectly—Product C | | 3 | 2 | 2 |
| COS Errors | | 4 | 5 | 1 |

# Figure 14.4
## Scenario 2: Before

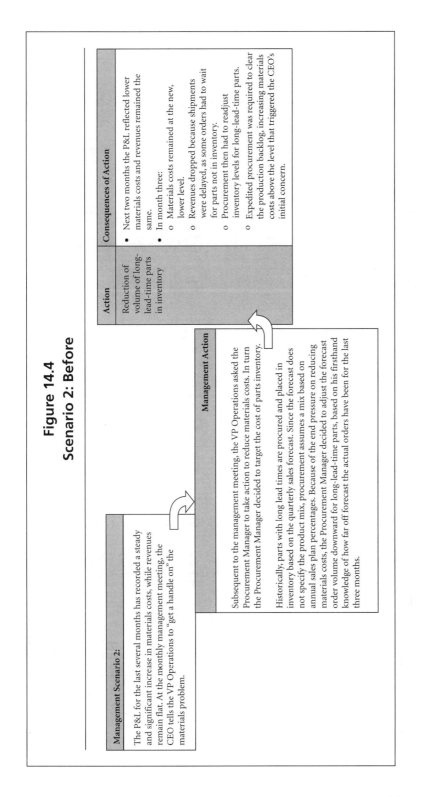

**Management Scenario 2:**

The P&L for the last several months has recorded a steady and significant increase in materials costs, while revenues remain flat. At the monthly management meeting, the CEO tells the VP Operations to "get a handle on" the materials problem.

**Management Action**

Subsequent to the management meeting, the VP Operations asked the Procurement Manager to take action to reduce materials costs. In turn the Procurement Manager decided to target the cost of parts inventory.

Historically, parts with long lead times are procured and placed in inventory based on the quarterly sales forecast. Since the forecast does not specify the product mix, procurement assumes a mix based on annual sales plan percentages. Because of the end pressure on reducing materials costs, the Procurement Manager decided to adjust the forecast order volume downward for long-lead-time parts, based on his firsthand knowledge of how far off forecast the actual orders have been for the last three months.

**Action**

Reduction of volume of long-lead-time parts in inventory

**Consequences of Action**

- Next two months the P&L reflected lower materials costs and revenues remained the same.
- In month three:
  - o Materials costs remained at the new, lower level.
  - o Revenues dropped because shipments were delayed, as some orders had to wait for parts not in inventory.
  - o Procurement then had to readjust inventory levels for long-lead-time parts.
  - o Expedited procurement was required to clear the production backlog, increasing materials costs above the level that triggered the CEO's initial concern.

# Figure 14.5
## Product Delivered Tracker

| Product Delivered Tracker | M1 | | M2 | | M3 | |
|---|---|---|---|---|---|---|
| | Plan | Actual | Plan | Actual | Plan | Actual |
| *Output Measures* | | | | | | |
| *Product A (Original)* | | | | | | |
| Avg. margin per job | 50% | 42% | 50% | 42% | 50% | 42% |
| Avg. cycle time per job | 30 | 35 | 30 | 35 | 30 | 35 |
| # jobs/products delivered on time | 29 | 24 | 29 | 24 | 29 | 24 |
| Total products shipped | 29 | 26 | 29 | 26 | 29 | 26 |
| # jobs not meeting spec or customer expectation | 0 | 2 | 0 | 2 | 0 | 2 |
| # days jobs stalled or on hold | 0 | 6 | 0 | 6 | 0 | 6 |
| Average cost per job | $500,000 | 567,000 | $500,000 | 567,000 | $500,000 | 567,000 |
| *Product B (Complex)* | | | | | | |
| Avg. margin per job | 50% | 42% | 50% | 42% | 50% | 42% |
| Avg. cycle time per job | 30 | 35 | 30 | 35 | 30 | 35 |
| # jobs/products delivered on time | 29 | 24 | 29 | 24 | 29 | 24 |
| Total products shipped | 29 | 26 | 29 | 26 | 29 | 26 |
| # jobs not meeting spec or customer expectation | 0 | 3 | 0 | 2 | 0 | 2 |
| # days jobs stalled or on hold | 0 | 6 | 0 | 6 | 0 | 6 |
| Average cost per job | $500,000 | 567,000 | $500,000 | 567,000 | $500,000 | 567,000 |
| *Product C (New)* | | | | | | |
| Avg. margin per job | 50% | 42% | 50% | 42% | 50% | 42% |
| Avg. cycle time per job | 30 | 35 | 30 | 35 | 30 | 35 |
| # jobs/products delivered on time | 29 | 24 | 29 | 24 | 29 | 24 |
| Total products shipped | 29 | 26 | 29 | 26 | 29 | 26 |
| # jobs not meeting spec or customer expectation | 0 | 2 | 0 | 2 | 0 | 2 |
| # days jobs stalled or on hold | 0 | 6 | 0 | 6 | 0 | 6 |
| Average cost per job | $500,000 | 567,000 | $500,000 | 567,000 | $500,000 | 567,000 |

## Figure 14.6
## Opportunity Pipeline Tracker

| | Estimated Units | Estimated Revenue |
|---|---|---|
| **Opportunities Total** | **236** | **$198,875,000** |
| Opportunities Total Stage One | 100 | $100,000,000 |
| Opportunities Total Stage Two | 57 | $41,000,000 |
| Opportunities Total Stage Three | 44 | $32,375,000 |
| Opportunities Total Stage Four | 35 | $25,500,000 |
| **Product A (Original) Total** | **48** | **$48,000,000** |
| Product A (Original) Stage Two | 21 | $21,000,000 |
| Product A (Original) Stage Three | 15 | $15,000,000 |
| Product A (Original) Stage Four | 12 | $12,000,000 |
| **Product B (Original) Total** | **11** | **$22,000,000** |
| Product B (Original) Stage Two | 4 | $8,000,000 |
| Product B (Original) Stage Three | 4 | $8,000,000 |
| Product B (Original) Stage Four | 3 | $6,000,000 |
| **Product C (Original) Total** | **77** | **$28,875,000** |
| Product C (Original) Stage Two | 32 | $12,000,000 |
| Product C (Original) Stage Three | 25 | $9,375,000 |
| Product C (Original) Stage Four | 20 | $7,500,000 |

Opportunity Mix Trend

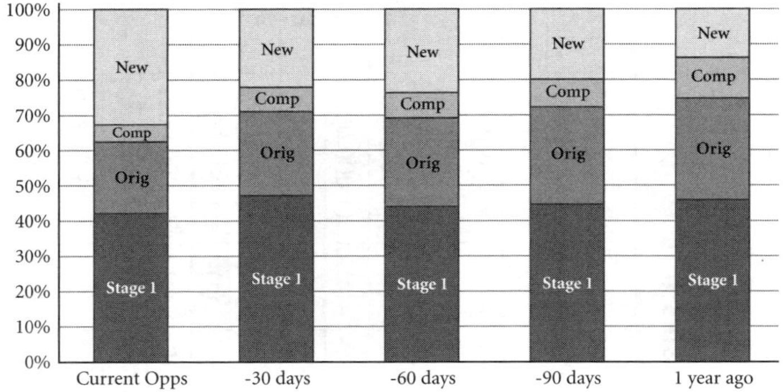


Stage 3 Opportunities Mix Trend

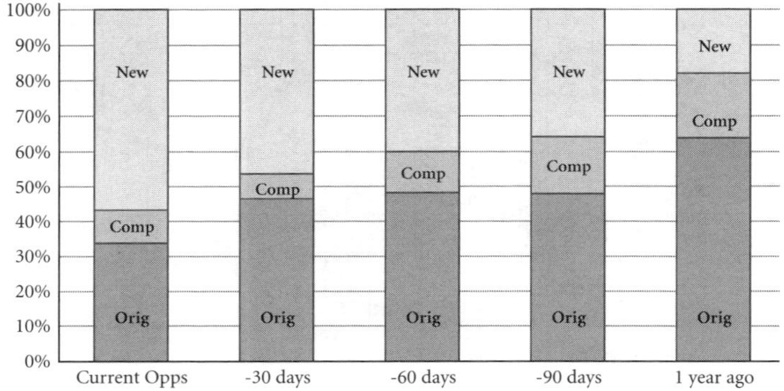

# Figure 14.7
## Belding Sales Tracker

| PERFORMANCE INDICATOR | | M1 | | M2 | | M3 | |
|---|---|---|---|---|---|---|---|
| | | Units | Revenue | Units | Revenue | Units | Revenue |
| **Sales—Product A (Original)** | | | | | | | |
| Region | Plan | 6 | 6,000.00 | 6 | 6,000.00 | 6 | 6,000.00 |
| | Actual | 6 | 6,000.00 | 5 | 5,000.00 | 6 | 6,000.00 |
| | Gap | 0 | 0 | (1) | (1,000,000) | 0 | 0 |
| | Cum | 0 | 0 | (1) | (1,000,000) | (1) | (1,000,000) |
| Region | Plan | 6 | 6,000.00 | 6 | 6,000.00 | 6 | 6,000.00 |
| | Actual | 6 | 6,000.00 | 5 | 5,000.00 | 6 | 6,000.00 |
| | Gap | 0 | 0 | (1) | (1,000,000) | 0 | 0 |
| | Cum | 0 | 0 | (1) | (1,000,000) | (1) | (1,000,000) |
| Region | Plan | 6 | 6,000.00 | 6 | 6,000.00 | 6 | 6,000.00 |
| | Actual | 6 | 6,000.00 | 5 | 5,000.00 | 6 | 6,000.00 |
| | Gap | 0 | 0 | (1) | (1,000,000) | 0 | 0 |
| | Cum | 0 | 0 | (1) | (1,000,000) | (1) | (1,000,000) |
| **Sales—Product B (Complex)** | | | | | | | |
| Region | Plan | 3 | 6,000.00 | 3 | 6,000.00 | 3 | 6,000.00 |
| | Actual | 0 | 0 | 0 | 0 | 0 | 0 |
| | Gap | (3) | (6,000,000) | (3) | (6,000,000) | (3) | (6,000,000) |
| | Cum | (3) | (6,000,000) | (6) | (12,000,000) | (9) | (18,000,000) |
| Region | Plan | 3 | 6,000.00 | 3 | 6,000.00 | 3 | 6,000.00 |
| | Actual | 0 | 0 | 0 | 0 | 0 | 0 |
| | Gap | (3) | (6,000,000) | (3) | (6,000,000) | (3) | (6,000,000) |
| | Cum | (3) | (6,000,000) | (6) | (12,000,000) | (9) | (18,000,000) |

# Figure 14.8
## Scenario 3: Before

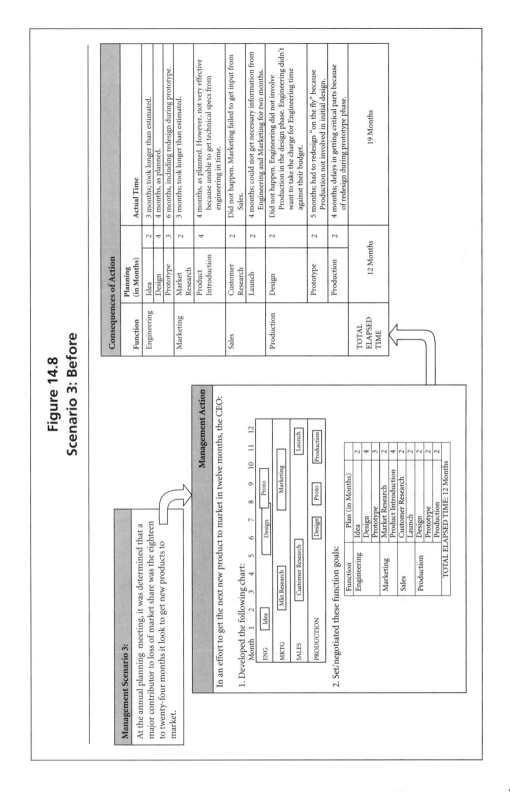

**Management Scenario 3:**

At the annual planning meeting, it was determined that a major contributor to loss of market share was the eighteen to twenty-four months it took to get new products to market.

**Management Action**

In an effort to get the next new product to market in twelve months, the CEO:

1. Developed the following chart:

| Month | 1 | 2 | 3 | 4 | 5 | 6 | 7 | 8 | 9 | 10 | 11 | 12 |
|---|---|---|---|---|---|---|---|---|---|---|---|---|
| ENG | Idea | | | | | Design | | | Proto | | | |
| MKTG | | Mkt Research | | | | | | Marketing | | | | |
| SALES | | | Customer Research | | | | | | | | Launch | |
| PRODUCTION | | | | | | | | Design | | Proto | | Production |

2. Set/negotiated these function goals:

| Function | Plan (in Months) | |
|---|---|---|
| Engineering | Idea | 2 |
| | Design | 4 |
| | Prototype | 3 |
| Marketing | Market Research | 2 |
| | Product Introduction | 4 |
| Sales | Customer Research | 2 |
| | Launch | 2 |
| Production | Design | 2 |
| | Prototype | 2 |
| | Production | 2 |
| TOTAL ELAPSED TIME: 12 Months | | |

## Consequences of Action

| Function | Planning (in Months) | | Actual Time |
|---|---|---|---|
| Engineering | Idea | 2 | 3 months; took longer than estimated. |
| | Design | 4 | 4 months, as planned. |
| | Prototype | 3 | 6 months, including redesign during prototype. |
| Marketing | Market Research | 2 | 3 months; took longer than estimated. |
| | Product Introduction | 4 | 4 months, as planned. However, not very effective because unable to get technical specs from engineering in time. |
| Sales | Customer Research | 2 | Did not happen. Marketing failed to get input from Sales. |
| | Launch | 2 | 4 months; could not get necessary information from Engineering and Marketing for two months. |
| Production | Design | 2 | Did not happen. Engineering did not involve Production in the design phase. Engineering didn't want to take the charge for Engineering time against their budget. |
| | Prototype | 2 | 5 months; had to redesign "on the fly" because Production not involved in initial design. |
| | Production | 2 | 4 months; delays in getting critical parts because of redesign during prototype phase. |
| TOTAL ELAPSED TIME | 12 Months | | 19 Months |

# Figure 14.9
## Scenario 3: After

| | Performance Monitored and Data Analyzed | Actions Taken: Month 1 | Actions Taken: Months 2 and 3 | Actions Taken: Months 4 to 15 |
|---|---|---|---|---|
| 1. Value Creation Management Team | 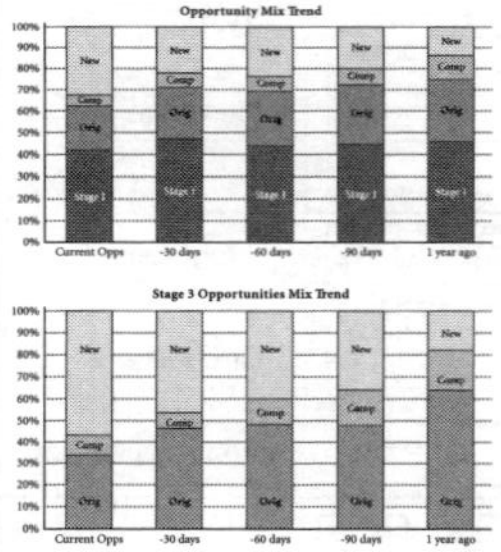 | • During the annual review and planning cycle, it was determined that a major contributor to loss of market share was the eighteen to twenty-four months it currently took to bring new products to market.<br><br>• The New Product Development and Launch process goal was set at twelve months' cycle time to bring a new product to market. The Product Launched Primary Processing System Management Team was given the task to reach the goal in time to impact this year's new product project portfolio. | • Monitors the progress of the improvement project | • Monitors the performance of the new process |
| 2. Product Launched Processing Sub-System Management Team | 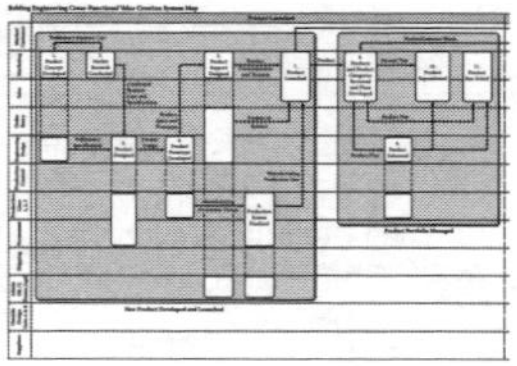 | • A cross-functional design team was formed to perform disconnect analysis and develop a process design that could meet the twelve-month cycle time goal. | • New process design approved and implementation plans developed and initiated | • Monitors the performance of the new process<br>• Makes refinements to the design as needed<br>• Conducts a post-mortem on the improvement project |
| 3. Product Manager | | • Initiates the next product using the existing process. | • Migrates the project to the new process for the remainder of the project<br>• Initiates next project using the new process | • First new product launched in 15 months<br>• Subsequent products launched in 12 months or fewer |
| 4. Functions That Participate in the New Product Development Process | | • Execute the project using existing process. | • Implement the new process; capture any issues as they go | • Implement refinements to new process |

# Figure 14.10
## Scenario 4: Before

**Management Scenario 4:**
- This year's budget was finalized during Q4 last year, after much discussion about strategy and how functions were to support the strategy.
- However, during January and February of this year, it was clear that assumptions about the revenues were overly optimistic.

| Management Action |
| --- |
| In March, all functions were ordered to cut their budgets for the remainder of the year by 10 percent. Subsequently,<br>- Each function independently cut programs and initiatives that would result in a 10 percent reduction in their individual budgets.<br>- A new corporate budget was issued for the remaining three quarters of the year that reflected a 10 percent reduction in planning expenditures. |

### Consequences of Action

| Function | Action in Response to 10 Percent Budget Cuts Across the Board | Consequences to Belding of Individual Function Action |
| --- | --- | --- |
| Finance | Held up introduction of new Oracle system | Continued lack of key management information in Engineering and Production |
| Engineering | Did not implement "partnership" program with outside design units | Outside design units continue to not understand and to not meet Belding design standards |
| Sales | Cut back on sales rep new hires | Turnover during the year resulted in several "open" sales territories for up to six months, impacting revenues |
| Procurement | Suppliers Certification Program put on hold | Less technically competent sales reps |
|  | Inventory optimization program on hold | Material shortages continue to plague Production |
| Production | Hold on capital expenditures to support new products | New products put on hold at prototype stages because of lack of production capability |
| Shipping | Plans for new automation that would impact packing time and in-transit damage put on hold | No improvement in:<br>- Time to receive orders<br>- Damage during shipping<br>Results in customer complaints and costly on-site repairs |

**Figure 14.11**
**First-Level Priority Resets**

| Processing Sub-Systems | Old Budget* | New Budget* | % Change | Rationale |
|---|---|---|---|---|
| Launched | $37 | $37 | 0 | New product goals critical. No change. |
| Sold | $106 | $95 | ($10.4) | Despite this cut, should be able to maintain adequate sales growth with careful management. |
| Delivered | $157 | $138 | (12.1) | With this cut, should still be able to deliver budget growth. Will hold planned improvements until next year. |
| Total | $300 | $270 | (10.0) | Required to meet earnings target. |

* in millions of $

**Figure 14.12**
**Second-Level Priority Resets**

| Function | Launched | | Sold | | Delivered | | Total | | % Budget Reduction | Rationale |
|---|---|---|---|---|---|---|---|---|---|---|
| | Old $* | New $* | Old $* | New $* | Old $* | New $* | Old $* | New $* | | |
| Admin | 2 | 2 | 3 | 1 | 5 | 2 | 10 | 5 | (50.0) | Full support of Launch. Maintenance support for Sold and Delivered. |
| Marketing | 10 | 10 | 20 | 14 | | | 30 | 24 | (20.0) | Full support of Launch. Trim demand generated programs for Sold. |
| Sales | 2 | 2 | 83 | 80 | | | 85 | 82 | (3.5) | Full support of Launch. Delay aggressive hiring plan for rest of the year. |
| Engineer | 20 | 20 | | | 30 | 25 | 50 | 45 | (10.0) | Full support of Launch. Trim plans to upgrade outsourcing partners in Delivered. |
| Procure | 1 | 1 | | | 29 | 25 | 30 | 26 | (133.3) | Full support of Launch. Trim plans to upgrade supplies in Delivered. |
| Production | 1 | 1 | | | 84 | 79 | 85 | 80 | (5.9) | Full support of Launch. Trim plans to upgrade shipping process in Delivered. |
| Shipping | 1 | 1 | | | 9 | 7 | 10 | 8 | (20.0) | Full support of Launch. Trim plans to upgrade shipping process in Delivered. |
| Total | 37 | 37 | 106 | 95 | 157 | 138 | 300 | 270 | (10.0) | |
| % Budget Reduction | 0 | | (10.4) | | (12.1) | (10.0) | | | | |

*in millions of $

Figure 14.13
Third-Level Priority Resets

| Function | Budget by Processing Sub-System* | | | Total |
|---|---|---|---|---|
| | Launched | Sold | Delivered | |
| Admin | 2 | 1 | 2 | 5 |
| Marketing | 10 | 14 | | 24 |
| Sales | 2 | 50 | | 82 |
| Engineering | 20 | | 25 | 45 |
| Procurement | 1 | | 25 | 26 |
| Production | 1 | | 79 | 80 |
| Shipping | 1 | | 7 | 8 |
| Total | $37 | $95 | $136 | $270 |

*in millions of $

## Figure 14.14
## Scenario 5: Before

**Management Scenario 5:**

At the last quarterly offsite, the VP Administration made a presentation regarding the number of improvement initiatives currently under way at Belding. As examples of the issue, the VP cited the following:

☐ There were six projects initiated by Corporate, including studies of accounting practices, executive compensation, and overtime policies.
☐ There were several projects initiated by Corporate, including:
  o Improving the spirit of innovation
  o Changing the corporate culture to make employees less risk averse
  o Improving earnings forecasts
☐ There were twenty projects mandated by various levels of government agencies.
☐ Within the various Belding functions there were countless improvement projects, including:
  o Twelve Six Sigma projects in Operations
  o Metrics development projects in Engineering and Shipping

The VP Administration then added:
☐ This list did not even include the continual product-related changes being made to "stay in business."
☐ A quick "ballpark" estimate was that these projects could consume as much as X hours of management time annually, or roughly 15 percent of all management time in a year, based on the assumption the average manager worked fifty hours a week.

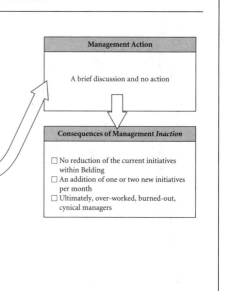

**Management Action**

A brief discussion and no action

**Consequences of Management *Inaction***

☐ No reduction of the current initiatives within Belding
☐ An addition of one or two new initiatives per month
☐ Ultimately, over-worked, burned-out, cynical managers

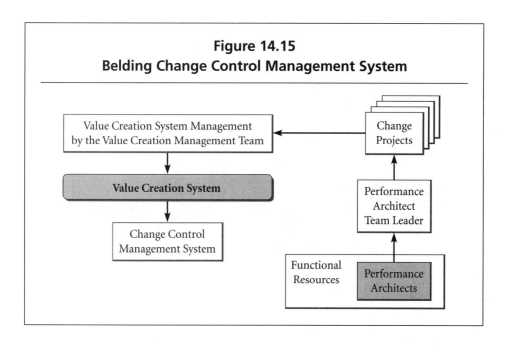

**Figure 14.15**
**Belding Change Control Management System**

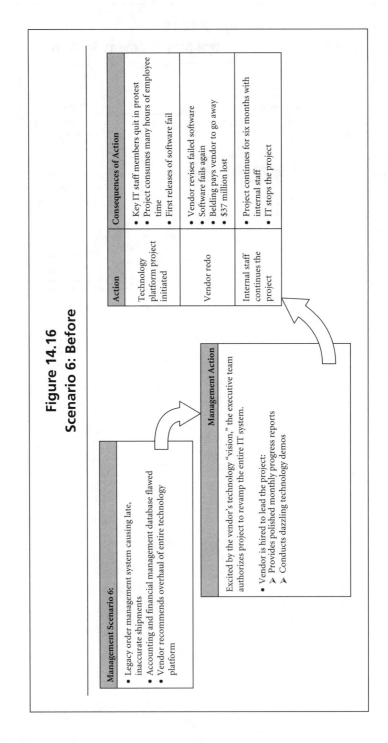

**Figure 14.16**
**Scenario 6: Before**

**Management Scenario 6:**

- Legacy order management system causing late, inaccurate shipments
- Accounting and financial management database flawed
- Vendor recommends overhaul of entire technology platform

**Management Action**

Excited by the vendor's technology "vision," the executive team authorizes project to revamp the entire IT system.

- Vendor is hired to lead the project:
  - Provides polished monthly progress reports
  - Conducts dazzling technology demos

| Action | Consequences of Action |
|---|---|
| Technology platform project initiated | • Key IT staff members quit in protest<br>• Project consumes many hours of employee time<br>• First releases of software fail |
| Vendor redo | • Vendor revises failed software<br>• Software fails again<br>• Belding pays vendor to go away<br>• $37 million lost |
| Internal staff continues the project | • Project continues for six months with internal staff<br>• IT stops the project |

## Figure 14.17
## Scenario 6: After

| | Performance Monitored and Data Analyzed | Actions Taken: Month 1 | Actions Taken: Months 2 and 3 | Actions Taken: Months 4 through 15 |
|---|---|---|---|---|
| 1. Value Creation Management Team | | • During the annual review and planning cycle, the company's IT systems were identified as causes of poor performance in Order management and in Financial management<br>• The Value Creation Management Team charters two cross-functional teams to examine the existing process (i.e., Order Fulfillment, Accounts Payable, and Receivables) and identify disconnects including any that relate to technology | • With help of technology experts, the Value Creation Management Team establishes a future vision for business performance | • Business case 2 is approved, and implementation plans are developed and initiated<br>• Performance of the new process monitored |
| 2. Steering Team (Processing Sub-System Management Teams from Delivered, IT, Finance) | | • Provides resources to the teams | • Based on the vision, the management team sets business requirements for the processes and enabling technologies<br>• Teams establish budget (business case 1) for the redesign work | • Business case 2 is reviewed and forwarded to the Value Creation Management Team for approval<br>• Implements new processes and enabling technologies<br>• Conducts a post-mortem on the improvement effort |
| 3. IT | | • Participates in process analysis | • Guides the executives in identifying and evaluating potential technology options to optimize business performance<br>• Provides participants for the redesign teams | • Builds the technologies solutions required by the redesigned process<br>• Hires and manages the technology vendor |
| 4. Cross-Functional Process Design Teams | 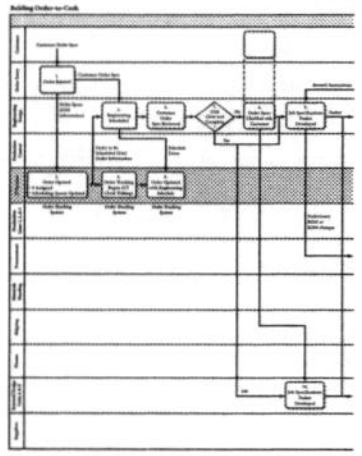 | • Each cross-functional design team performed disconnected analysis and identified disconnects caused by or related to technology | • The cross-functional teams conduct integrated process and technology redesign<br>• IT sets functional requirements based on the process designs<br>• Teams propose business case 2 for the proposed solutions, with cost/benefit analyses | • Develops implementation plans<br>• Monitors the performance of the new process<br>• Makes refinements to the design as needed |

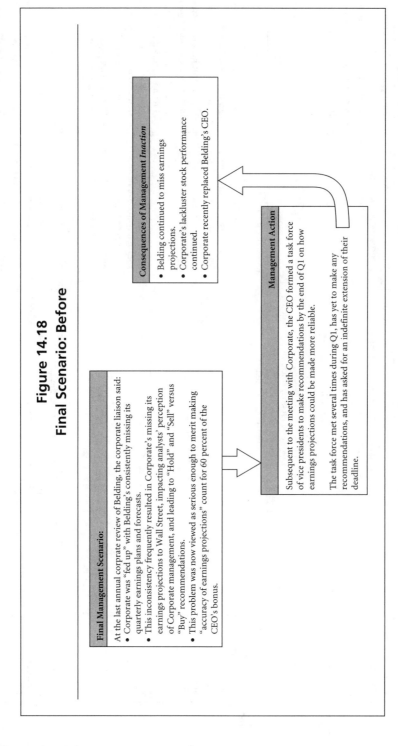

**Figure 14.18**
**Final Scenario: Before**

**Final Management Scenario:**

At the last annual corprate review of Belding, the corporate liaison said:

- Corporate was "fed up" with Belding's consistently missing its quarterly earnings plans and forecasts.
- This inconsistency frequently resulted in Corporate's missing its earnings projections to Wall Street, impacting analysts' perception of Corporate management, and leading to "Hold" and "Sell" versus "Buy" recommendations.
- This problem was now viewed as serious enough to merit making "accuracy of earnings projections" count for 60 percent of the CEO's bonus.

**Consequences of Management *Inaction***

- Belding continued to miss earnings projections.
- Corporate's lackluster stock performance continued.
- Corporate recently replaced Belding's CEO.

**Management Action**

Subsequent to the meeting with Corporate, the CEO formed a task force of vice presidents to make recommendations by the end of Q1 on how earnings projections could be made more reliable.

The task force met several times during Q1, has yet to make any recommendations, and has asked for an indefinite extension of their deadline.

# Figure 14.19
## Revenue and Earnings Tracker

| | Factor | Jan Plan | Jan Fcst | Jan Act | Feb Plan | Feb Fcst | Feb Act | Mar Plan | Mar Fcst | Mar Act | Apr Plan | Apr Fcst | Apr Act | May Plan | May Fcst | May Act | Jun Plan | Jun Fcst | Jun Act |
|---|---|---|---|---|---|---|---|---|---|---|---|---|---|---|---|---|---|---|---|
| Customer Committed | Cycle Time (Days) | 30 | 30 | 30 | 30 | 30 | 30 | 30 | 30 | 30 | 30 | | | 30 | | | 30 | | |
| | # Proposals Submitted | 200 | 200 | 200 | 200 | 200 | 200 | 200 | 200 | 204 | 200 | | | 200 | | | 200 | | |
| | Close Ratio | 50% | 50% | 49% | 50% | 49% | 50% | 50% | 50% | 50% | 50% | | | 50% | | | 50% | | |
| | Ave Sale Size | $1M | $1M | $1M | $1M | $1M | $1M | $1M | $1M | $1M | $1M | | | $1M | | | $1M | | |
| | Sales | $100M | | $98M | $100M | $98M | $105M | $100M | $100M | | $100M | | | $100M | | | $100M | | |
| Customer Delivered | Cycle Time (Days) | 30 | 30 | 30 | 30 | 30 | 30 | 30 | 30 | 30 | 30 | | | 30 | | | 30 | | |
| | # Orders Entered | 100 | 100 | 98 | 100 | 98 | 105 | 100 | 102 | | 100 | | | 100 | | | 100 | | |
| | Ave Sale Size | $1M | $1M | $1M | $1M | $1M | $1M | $1M | $1M | | $1M | | | $1M | | | $1M | | |
| | Ave Mfg Cost per Unit | $400K | $400K | $400K | $400K | $400K | $400K | $400K | $410K | | $400K | | | $400K | | | $400K | | |
| | Order Yield | 100% | 100% | 100% | 98% | 98% | 99% | 100% | 100% | | 100% | | | 100% | | | 100% | | |
| | Revenue 1 | $100M | $100M | $96M | $100M | $96M | $104M | $100M | $102M | | $100M | | | $100M | | | $100M | | |
| | Contribution 1 | $60M | $60M | $66.2M | $60M | $55.2M | $61.36M | $60M | $60.18M | | $60M | | | $60M | | | $60M | | |
| Product Receivable | Cycle Time (Days) | 30 | 30 | 30 | 30 | 30 | 30 | 30 | 30 | 30 | 30 | | | 30 | | | 30 | | |
| | $ Invoiced | $100M | $100M | $96M | $100M | | | $100M | $102M | $103M | $100M | | | $100M | | | $100M | | |
| | Erosion | $2M | $2M | $1M | $2M | $1M | $1M | $2M | $1M | $2M | $2M | | | $2M | | | $2M | | |
| | Cash | $98M | $98M | $95M | $98M | $95M | $95M | $98M | $101M | $103M | $98M | | | $98M | | | $98M | | |
| Accounts | Revenue 2 | $98M | $98M | $95M | $98M | $95M | $103M | $98M | $101M | $103M | $98M | | | $98M | | | $98M | | |
| | Contribution 2 | $58M | $58M | $54.2M | $58M | $54.2M | $58M | $54.2M | $60.36M | $58M | $58M | | | $58M | | | $58M | | |
| Quarterly Performance | Revenue Plan (Month) | $98M | | | $196M | | | $294M | | | $98M | | | $196M | | | $294M | | |
| | Revenue Plan (QTD) | $98M | | | $95M | | | $99M | | | | | | | | | | | |
| | Revenue Forecast (Month) | $98M | | | $190M | | | $300M | | | | | | | | | | | |
| | Revenue Forecast (QTD) | $98M | | | $103M | | | $300M | | | | | | | | | | | |
| | Revenue Actual | $95M | | | $25M | | | $25M | | | $25M | | | $25M | | | | | |
| | UAE Plan | $25M | | | $25M | | | $25M | | | $25M | | | $25M | | | | | |
| | UAE Actual | $24M | | | $33M | | | $33M | | | $33M | | | $33M | | | $33M | | |
| | Earnings Plan | $33M | | | $33M | | | $30.2M | | | $33M | | | $33M | | | | | |
| | Earnings Forecast | $33M | | | $35.36 | | | | | | $35.18 | | | | | | | | |
| | Earning Actual | $30.2M | | | | | | | | | | | | | | | | | |

# Figure 14.20
## Belding Performance Indicators Model

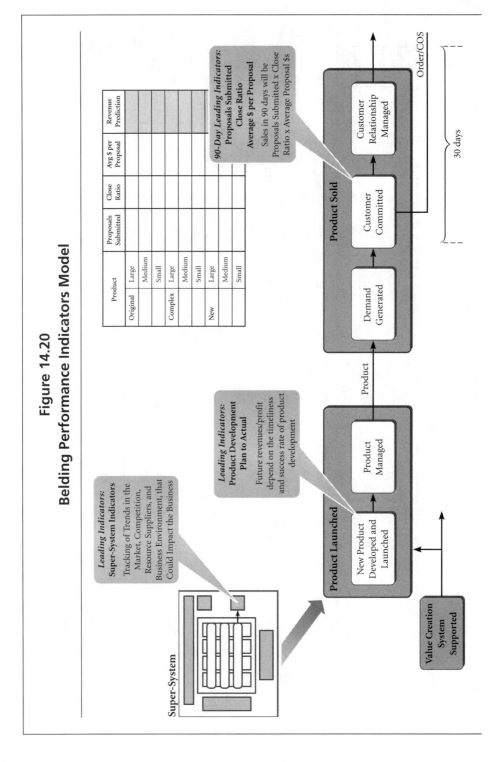

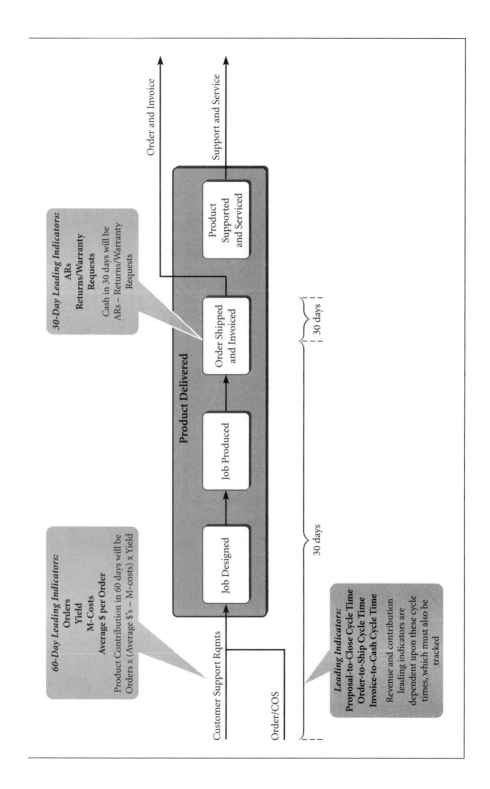

**60-Day Leading Indicators:**
**Orders**
**Yield**
**M-Costs**
**Average $ per Order**

Product Contribution in 60 days will be
Orders x (Average $'s – M-costs) x Yield

**30-Day Leading Indicators:**
**ARs**
**Returns/Warranty**
**Requests**

Cash in 30 days will be
ARs – Returns/Warranty
Requests

*Leading Indicators:*
**Proposal-to-Close Cycle Time**
**Order-to-Ship Cycle Time**
**Invoice-to-Cash Cycle Time**

Revenue and contribution
leading indicators are
dependent upon these cycle
times, which must also be
tracked

Customer Support Rqmts

Order/COS

Job Designed

Job Produced

Order Shipped
and Invoiced

Product
Supported
and Serviced

**Product Delivered**

30 days

30 days

Order and Invoice

Support and Service

Geary Rummler always had hope that organizations are being run by ethical, rational individuals who care deeply about their customers, their employees, and their community. He spent his life creating highly structured models for leaders to understand their organizations and to make them better. The criticism by some observers was that his models were sometimes too complex and could be difficult to apply, but his response was always that it's organizations that are complex and horrendously hard to design and manage; even the most complex of his models barely represented all the interacting variables of real organizations. To design and manage organizations is a serious, arduous role that he tried never to underestimate.

Geary once wrote a book entitled *Serious Performance Consulting*.[1] It was meant to impart a methodology and tools to people who provide consulting services to organizations. The meaning of the title was that his approach was always intended to produce measurable long-term positive results—hence a serious approach to consulting rather than a Band-Aid® or temporary effect. When we teach a classroom training program based upon the book, we always make a point to participants that in order to be a serious performance consultant, one must have a serious client. That is, one must be working for a senior executive who wants to make a positive long-term difference, or all the well-intended consulting techniques won't mean a thing.

One simple way of sorting out the individuals who sit at the top of organizations is to put them into two camps. One type is the serious leader, someone who wants to make a difference. The other type is the political operator, who wants to look good and do well for himself or herself. Sometimes it is possible for a leader to accomplish both—look good and lead well—but what matters more is how the person handles all the myriad decisions, large and small: Are the decisions for the good of the organization or the good of the leader?

It is true that Rummler's work was predicated on the existence of a serious, rational person at the helm of an organization. The reality is not always up to the ideal. What we have seen is that a single leader is capable of destroying all the good that an organization has to offer and of doing it in record time. We once watched in dismay as a very well designed company with effective management was taken over by a new owner. That person said all the right things, about vision and quality and "standing shoulder to shoulder." But it eventually became evident, as salaries were cut, resources diminished, products cheapened, that this leader's chief concern was how much money got into his pocket. Once employees figured that out, of course, the best ones dove out the door as fast as possible, and so this company, which took years of careful design and management to achieve success, was trashed in a matter of months.

So leadership can trump rational design. Leadership can trump everything. Nothing in this book would prevent a willfully bad manager from managing badly. But what we are hoping for is a few serious leaders to get excited about the concepts, methods, and tools in this book, to take up the endeavor to become a 3-D Enterprise. It takes a strong, serious leader but is well worth it.

**E N D N O T E S**

## INTRODUCTION

1. James C. Collins and Jerry I. Porras. *Built to Last: Successful Habits of Visionary Companies.* (New York: HarperBusiness Essentials, 1994, 1997, 2002).

2. Gary Hamel. *Leading the Revolution: How to Survive in Turbulent Times by Making Innovation a Way of Life.* (Rev. ed.) (Boston: Harvard Business Press, 2002).

3. Geary A. Rummler, Alan J. Ramias, and Richard A. Rummler. *White Space Revisited: Creating Value Through Process.* (San Francisco: Jossey-Bass, 2009).

## CHAPTER 2: THE VALUE DIMENSION

1. Michael E. Porter. "What Is Strategy?" *Harvard Business Review, 74*(6), November 1, 1996. See also Michael E. Porter. "What Is Strategy?" *HBR OnPoint Enhanced Edition, Harvard Business Review*, March 3, 2009.

## CHAPTER 3: THE RESOURCE DIMENSION

1. Vamik D. Volkan, M.D. *The Need to Have Enemies and Allies: From Clinical Practice to International Relations.* (New York: Jason Aronson, 1988).

2. Geary A. Rummler and Alan P. Brache. *Improving Performance: How to Manage the White Space on the Organization Chart.* (San Francisco: Jossey-Bass, 1990). Revised and updated edition published by Jossey-Bass, 1995.

3. Robert J. Herbold. *The Fiefdom Syndrome.* (New York: Currency Doubleday, 2004, pp. 3–4).

## CHAPTER 7: DEMONSTRATING HOW

1. Geary A. Rummler, Alan J. Ramias, and Richard A. Rummler. *White Space Revisited: Creating Value Through Process.* (San Francisco: Jossey-Bass, 2009).

2. For those familiar with our seven-phase process improvement methodology called the Rummler Process Methodology, this four-phase model might seem like a change in direction. But the intention is simply to provide a simple front-end to the Executive PIP that still matches the more robust seven-phase RPM model. Here is how the two sets of phases line up:

| Rummler Process Methodology (RPM) | Executive PIP |
|---|---|
| Align Phase<br>• Project Definition<br>• Project Organization | Phase 1<br>• Gather performance data<br>• Conduct interviews<br>• Map the business process |
| Analysis Phase<br>• Process Analysis<br>• Strategy Development | Phase 2<br>• Review the "is" process<br>• Identify disconnects<br>• Prioritize the disconnects |
| Design Phase<br>• Process Design and Testing<br>• Process Management Design and Testing<br>• Change Assessment and Planning | Phase 3<br>• Develop solutions<br>• Create high-level implementation plan |

| Rummler Process Methodology (RPM) | Executive PIP |
|---|---|
| Commit Phase | Phase 4<br>• Hand over project to design team<br>• Oversee project as steering team |
| Build Phase<br>• Detailed Design<br>• Develop<br>• Test<br>• Solution Preparation | |
| Enable Phase<br>• Prepare<br>• Internal Launch | |
| Adopt Phase<br>• Cut Over<br>• Stabilize<br>• Operate | |

3. Rummler and Brache, *Improving Performance.*


## CHAPTER 8: EVOLUTION OF A MANAGEMENT SYSTEM

1. Rummler, Ramias, and Rummler, *White Space Revisited.*


## CHAPTER 10: PERFORMANCE MANAGED

1. We hesitate to use the popular term "dashboard" because in so many places this has become an overly simplistic green-yellow-red indicator board that is not effectively linked to performance at the multiple levels we are recommending.


## CHAPTER 11: WHAT IT WILL TAKE

1. Volkan, *The Need to Have Enemies and Allies.*

2. Rummler, Ramias, and Rummler, *White Space Revisited.*

## CHAPTER 14: RETURN TO BELDING ENGINEERING

1. For those who want to understand the specifics of the revenue and earnings tracker for managing Belding's business in a proactive manner, here is an explanation that is keyed to Figure 14.19:

   Referring to the highlighted cells in the tracker, the "planned" data is loaded into the tracker as follows:

   1. Referencing the underlying value chain factors shown in Figure 14.19, data are entered reflecting assumptions about what will happen in January for the Customer Committed segment of the value chain. That is:

      a. The average cycle time for a prospect to move from "proposal submitted" to "sale closed" and order entered will be thirty days.

      b. Two hundred proposals will be submitted to prospects during the month.

      c. One hundred proposals will be accepted, meaning the "close ratio" will be 50 percent.

      d. The average size of sales made in January will be $1 million.

      e. One hundred accepted proposals, at $1 million each, leads to projected sales for January of $100 million.

   2. Now these sales of $100 million must be tracked through the next segment of the value chain, which is Product Delivered. This work will be done in February, and these data are entered as follows:

      a. The average cycle time for an order to move from "entered" to "shipped" will be thirty days.

      b. One hundred orders will be submitted during the month.

      c. The average sale size of each order is $1 million.

      d. The average cost to manufacture each order is $400,000. (This means an average of $600,000 contribution to profit from each order.)

      e. The order yield is 100 percent. (This means that all one hundred orders that entered the system also exited. No orders were delayed, scraped, etc.)

f. Shipping one hundred orders worth $1 million each means that Belding can claim gross revenues (Revenue 1) of $100 million at this point.

g. The contribution to Belding profits by Production (Contribution 1) is $60 million. ($100 million in orders, less $40 million in manufacturing costs, gives us $60 million contribution.)

3. But this gross revenue of $100 million must be tracked through the final segment of the value chain (technically, still part of Delivered), identified as Accounts Receivable. These data look like this:

a. The average cycle time for an invoice to be paid is thirty days.

b. $100 million were invoiced (one hundred shipped orders at $1 million each).

c. Adjustments, warranty claims, and so on, lead to an "erosion" of the accounts receivable by $2 million.

d. $100 million invoice, minus $2 million in erosion, leaves us with cash receipts of $98 million.

e. The actual receipt of $98 million requires us to recognize that the net revenue (Revenue 2) is now $98 million.

f. In the same way, Contribution 1 is now reduced to $58 million.

These same "planned" steps are followed for each month of the year. The assumptions about the various factors shown in the tracker (e.g., cycle times, # proposals submitted, average sale size, manufacturing costs, and erosion) will vary by month, depending on "actual" performance history and anticipated external events, such a seasonal fluctuations, new competitors, and so on.

The "actual" columns are straightforward. They reflect whatever the reality was for each period.

The "forecast" columns are updated data entered within sixty days of a period. These data represent the latest projections, based on more current data. For example, when this preliminary plan was put together in December of last year, the anticipated close ratio for September of this year was 45 percent. However, in July, Belding executives know that there is going to be a price change in August that they anticipate will increase the close ratio in September to 60 percent. So the forecast for September should reflect a change in assumptions about the "close ratio" (up) and the "average sale size" (down).

The bottom section of the revenue and earnings tracker reflects (appropriately enough) the Belding bottom line, for each quarter. It works like this.

- *Revenue*
  - The planned revenue is summarized for each month. Then it is accumulated for the quarter. (Quarter-to-date or QTD rows.) So it is very clear how revenues are progressing each month toward quarterly goals.
  - The same is done for revenue forecast and actual.
- *Unallocated Expenses (UAE)*
  - UAE are all indirect Belding expenses that have not been directly captured as part of manufacturing costs in Delivered (e.g., Sold costs, overhead). These data do not come from this tracker, but must be entered from expense budget figures maintained by Finance.
- *Earnings*
  - This figure is derived by subtracting the UAE figure for the period from the Contribution 2 figure for that period. Going back to our example, in the month of March, a planned UAE of $25 million (data from Finance) is subtracted from a planned Contribution 2 of $58 million, to arrive at planned earnings for the month of $33 million.

## AFTERWORD

1. Geary A. Rummler. *Serious Performance Consulting: According to Rummler.* A publication of the International Society for Performance Improvement. (San Francisco: Pfeiffer, 2007).

# INDEX

NOTE: Boldface page locators refer to charts, tables, and diagrams.

Belding case study, transformation (*continued*)

Calendars in, **97, 114,** 158, **170–171, 172–174;** performance planning system in, 91–102; "plan differently" step in, 91–102; problems list in, 58; process improvement project in, 73, 75–84, 94; Stage I management in, 73–84, 94, 99–101, 122–121; Stage I tools in, 143–145, **146–153;** Stage II management in, 91–99, 101–102, 103–104, 123–125; Stage II tools in, 155–161, 162–190; "support performance" step in, 115–121; "sustain" step in, 127–139; tracking systems in, **107–112,** 123, 158–159, **175–176, 177–179;** value creation architecture development in, 70–74. *See also* Order-to-Cash process (Belding)

Belding case study, transformation scenarios: Scenario, final, in, 51–52, **218–221;** Scenario 1 in, 191–194, **201–204;** Scenario 2 in, 194–196, **205–208;** Scenario 3 in, 196–197, **209–210;** Scenario 4 in, 197–198, **211–214;** Scenario 5 in, 198–199, **214–215;** Scenario 6 in, 199–200, **216–217**

"Big room" sessions, 60

Blockbuster, 24

Bonuses: for cross-functional process work, 84, 125; for heroics, 137; in resource-dominated organizations, 32, 137. *See also* Compensation; Consequence system; Rewards

Brache, A., 31, 81

Budgeting: in resource-fixated, siloed organization, 7, 11, 47–49, 197, 198; in Stage I management system, 87, 100–101; in Stage II management system, 92, 197–198, **212–214;** trackers for, 197, **212–214**

Business: components of, 8–9; key requirements of, 4–5; Value Creation System of, 17–18

Business performance: dimensions of, 9; process performance and, 87; tracking, 200, **212,** 228–229$n$. 1

Business Process Framework map, 72, 145, **150–151**

## C

Capacity, in Human Performance System, 115, **117, 121**

Case study. *See Belding headings*

Champion of value, 128–129

Change: large-scale, 130–132; methodologies of, 135–136; Performance Architects' role in managing, 132–135; philosophies of, 136; proactive value improvement initiatives for, 130–131; resistance to, in resource-fixated, siloed organizations, 28, 31–34; siloed functions as barriers to, 24, 30; sustaining the 3-D Enterprise and, 127–139; value engineering for, 131. *See also* Improvement initiatives; Transformation

Change control management system, 132–136; improvement initiatives and, 133–136, 198–199; Performance Architects' role in, 132–133, 198; role of, 132

Change Initiative Tracking Map, 134

Change initiatives. *See* Improvement initiatives

based on, 9; visibility of, 7–8; work system defined by, 6

Functional silos: accountability and, 11; in Belding case study, 35–54; change initiatives in, 133, 135; cross-functional processes and, 45–47; infrastructure changes and, 131–133; IT organization and, 6; management challenges with, 25–28; managerial practices and, 35–54; organizational culture and, 6, 30, 128; and organizational evolution, 23–25; performance management and, 39–52; performance measures and, 39–40; performance planning and, 36–39, 94; persistence of, 30–34, 94, 128, 131–132, 138–139; process improvement and, 69–70; resource buckets defined by, 6, 29; resource-dimension dominance and, 23–34. *See also* Territory-building

## G

GE, 60

GM, 24

Goals, enterprise: cascading, 91–93; cross-functional processes and, 13–14; in resource-fixated organization, 39; Stage II management system for, 89, 91–102, 103–126; sub-system alignment for, 87, 89, 91–99

Goals, functional: in resource-fixated organization, 39, **92**; in two-dimension organization, 92–93

Goals, sub-functional, 39

Government agencies, Value Creation System in, 18–19

Group cohesion, 30

Guardian of continuing value, 129

## H

Herbold, R. J., 32

Heroics, 137

Horizontal management teams, 94–99, 113, 114–115, 123–125

Horizontal organization: in Stage I management system, 86, 99; in Stage II performance planning system, 93–102; vertical organization *versus,* 31–32

Human Performance System (HPS), 115–121; alignment of, with systems, 119; elements of, 115–116, **117**; graphic depiction of, **116**; implementing and managing, **120–121**; managerial tasks in, 116–121, **117**

## I

Improvement initiatives: change control management system for, 133–136, 198–199; methodology for, 135–136; Performance Architects' role in managing, 132–135, 198; proactive *versus* small-scale, 130–131; siloed approach to, 49–50, 198; sub-optimization potential of, 70, 133, 134, 198. *See also* Process improvement

*Improving Performance* (Rummler and Brache), 31

Information Technology (IT) function: failed implementations of, 50–51, 119, 199–200; in resource-fixated, siloed organizations, 6, 25–27, 32–33, 50–51, 199–200; 3-D approach to initiatives of, 199–200

Infrastructure changes, 131–133

Inputs, in Human Performance System, 115, **117, 120**

Instrument panels. *See* Dashboards
Internal processing system, 161
Inventory management, 43–44, 194–196

## J

Japanese quality improvement tools, 41, 136
Job aids, for managers, 138
"Job Designed" Measures Chain, 156, **166–167**
"Job Designed" Process Map, **164–165**
"Just do it!" approach, 42, 135

## K

*Kaizen,* 136
Knowledge, in Human Performance System, 115, **117, 121**
Kodak, 24

## L

Large organizations: evolution of silos and, 23–25; internal processing system for, 161; sustaining value in, 130; Value Creation Systems in, 19
Large-scale change, 130–132
Launched sub-system. *See* Product/Service Launched sub-system
Leadership: rational *versus* political, 223–224; for sustaining the transformation to 3-D organization, 128–131; for transformation to 3-D organization, 58–59. *See also* Chief executive officer; Managers; Senior executives
Line managers, performance support responsibilities of, 118–119
Loss, sense of, 59–60

## M

Management, resource-fixated, 7–8; in Belding case study, 35–54; causes and reinforcers of, 28–34; consequences of, 9–11, 31–34; performance management in, 39–52; performance planning system in, 36–39. *See also* One-dimensional organization; Resource-dimension dominance
Management Bridge Room, 134
Management dimension: defined, 9; in 3-D model, 52–54
Management Domain Chart, 95, **96,** 157–158, **185–189**
Management guides, 159, **182–183, 190**
Management Planning Calendar, **97,** 158, **170–171**
Management Planning Sequence, **92**
Management system: critical actions for, 54; evaluation of, 113; evolution of, 85–89; Performance Managed component of, 103–126, 156–161, **168–190**; Performance Planned component of, 52–54, 91–102, 115, 156–161, **168–190,** 198; for process improvement, 83–84; Stage I, 86–89, 94, 99–101, 122–121; Stage I tools for, 143–145, **146–153**; Stage II, 89, 91–102, 103–126; Stage II tools for, 155–161, 162–190; summary of, 125–126; for two-dimensional management, 52–54, 64, 85–89, 103–126; visibility and control of, 15–16. *See also* One-dimensional organization; Performance management system; Process management; 3-D Enterprise; Two-dimensional management

Planning: in resource-fixated organization, 11, 36–39. *See also* Budgeting; Performance planning system

Political operators, 223–224

Porter, M., 16, 19

Power, resource control as, 29

Procedures, 16–17

Process(es): definition of, 14–17; functional view of, 23; procedures *versus,* 16–17; resource-fixated view of, 39; senior management control of, 15–17; strategic importance of, 16–17; in Value Creation Hierarchy, 68, 69; in Value Creation System, 18. *See also* Cross-functional processes

Process architecture design, 64

Process experts, 17

Process improvement: in Belding Level I transformation, 81–84; change control management system for, 133–136; choosing a methodology for, 77; critical business issue for, 76–77, 81; as evolutionary step toward two-dimension management, 85–89; Executive PIP for, 75–84, 135; at Level 5 (performer) level, 69–70; management system for, 83–84; methodology for, 135–136; Performance Architects' role in, 132–135, 198; Rummler methodology for, 75–76, 77, 86, 135; specialist involvement in, 75, 82. *See also* Executive PIP; Improvement initiatives

Process management: functional silo approach to, 45–47; myopic approach to, 3–4; proliferation of, 95; senior executives' responsibility for, 15–17, 73–74, 75–76, 86–87; in Stage I management system, 86–89, 99–101,

122–121; in Stage II management system, 89; systems view of, 4–5. *See also* Management system; Two-dimensional management

Process Management Teams (PMTs): development of, in Belding case study, 122–123, 124–125; for Level I single-process management, 86–87, **88,** 94, 99–101; for Level II horizontal management, 95, 113; meetings and reviews of, 122–123; members of, 86, 94; responsibilities of, 86–87, 113; schedule of activities of, **88**

Process movement, 3–4

Process owners, 94, 192, 193

Process ownership: of executives, 82–83; resource control and, 29

Procurement function, in Belding materials cost scenario, 43–44, 194–196

Procurement Manager, 43–44, 194, 196

Product Delivered management team: late-deliveries problem handled by, 191–194; materials cost problem handled by, 194–196

Product Delivered sub-system tracker, 191–192, 194, **202–203, 206–207**

Product delivery, customer complaints about, 40–43, 191–194

Product launch failure, 10

Product/Service Delivered sub-system: customer service in, 19; defined, 18, 67; horizontal alignment of, 91–99; horizontal management teams for, 94–99, 113, 114, 124

Product/Service Launched sub-system: defined, 18, 67; horizontal alignment of, 91–99; horizontal teams for, 94–99, 113, 114, 124

Product/Service Sold sub-system: defined, 18, 67; in government agencies, 19; horizontal alignment of, 91–99; horizontal teams for, 94–99, 113, 114, 124

Product Sold management team: horizontal organization of, 94–99, 113, 114, 124; materials cost problem handled by, 195

Production function: in Belding cost-cutting scenario, 48; in Belding New Product Development process, 45, 46

Profits, decline in, 36

Project management offices (PMOs), 133

Project planning methodologies, 133

Project team, process improvement, 77, 82

Promotion criteria, 10, 29, 137

## Q

Quality awareness campaign, 41, 42

## R

Recognition, 137

Reorganization, failure of, 9

Resource buckets. *See* Functional resource buckets

Resource dimension, 23–34; defined, 9; in performance planning, 52, 91–93, 100–101; in performer level of Value Creation Hierarchy, 69; tangibility of, 28; in 3-D model, 52–54; visibility of, 7, 33, 52

Resource-dimension dominance: Belding case study scenarios in, 40–52, 191–203; in business management education, 128; consequences of, 9–10, 31–34; functional silos and, 23–25, 30–34; impact of, on management, 10, 25–28,

29, 30, 31–34; managerial practices of, 35–54; one-dimensional organization and, 7–8, 9–11; persistence of silos and, 30–34, 128, 131–132, 138–139; process improvement and, 69–70; reasons for, 6–8, 11, 28–34; short-term returns and, 5, 7. *See also* Functional resource buckets; Management, resource-fixated; One-dimensional organization

Resource management: in context of Value Creation System, 11, 91–102, 197–198; in one-dimensional organization, 7–8, 9–11, 35–54; in Stage I performance planning system, 100–101; in Stage II performance planning system, 91–102. *See also* Budgeting; Functional resource buckets; Management, resource-fixated

Revenue and Earnings Tracker, 200, **219,** 228–229*n*. 1

Rewards: in resource-fixated organizations, 10, 29, 32; to sustain 3-D culture, 136–137; in two-dimensional management, 84, 94. *See also* Bonuses; Compensation; Consequence system

Rework Tracker, 191–192, **202–203**

Rummler, G., 31, 77, 81, 223–224

Rummler Process Methodology (RPM), 75–76, 77, 86, 135, 226–227*n*. 7:2

## S

Sales function: in Belding cost-cutting scenario, 48; in Belding New Product Development process, 45, 46

Sales Manager Instrument Panel, 106, **110–112,** 113

Sales Tracker, 194, 197, **208–209**

Senior executives: impact of functional silos on, 32; on Process Management

Team, 86–87; process responsibility of, 15–17, 73–74, 75–76, 86–87; process work of, 75–84; on Value Creation Management Team, 95, 124–125; "value engineering" responsibilities of, 131. *See also* Chief executive officer; Leadership; Managers

"Sensing" session, 60, 71

*Serious Performance Consulting* (Rummler), 223

Service launch failure, 10. *See also* Product/Service Launched sub-system

Shipping function, in Belding cost-cutting scenario, 48

Silos. *See* Functional silos

Six Sigma, 49, 132, 133

Six Sigma Black Belts, 75

Skills, in Human Performance System, 115, **117, 121**

Small-scale improvement, 130–131

Sold sub-system. *See* Product/Service Sold sub-system

Stage I management system. *See* Management system; Order-to-Cash process (Belding)

Stage II management system. *See* Belding case study, transformation; Management system; Performance management system; 3-D Enterprise

Stakeholders. *See* Customers; Financial stakeholders; Value

Stovepipes. *See* Functional silos

Strategy: process and, 17–18; super-system map for, 144; value dimension and, 131

Structure, organizational, resource fixation and, 11

Sub-optimization: due to resource-fixated, siloed management, 32–34, 39, 69–70;

improvement initiatives' potential for, 70, 133, 134, 198; reward system and, 137. *See also* Failure

Sub-processes, in Value Creation Hierarchy, 68, 69

Sub-systems: cross-functional map of, 156, **164**; defined, 17–18; horizontal alignment of, 87, 89, 91–99; horizontal teams for, 94–95. *See also* Product/Service Delivered; Product/Service Launched; Product/Service Sold

Succession planning, 137

Super-system: defined, 66, 71; internal processing system alignment with, 161; maps of, 70, 71, 143–144, **146**

Support systems. *See* Human Performance System; Performance support

Sustaining, the 3-D Enterprise, 127–139; leadership for, 128–131; management support for, 138; systemic changes for, 131–137

Swimlane charts. *See* Cross-functional process maps; Cross-Functional Value Creation Map

Systems, organizational: changes in, to support the 3-D Enterprise, 131–137; failure to manage with view of, 4, 119

## T

Territory-building and territory-protecting, 29, 32–34; in Belding New Product Development process, 47; process goals and, 93. *See also* Functional silos

3-D concept: aspects of, 1, 3–11; performance management model of, 52–54

Value Creation Management Team: change control management role of, 133, 134; cost-cutting involvement of, 197–198; IT initiative involvement of, 199–200; materials cost problem handled by, 194–195; members of, 95; New Product Development process involvement of, 196–197; responsibilities of, 95, 97, 98, 113, 124; revenue and earnings tracking by, 200; role confusion in, 125

Value Creation System (VCS): caveats to, 18–20; components of, 17–20, 67; decisions about, 67–68; graphic depiction of, **20, 67**; horizontal management teams for, 94–95; in non-profit and government organizations, 18–19; Performance Architects' role in managing, 132–133; resource management in context of, 11, 91–102; role of, 9, 17, 64. *See also* Product/Service Delivered sub-system; Product/Service Launched sub-system; Product/Service Sold sub-system

Value dimension, 13–21; critical questions about, 14; defined, 9; graphic depiction of, **21**; horizontal organization and, 31–32; importance of, 9–11, 13–14; invisibility of, 6, 33, 63; in performance planning, 91–93; resource-dimension dominance over, 5–8, 9–10, 23–34, 47, 63–64; stakeholder imbalances in, 5; steps in understanding and managing, 14; strategy and, 131; in 3-D model, 52–54; understanding and making visible, 14–21, 59, 63–74

Value engineering, 131

Value improvement initiatives, 130–131

Value Machine (value-producing machine): components of, 8–9; graphic depiction of, **8**; importance of, 9–11, 64–65

Value-Resource Detail Chart, 72, 145, **152–153**

Value-Resource Map, 155, **162**

Variations, identification and diagnosis of, 104, 122–123, 191–203

Vertical organization, 31–32; in Belding case study, 36–39; performance planning in, 36–39. *See also* Functional silos

"Visionary dictatorship" leadership, 58–59

Volkan, V., 30, 128

# W

Welch, J., 60

White-space management: horizontal teams for, 95, 124–125; senior executive involvement in, 17, 124–125

*White Space Revisited* (Rummler, Ramias, Rummler), 77, 86, 132, 135, 139

Work, value-adding: imbalance between resources and, 5–8, 9–11; invisibility of, 6, 8, 39, 63; Value Creation System and, 9. *See also* Value Creation System; Value dimension

Work organization, 14–16

Work-out sessions, 60